WHERE THE ROAD ENDS

The author today with his wife Iris.

HOWARD MURPHET was born in 1906 in Tasmania, Australia, and educated at the University of Tasmania, Hobart. During the Second World War he served with the Eighth Army from El Alamein to Tunis, took part in the invasion of Sicily and Italy and, later, with the British Second Army in the D-Day invasion of Normandy. He was also in charge of the British Press Section at the Nuremberg Trials for some time.

After a period as a Public Relations Officer in the chemical industry he visited India in 1964 to study Yoga and Eastern Philosophy. His first stay in India (1964–70) deepened his consciousness of the *Avatar*-like qualities of Sai Baba and led to his return to India in 1974 and many times since, most recently in 1992.

Also by Howard Murphet:

Yoga for Busy People

Yankee Beacon of Buddhist Light
(first published as *Hammer on the Mountain*)

Sai Baba: Man of Miracles

Sai Baba Avatar (published by Birth Day Publishing Co.)

When Daylight Comes

Sai Baba: Invitation to Glory
(also published in USA as *Walking the Path with Sai Baba*)

Beyond Death — The Undiscovered Country

WHERE THE ROAD ENDS

From self through Sai to SELF

Howard Murphet

Where the road ends God is attained
and the pilgrim finds he has journeyed
from himself to himSelf.
SAI BABA

4026 River Road
Faber, VA 22938 USA

2nd U.S. edition, 1998

First published in Australia by Butterfly Books, 1993

Library of Congress Catalog No. 94-76983
WHERE THE ROAD ENDS: from self through Sai to SELF

Cover Illustration: A composite of photographs showing Sathya SaiBaba giving darshan at His ashram at Puttaparthi. ©Michael Cook

ISBN 0-9629835-3-5

Printed in the United States of America by McNaughton & Gunn, Inc.

DISTRIBUTED BY
SATHYA SAI BOOK CENTER
OF AMERICA
305 W. FIRST STREET
TUSTIN, CA 92780, USA
714-669-0522

This book is dedicated with veneration and devotion to Sri Satya Sai Baba, without whose inspiration and divine inner guidance it could never have been written.

Contents

Birth Of A Book
(with Acknowledgements)

I thought that my voyage had come to its end, that the path before me was closed, that provisions were exhausted and the time come to take shelter in a silent obscurity. But I find that Thy will knows no end in me, and when old words die out on the tongue, new melodies break forth from the heart, and where the old tracks are lost, new country is revealed with its wonders.

RABRINDINATH TAGORE

BEFORE I CAME into Sai Baba's private interview, near the end of 1989, I had accepted unhappily the prospect of a silent rest from the labours of writing, which had been my life and joy for many years. As Swami knew, through retinal haemorrhages into both eyes, I was quite unable to read or write. All I had was minimal peripheral vision in one eye. But in a firm, commanding voice he said, "You must write the book that's in there." He patted my chest. "Go home and write it and bring it back to me in two years."

My wife and two friends who were present in the room looked startled at this royal command. "May he have a co-author to help him?" asked my wife.

"No," replied Swami. "He must write his own book. I will give him all the help he needs."

I knew that I must somehow carry out this task set me by my divine Master. But how? For many years my writing had been born of a happy partnership between me and an old typewriter. The art of prose writing demanded that I work with words and phrases on the written page, polishing towards perfection or as near to it as attainable. To reach a satisfactory standard in prose expression through auditory means would be quite impossible for me. Yet I must make the attempt.

The Lord Sai's help is often given through the hands of others. I saw the first signs of this when a dictaphone and other equipment necessary almost fell into my lap. This was mainly through the help of some occupational therapists at Concord Hospital, Sydney. In the main I want to thank Marcia Davies there for starting me off on this new, unfamiliar road to creative writing.

The author with Satya Sai Baba who blesses the manuscript of this book.

At first it seemed so hopelessly cumbersome that I almost lost heart. Many drafts came through the dictaphone onto cassettes before it began to sound anything like acceptable. But would I be able to get it onto paper in type large enough for me to edit? Several ladies, Sai devotees with secretarial skill and modern technical equipment, offered to help in this. They were like angels sent directly by Lord Sai. My thanks go to them all. One in particular who came forward, telling me that she was purchasing laser printing equipment specially for the work, was Frances Pearce, herself an experienced author. She would transcribe the cassettes into words of a size and clarity that I could read and sub-edit on paper. Her confidence and genuine desire to give this wonderful Sai service swept away my doubts and defences. My heartfelt gratitude to Fran is beyond all expression.

In the event, we found that to put the book into words large enough for me to read, even with the laser printing, would probably deplete Australia's paper supplies. At this juncture, to solve a problem, another Sai helper with secretarial experience came forward. This was Stephanie Bugmann of our own Satya Sai Centre in the Blue Mountains. Sentence by sentence, with great patience, she read to me the printed chapters from Fran, making any alterations I required. In this way I was able to edit the book by ear. I am very grateful to Stephanie for her patience and skill in this work.

Finally, before the chapters went back to Fran for the final print-out, my wife, Iris, read the edited version to me for checking and the best fine-tuning I could manage for my first spoken book. My very deep gratitude goes to my wife. Without her help in research, in speaking quotations and other matter onto reference tapes and her continual support in many ways, I certainly could never have written the book.

Finally I would like to express my sincere thanks to all those friends, too numerous to name, who have helped me in this fulfilling and rewarding task of serving as an instrument of Bhagavan Sri Satya Sai Baba.

What is it about?

When Sai Baba touched the area of my heart with the magic wand of his hand and said, "It's all in there. Write it," I felt sure that he meant me to express what had been simmering inside me for some time. In this, my fourth book about Sai Baba, I must attempt two things, neither of them easy. One was that I must tell about my odyssey to him. Autobiographies are only of interest about people who have become famous and thus raised curiosity about their lives in the public mind. So this must not be a full-blown autobiography. It must give the salient points in a life that has been a search and a preparation. A search for life's meaning and a preparation for the work to be done when the Light of meaning begins to dawn. In this way the voyage of discovery, though unique in its details, as every life is, may reveal the essence of everyman's journey. Hopefully, it may help each reader to understand his own search for the meaning of life's mystery. In a sense it is a part of man's pilgrimage from what he is to what he hopes to be.

Finding the insight that will pierce through the debris of daily events to find the myth of inner meaning in one's own life is no easy task. Any degree of success achieved in this is undoubtedly through the grace of God. The second task was no less difficult. It was to show how, after I came to Sai Baba, he gradually revealed himself to me as God. It was to show how in his unique and wondrous way he draws people around him from all parts of the world. It should endeavour to show how he brings greater and deeper understanding of life's purpose and a higher degree of happiness to the individual and thereby to the life of mankind. It would hope to throw some light on his cosmic, universal revelation and his significance in the forward evolution of humanity.

Myths, legends and fables

The deeper meanings of some myths, legends and fables can throw light on man's own life journey. Some reference is made to three of these throughout the text of the book, so I will give an outline of these stories here for the benefit of the reader who is not acquainted with them.

One is the medieval European myth of Parsifal. This myth belongs to the days of King Arthur and the Round Table. Folklore of different nations has changed the details a good deal, but fundamentally the story remains the same. It concerns one man's quest for the Holy Grail. Originally this meant the chalice of the Last Supper before the Crucifixion of Christ, but it had acquired a wider significance. It symbolised the chalice that contains the precious, mysterious inner meaning of life, that which will bring enlightenment to man's darkness. It has been called the pearl of great price for which all souls hunger.

The hero of the tale is an unsophisticated country youth named Parsifal. Early in his quest he finds the Grail castle, the place where the Grail is kept, and has a vision of the chalice but the vision vanishes immediately and Parsifal is left with nothing but the Grail hunger. The word 'Grail' is related in its root to the word 'gradual', which implies that the finding of the Grail is a gradual process. This is a lesson that Parsifal learns. As a valiant knight, he becomes a member of the Round Table. He travels a great deal in his search, having many adventures, slaying dragons, overthrowing other knights, helping damsels in distress. For a time he even forgets about his search but, being reminded of it, he sets out again with great determination. If he finds it, this time he will ask the right question so that instead of vanishing the Grail will crown his life with true spiritual success.

His arduous, intense search is finally rewarded. He sees and enters the Grail castle. Within the castle are many knights and ladies, the chief of them being one called the Fisher King. He has been deeply wounded by a taste of the highest truth before he is ready to assimilate it. Now all he can do is fish, which symbolises working on himself through some creative activity. Through his suffering, the whole neighbourhood is unhappy, poor, unproductive. Some versions of the story say that Parsifal's question must be, "What ails thee, brother?" to the Fisher King. Such a question reveals the compassion that will save the world. But the most important question he must ask is, "Whom does the Grail serve?" Then he receives the answer, "The Grail serves the Grail King who has resided in the innermost room of the castle since time immemorial."

The Grail King is a symbol of man's inner God. When Parsifal assimilates this answer, his quest is over, he has reached salvation. Furthermore, the Fisher King is healed and the whole neighbourhood, symbolising humanity, becomes happy, peaceful and prosperous.

Another story that holds at its deepest levels of meaning the story of mankind is Homer's classical legend of Odysseus. On the surface, this is the story of the hero's monumental struggles and difficulties to reach his precious island home after years spent at the Trojan Wars. Esoterically, it is the story of a soul after it has heard the call from its true spiritual home. It turns its back on the blind conflicts of the world, symbolised by the Trojan Wars, and sets its sights on the home of peace and bliss that it left long ago.

But this conscious journey to the longed-for destination is fraught with many difficulties and obstacles. An early one is the conquest of the Cyclopean giant, a symbol of the individual's own brute nature. In another adventure he is held prisoner for many years by the possessive love of the sea-nymph Calypso. Only by divine grace, represented by the Olympian gods, is he able to cut this binding tie and continue on his homeward journey.

But there are many more obstacles on the homeward voyage. One of them is the witch, Circe, who turns some of his men to pigs. Odysseus was due for the same fate, had he not overpowered the witch and made her serve him. Then she helps him on his way with great resourcefulness. We can take Circe as a symbol of man's lower mind, which will serve the lower animal nature but can be made to serve the high spiritual aspirations. The spiritual power in the human being can turn black into white magic.

The hero has to descend to the dangerous lower world, the nether world, to receive final directions for his homeward journey. The soul must sink to the lowest before it can reach the highest. Sai Baba teaches that only from the firm springboard of earth, not from any of the intermediate planes, can man make the great leap to Liberation in the spiritual realm beyond the manifested universe. Perhaps this truth is represented in Odyssseus' essential visit to the lowest plane.

Among the hero's last adventures is his temptation in passing the isle of the Sirens. These sweetest of sweet singers represent the false prophet. Their songs are the sweet enticing words of false teachers who seem on the surface to be giving the truth but basically their teachings are false and will lead to delusion, death and destruction. Odysseus passes through and away from this temptation by being lashed to the mast of his ship. This could symbolise the firm mast of eternal truth expounded by the *paramguru* or true spiritual teacher.

Even when the hero reaches the shores of his own island, he could not have broken through the barrier to his home without the assistance of divine grace given in the form of the goddess Athena, the divine form that the hero worships. She dresses him as a beggar and enhances his courage and confidence that enable him to overcome his final enemies and break through to the inner sanctuary of his true home. In like manner, when the soul comes to the outer court of its home, it must be divested of its final possessions and approach the door with the courage and confidence of Truth. Then the grace of God, divine love in action, will aid it to break through the final barrier to the innermost temple of eternal peace and joy.

Finally there is the parable of the prodigal son. In this well-known fable, a son receives the heritage that is his birthright and goes forth from the shelter of his home into the world. There he goes through all the ups and downs that are a part of worldly life. He enjoys all the sensory pleasure of the fleshpots and suffers the pains that these inevitably bring. Eventually, having squandered his heritage, he sinks to the very lowest. On the very edge of starvation, he suddenly remembers his father's home and contrasts its peace and joy with his life of suffering in the world. Having learned the hard lessons that material life gives, he decides to return home.

The fable does not relate the events of that return journey but describes the joy of his arrival when his waiting father sees him from a long way of and goes out to meet him. With great love and rejoicing, the father welcomes his son back into his family home.

This, in fable form, is the story of the human soul's journey. Leaving its spiritual home, the Godhead, in the form of a monad of consciousness, it travels the journey of necessity through the material kingdoms for a very long period of time, a whole series of what we call human lifetimes. Then, having learned the hard, necessary lessons of earth life, the memory of its true home comes to it like a faint, far-off bugle call. Then it begins its return journey homeward. Whether the homeward journey be long or short, one lifetime or several, near its end the love of God comes out to meet and welcome the returning pilgrim soul and bear it with joy and rejoicing into its eternal spiritual home.

It has been a circuitous journey, beginning and ending in the same place, but the prodigal son, or pilgrim soul, that went forth as a speck of primitive consciousness returns as a fully evolved being of divine consciousness. It now knows itself as being one with God and is ready to share in the life of the divine.

Mandorla

This word from medieval Christian theology will not be found in the average modern English dictionary. It is the name of a geometrical figure found in some Christian cathedrals. The figure consists of two intersecting circles. The portion shared by the two circles is in the shape of an almond and that is how the figure acquires its name. *Mandorla* is the Italian word for almond. The almond may be large or small, depending to what extent the two circles overlap each other. Actually the figure is an excellent representation of a great truth of our earthly existence. One circle represents the material world, the other the spiritual realm. We should live our lives in the almond-shaped intersection of the two circles. If he is entirely in the one circle of earth, man is living the dark animal life within the brain. He cannot, however, live entirely in the circle of spirit and still keep his feet on earth. Whenever a mandorla is shown in the great cathedrals either the figure of Jesus or the Virgin Mary is placed in the almond of the two intersecting circles. Even the greatest Avatar of God must live in the mandorla, for he must have a material body and bear the burden of earthly nature while he is here. But the overlap of the circle of spirit will be very great for him.

As a man makes progress on the spiritual path, the mandorla or almond of his existence will increase in size, but if the shining circle of spirit overlaps the dark circle of earth completely, as in the case of Self-realisation, the individual will no longer keep his feet on earth. We look at some exceptions to this and discuss the reasons for the exceptions in the text of the book.

Man in his journey towards God may have passing glimpses of the divine within the dark shadows of his life. This may come in the form of Light, bliss, a sudden uplift of consciousness or in several other ways. It can be regarded as a momentary dip of the circle of spirit more deeply into the dark circle of earth. The aim of the searcher, the pilgrim soul hungry for Light, is to bring the circle of the spiritual world further and further into the circle of earth until his almond-shaped segment, his mandorla, is as large as it can be while he must still keep one foot on the earth.

PART ONE

CHINKS IN THE WALL OF *MAYA*

(The phenomenal universe)

When all around is darkness,
How can I know there's light?
I know because I've glimpsed it,
A radiance sweet and rare,
Through chinks between the moments,
Through molecules of air.

1. Window In Heaven

But trailing clouds of glory do we come
From God, who is our home:
Heaven lies about us in our infancy!

WORDSWORTH

FROM WHEREVER MY journey to earth might have begun, I arrived in Tasmania, Australia, on November 4th, 1906. I have no doubt, however, that Wordsworth touches a truth about recollections of early childhood, for the years of my youth were haunted by vague memories of some glorious place far away. Sometimes the memories seemed to be calling me and would have taken me back, five or six years later, had not some stronger power held me firmly on earth. I understand now, though of course I had no idea then, why I was meant to live this life. About half a century later, Sai Baba revealed to me the two main purposes of my life, both equally important. And they are what this book is really about.

My near brush with death happened on my father's farm in Northern Tasmania. I was playing with my sister Rita, seventeen months my senior, in a green meadow sloping down from the gate of our farmyard. We were beyond the watchful eye of our mother, busy no doubt in the farmhouse. We could see our father some distance away across the fields engrossed in some harvesting job with his farm labourers. It would be safe, we thought, to go and play by the forbidden willow-encircled pond. We had been warned that the pond was deep and dangerous but its dark still waters, rising just below the bank in some places, were a great temptation for the game of boats. So we began to play, using whatever suitable sticks we could find to represent our boats. All might have been well had not my boat got stuck behind a small floating log, near to the bank but not near enough to reach. My child mind figured out that the floating log would have the buoyancy to hold me up if I stepped on it. This would be the way to retrieve my stuck boat. So I stepped on it and, as it was small, it gave way immediately under my weight. Down I went through the dark brackish waters to the muddy bottom, some nine feet below. I rose to the surface, gasped air in terror, then sank again. It may have been the third time that my face broke the water that I saw a small root of a willow projecting from the bank within my reach. I grasped it and tried to pull myself up the steep slippery bank.

I became aware of my sister running around the pond, like a wild thing, screaming and beating on a tin can she was carrying, but my father was too far away to hear her clamour, and my mother was out of earshot behind walls. There was no-one to help me but as my hands slipped on the wet willow root and my bare feet could find no hold on the steep wall of the bank, and I felt I was sliding back to a dark watery death, some mysterious help came from below. It was as if unseen hands were pushing me upwards until I was clear of the water and standing on the bank. My sister stopped her clamour and stood staring at me as if she were looking at a miracle. Then, with brackish water streaming from my clothes, I started to run up the grassy hill towards home. With the great shock of my near shave with death, I was screaming even louder than my sister had. My bare foot must have trodden on a bee, busy sucking nectar from a clover flower. He stung me on the middle of the sole and the pain of it made me shout and cry louder than ever. Before I reached the top of the hill, my mother suddenly appeared there and ran down the hill to meet me. Soon I was enfolded in her protective arms and being taken back to the farmhouse to be dried and comforted. My mother, so shaken by my near brush with death, could only say, "You must never go near waterholes or rivers until you learn to swim." As she was my goddess of Love, she was permitted such paradoxical remarks.

To my young eyes she was the very embodiment of beauty too, with tender grey eyes set wide apart and a small straight nose leading down to a soft mobile mouth and a cleft chin. As these were the days before World War I that revolutionised women's fashions, she wore voluminous Edwardian skirts flaring out from a corsetted waist. At the age of about thirty-three years she was to my eyes so beautiful that I wondered why she had not been chosen as Queen of the British Empire instead of the present Queen. My mother, whose name was Caroline, was a daughter of John Presnell of Ross in central Tasmania. A lay preacher and pillar of the Methodist Church of that small town, he taught his family to live according to the strict Christian precepts as laid down by the great evangelist John Wesley. Of John Presnell's large Victorian family, my mother was probably his best pupil. Sai Baba has said that the mother should be the child's first *guru* or spiritual teacher, and this my mother certainly was, to the best of her knowledge and ability.

From her we learned of the great Father God in Heaven who watched over us every moment of the day and night. We learned too of his only son Jesus Christ who had spent time teaching on earth and been cruelly crucified on a cross. He had died in this way that our sins might be forgiven by the Father. If in our daily prayers we asked for our sins to be forgiven in the name of Jesus Christ, the Father would forgive us and wash away the stains of our sins. Inside of us there was the still, small voice of conscience, which told us how to behave. If we followed this instead of doing just what we wanted and if we sought God's forgiveness when we made mistakes, we would after death go to Heaven to be with the angels who hovered around the throne of God playing on golden harps and living lives of great happiness. We liked the idea of being angels because they had wings and could fly where they wished like the birds. On the other hand, if we disregarded the commandments of God, as taught in the Bible, and lived sinful, unrepentant lives, we would go at death to a place that did not bear thinking about. This was a place where sinners suffered the torments and agony of eternal flames. It was called Hell. This was a place to be avoided at all costs. So, knowing that God had his all-seeing eye on us, we did our best to be good and prayed for forgiveness every evening before we went to bed in case we had slipped up somewhere. Because I often felt like a stranger on earth, as if I did not really belong here but had been dropped from some other place, I thought that I perhaps had come somehow from Heaven. Heaven did seem somehow to lie about me in my childhood. This was certainly not part of my mother's theology. She told us that our souls had been made by God at the time we were born on earth. I wonder, however, if my elusive, haunting memories were not perhaps connected with a strange vision I had some time later when I was about seven years old.

Rita, my sister, and I were playing on Sunday afternoon just behind the farmhouse on the edge of a field of oats. The oats were fully grown, tall, green, with silvery heads. They would soon be ready for harvesting and we knew better than to run into them and tread some of them down. But we made a wonderful discovery: a path that led into the oat crop. It was a narrow path just wide enough for one person to walk at a time. So we set off on it in Indian file. The ground beneath us was bare, the ears of the oats stood just above our heads. The path did not go straight but wound in different directions. We knew it would not have been man-made. "Perhaps the fairies made it," my sister said. If so, I thought, it could lead to some enchanted spot. A tinge of apprehension touched my mind but curiosity lured us both onward. The path seemed endless and then suddenly it led us into a bare space, a space as large as a medium-sized room, with not one stalk of oats or blade of grass growing on it. The bare, reddish-brown earth looked warm and inviting. So in the middle of this fairytale room, we threw ourselves down and lay on our backs looking up at the cloudless blue sky above us. Not a word was spoken between us, while the sun shone down and the peaceful silence was broken only by the occasional rustle of the silvery ears above the green wall that surrounded us on all sides.

As I gazed upwards into the blue, absorbed in the beauty of this dome-like roof of the world, suddenly a window appeared in the roof. Beyond the window was a glorious scene that made me feel I was looking into Heaven. There was a radiant light shining on white or light-coloured buildings in the background. In the foreground were figures moving about as if in a street scene. Their robes were of rich colours with red and gold predominating. I could see some of their faces which to me looked wise, benign and somehow noble. I remember too that there was a soft drift of heavenly music coming through the window and reaching my ears as I lay on my back among the silent oats. A wave of bliss flooded through me as time stood still. Then as suddenly as it had come, the window disappeared, leaving nothing but the clear blue of the sky. But I knew that the radiant, heavenly scene in the sky had been as real while it lasted as the oats around me and the warm earth beneath my back. Was it really Heaven I had been looking into, I wondered, but I had not seen the golden throne of God, and the figures moving about did not have wings, as angels should, according to my mother.

My sister, lying a few feet away, had fallen asleep. The afternoon was growing colder as the sun sank towards the horizon. I called to my sister that it was time to go home. As she stood up, smiling sweetly, I did not tell her about my window in the sky, for perhaps I was afraid that she would say it was just a daydream. But I knew that it was real, just as real as the oats around us and the hills and mountains that lay beyond our farming district. We left the enchanted room and as the day was nearing its end, hurried back along the winding path. We went through the gate and into the big farmyard with stables and sheds and barns surrounding it, and ran into the house where our mother was busy preparing the evening meal. She asked us where we had been and we told her about the winding path and the enchanted room in the middle of the oats. She offered no explanation of this mystery, probably thinking that it was part of our childish imagination. But I did not tell her about my window in the sky, neither then nor ever. I probably thought that she would not believe its reality and I did not want my wonderful vision to be spoilt by anyone's disbelief.

I wondered if I could tell my father, whose arrival home was heralded by the sound of voices, harness and chains. I ran down the yard to greet him and watch the exciting drama of the horses being stabled and fed. I loved the warm, pungent smell of the stable, the sound of the horses munching their chaff. It made me feel part of the earth again and I did not tell my father about my window in the sky as I walked with him in the twilight up the cobbled slope to the farmhouse. I watched him take off his battered felt hat, revealing black hair beginning to thin above his high intelligent forehead. His eyes were warm and brown on either side of a prominent nose with flaring nostrils. Under the nose was a curling Edwardian moustache. I remember my father as a good comrade with whom I had hunted the kangaroo and possum in the wooded hills around, fished in the Meander River, played cricket in the orchard and helped in my own small way with jobs about the farm. I remember how on rainy days we would sit together in the barn watching the falling rain through the doorway while he told me stories. Some of these were about his boyhood and his family memories. His father, Samuel Murphet, had been one of four brothers, young men who with their father had come out from Cambridgeshire in England and taken up land in Tasmania. Their sons and grandsons had followed in their fathers' footsteps and now there was a goodly tribe of farming Murphets in different parts of the island. I too looked forward to following the same farming tradition, when the slow-moving years had taken me to my fourteenth birthday and I was legally able to leave school.

My father left discipline in my mother's capable hands. Sometimes, however, he would roar like a lion when we did something wrong and then immediately look ashamed of himself. But I remember one occasion when I was about four and, trying to help him in some job, caused him to hit his fingers with a hammer. He shouted that I was useless and called to my sister Rita to help him. She always had the practical skills of a boy. Buried deep in my subconscious, this childhood incident may have been the cause of the inferiority complex I carried with me for years. Though a handicap in many ways, this complex was conversely the spur that drove the horse of my willpower over many difficult fences. Though my gentle mother sometimes stung my bare legs with a swishing cane, I knew deep down that the hand of discipline was wielded from the heart of love. So I always forgave her quickly for hurting me and, indeed, loved her more than I did my father. In retrospect I wonder, however, if her moral code was too stern and rigid. The effects of her training and influence held me in firm traces through my adolescent years. When I did finally break from the confining harness, my revolt was at first guilt-ridden, always secret and sometimes unrestrained.

When I was ten years of age, my twin sister Leone was born. How twins can be born ten years apart is certainly a mystery, but many years later, in fact in 1970, when I told Sai Baba that I was going to America to see my sister, whom I had never previously mentioned to him, he was silent for a moment, then holding up two fingers twisted together he said that Leone and I were twin souls. This explained things that had puzzled me through the years: why, for example, she always seemed to know what I was thinking or feeling before I spoke; why she always seemed to know it by some psychic sense. Once, for example, her head felt the bump when my head hit the road in a motorcycle accident some twenty miles distant. No two people could have understood each other better than did Leone and myself. Physically she was not my replica in appearance but enough like me to trouble my adolescent years.

Her appearance on the scene of earth brought a change in my life. Suddenly I felt grown-up. I was to help my father on the farm as well as any farm labourer could or did. During the next few years while my mother remonstrated that I was being treated like a grown man, I learned to do practically everything on a farm, to work a team of horses, ploughing, cultivating, harrowing, sowing, even building haystacks. Of course I could ride a horse to round up cattle and work the dogs to round up the sheep. So before I could leave school officially and spend my life on the land, I had, to my own delight and my father's satisfaction, become a practical farmer. This was helped by the fact that for some six months leading into my final year at school the lady teacher of the one-teacher Westwood State School had married a farmer and resigned. Because the number of pupils at the school had fallen below the minimum required for a teacher to be sent, the Westwood State School remained closed. I hoped that it would remain so until I reached my fourteenth birthday, when I could leave forever the smell of ink and paper and chalk. It would be like leaving prison. But fate willed it otherwise. A new family with a number of school-age children moved into the district. The number of pupils rose to the required level and some time before the middle of my fourteenth year, the Education Department sent another teacher and the little weatherboard school beyond the far corner of our farm opened its doors again. The new teacher was destined not only to frustrate my dream of immediate freedom but to change the whole course of my life.

With the new phase of life about to begin, my secret window in Heaven faded into the background of my mind, but as my first glimpse of the Grail castle, through a chink in the wall of *maya*, it was my reassurance that a radiant reality existed beyond this world. And so, hidden beneath the scenes, the window no doubt remained a persistent influence on my life.

2. Widening Horizons

Let Knowledge grow from more to more,
But more of reverence in us dwell;
That mind and soul, according well,
May make one music as before.

TENNYSON

IT WAS ON the day that the new teacher read aloud a passage of English poetry in the little pine-lined schoolroom that the ship of my life changed its course. The twin spirits of Beauty and Truth stole in through the windows and took their permanent abode in my heart. My boyhood love of the farmyard smells was replaced by something else, something like a yearning for far-off things, haunting but intangible. It was past the middle of that fateful year of 1920 when the teacher, who had brought me the love of poetry, said something that made me jump almost out of my desk. "I would like you to sit for the Qualifying Examination at the end of this year," she said, then seeing my expression, she added, "I will help you with the extra study you will have to do to make up for lost time and I think you will have a good chance of passing." She was talking about the tough entrance examination to the State High School, that impressive temple of learning which I had once glimpsed without much interest while on a visit to the city of Launceston some fourteen miles away. Her unexpected faith in my abilities gave a pleasant lift to my self-esteem and a desire to meet the challenge. None of the homespun youngsters from this small country school had ever made such an attempt before. My mother, who was a great lover of learning, was delighted when I told her the news and my father dubiously agreed that I should try. I think his agreement was a result of my mother's influence. His farmer friends were stunned to a pipe-smoking silence when they heard the news but their wives talked for them, mainly to the effect that it was a foolish attempt and I would not have a chance of passing.

The next few months found me getting up very early to milk my quota of cows and reach the school about an hour before the regular opening time. My earnest, inspiring teacher would be there with much already written on the blackboard, as part of her coaching to try to make up for all I had missed during the many months that the school had been closed. I found myself enjoying the extra study. Finally, towards the end of November, the day of examination arrived. It was to take place at a big city school in Launceston. In its grounds among the wisecracking city kids, I felt very much the country yokel. My self-confidence was at a low ebb when the bell sounded for us to go into the examination room. When the ordeal was over, I found my mother waiting with horse and phaeton to drive me home. It was about a two-hour drive and, as the horse's hooves clopped up hill and down dale, I thought about the answers I had written. When my mother with anxious eyes asked me how I thought I had fared, I honestly replied that I did not know, but felt that the odds were against my passing.

One day during December, when the schools were closed for Christmas holidays, and harvesting was at its height on all the farms, I rode my bicycle up the long hill to the house where the mail and daily newspapers were collected. I knew that the results of the Qualifying Examination would be published that day. Nervously I opened the daily newspaper and searched through its columns. Then for the first time in my life I saw my own name in print. I had passed the examination. I was almost shouting with joy and a feeling of triumph as I cycled madly down the long hill towards home. Now having proved myself to the army of doubters, I could perhaps have done what my father wished and thrown away the books to join him on the farm. But the call to faraway, intangible things, like soft, mysterious voices from distant places, proved too strong. "I would just like to try the High School for a year or two and then come back to the farm," I told my father and my conscience. My staunch little mother with shy determination took me to the Headmaster of Launceston High School on opening day, then she left me alone in the enticing odour of new books, and the wisps of pungent smells from the science laboratory, at the doorway to a new world.

It was as if my reasoning faculties and imagination had previously been cramped up in a small room and found themselves suddenly released into an exhilarating wider world through the avenues of Mathematics, Science and English Literature. Through Maths, Chemistry and Physics I was in a new age of probing reason. Through the Classics I was wandering back through vistas of time to worlds previously undreamed of. Through English Literature I was in green pastures that are timeless.

After two years of this stimulating mind expansion, with the promise of more to come, I had no desire to return to the confined world of the farm, though I was always happy to go home on holidays. In the long Christmas vacations I eased my conscience by working doubly hard at the harvesting. I saved my father the wages of about one-and-a-half farm labourers, I told myself. I was always glad, however, when working holidays were over and the academic year began again.

At the age of sixteen I did not, in fact, return to the High School. Instead I became a pupil at the Launceston Church of England Grammar School where a friend of my father's, and my own boyhood hero, had just joined the teaching staff. This school, the oldest secondary school of continued existence in Australia, was proud of its traditions. The pupils took their academic studies more seriously than had my friends at High School and there was even more emphasis on cricket, football and other school sports. Moreover, character-building and the principles of honourable, ethical behaviour were given great emphasis.

At about this time, I myself began to feel the strong altruistic urge that is experienced by many teenagers. I wanted to spend my life in a career that would somehow do good for humanity. I must, I felt, play my part in lifting mankind above the mire of ignorance in which it was at present wallowing. My own search for meaning had taken me, during my High School days, to the churches of practically every denomination in the city of Launceston. Ultimate meanings still eluded me, but could there be any better avenue of search for both me and for mankind than religion? I was beginning to understand that, though the rational mind could take me to very wide horizons, the answers I sought always lay just beyond those horizons.

I was about seventeen when I told my headmaster that I wanted to become a minister of the Church of England. Being himself an ordained minister of that church, he seemed quite pleased. So during my last year at secondary school I began to receive, in addition to my academic studies, instruction in the doctrines and dogma, the creeds and rituals of the Anglican Church. But by the time I had passed my Matriculation Examination for the University of Tasmania, a doubt was filling my mind. I became aware that the rational training I had received through Science and Mathematics made it difficult for me to accept the religious teachings and practices of the Church. How could I lead people in a ritual that had no meaning for me? How could I teach them a theology in which I could not myself believe? No, I would simply be a hypocrite earning my living in the Church but doing no good for mankind, perhaps indeed only leading them into greater darkness. So I changed my mind about becoming a minister of the Church. My headmaster took my decision resignedly, while my father was pleased. He thought that I might now at long last return to the land. But how could I help to raise the level of humanity by turning the furrows to grow oats and barley? No, there was no turning back. But which way to turn, that was the question.

After considerable deliberation, I concluded that the best point of attack for bringing a revolutionary change in the thought and life of mankind was through children. Whereas the thought of adults was set into habits and patterns and was therefore difficult to change, the minds of the young could be easily moulded and turned into the right directions of thought and feeling. Surely education must be the right career for me. I would train to be a school teacher. This decision led me to the Teachers' Training College and the University of Tasmania, side by side on the Hobart Domain. As a student in these two institutions, I learned much about the art of teaching, while studying appropriate subjects in the University Arts Course. The main ones of these were Psychology, Logic, Ethics and Philosophy, Education, which was a study of the theory and practice of education during the last few centuries, the History of England and my greatest love in the academic world, English Literature. Studies in this latter subject were conducted at both the Teachers' College and the University; the two lecturers concerned were an important influence in my life.

One of these was the Principal of the Teachers' College, a lovable character named Johnson but always known affectionately as 'Johnno'. He was tall, elegant, silvery-haired with the drooping eyelids of genius. Somehow he seemed to be the very embodiment of English poetry and always had the apt quotation for every occasion. For example, once when he passed a group of women students chattering loudly on the stairs, I heard him quote from *King Lear*: "Her voice was ever soft, / Gentle and low, an excellent thing in woman." You could have heard a penny drop in the shamed silence that followed his remark. He greatly increased my love of poetry and I think every trainee teacher who came under his influence must have developed such a love. Under him we studied two of Shakespeare's plays and other gems of English Literature. He appointed me as editor of the College magazine and in many ways encouraged my creative writing. Thus he sowed some of the seeds of my ambition to become a writer.

Further, such seeds were sown and nurtured by the Professor of English Literature at the University. Whereas Johnno's attitude towards the writings of the great masters was reverential, Professor

Taylor's was iconoclastic. He had the fresh critical approach that stimulated original thinking among his students. His lectures were enjoyable and refreshing. The high awards he gave me in my regular essays and in the periodic examinations influenced me to try my hand as soon as possible as a professional writer. I could combine this with my school teaching career, I thought. Then while moulding the minds of youth I will be practising and perfecting the writing craft in order that some time in the future I would be able to write something worthwhile for mankind. What this something was, I had no idea at the time. But it had to be something that would bring a better understanding and a better way of life for many people.

Though the road to professional authorship proved to be more difficult and more disciplined that I had imagined, I did manage during my few years as a teacher to get my feet on the first rung of the ladder of professional writing by having some short stories and articles accepted by a few Australian journals. I also attempted some short lyrical poems but these, falling far short of the gems I loved, I kept hidden away. Eventually most of them were left to disintegrate in old boxes and chests in cellars and attics of my island home while I travelled the world. This, I think, is the fate they deserved.

As for my dream of shaking and moving the world through the classrooms of Tasmania, it proved to be no more than that, just a dream impossible of realisation. My University study in the subject of Education had shown me that systems of education had been always faulty, sometimes indeed criminally ignorant. They had led the new generations not towards enlightenment but into darkness where their parents lived. But now through the growth of the sciences, especially Psychology and the Social Sciences, I thought and hoped that things would be different. Young minds are naturally eager for knowledge, eager for an understanding of the mysteries of the world around them, eager for certain, sure guidance in the way to live. Surely now, I thought, teachers can offer their pupils what they long for and need, and teaching will become a noble profession. But, alas, it was not so. The system of education ignored the hunger and thirst of youth. It set the syllabus of subjects and standards targeted towards public examinations. The children had to be crammed with facts in order to spill them out copiously through their pens on the examination papers. For the future livelihood of both the pupil and the teacher a good standard of examination results had to be achieved. A child's natural desire for knowledge and inner development was deadened and killed. In brief, the purpose of the schools was to teach the pupils how to make a living, not how to live. The system had even worsened in the few years since I had been a boy at State School. Then at least there was the occasional Scripture lesson given by a minister from one of the churches. Now no attempt at teaching spirituality was made. Moreover, the pressing need to reach examination standards in required subjects left no time, no leisure to lead young minds along the pathways of Beauty, no time to open their eyes in wonder at the grandeur and strange mysteries of Nature, no time for anything that was really educational. It was a terrible disillusionment to find myself caught up in the mechanics of a factory where knowledge was fed in at one end, called the classroom, and came out at the other, called the examination room. By the end of my first year as a teacher, I had realised the futility of my altruistic dream, my dream of laying the foundation stones for a new world in the classrooms of Tasmania. The idea was laughable and, thank God, I still had my sense of humour. I would have resigned then but I was bonded to teach for four years to pay for my training at the Teachers' College and University.

Some years earlier a Hindu astrologer visiting Tasmania read my horoscope and told me that I would leave Tasmania and travel the world. I would find my star in the East, the star of my true destiny. When I asked him how long I would be away, he said that it had been twenty-five years since his last visit to Tasmania and that I would be away much longer than that. Now, as the end of my bonded years was in sight, I began to feel an urge to be off into that wide, untravelled world that awaited my exploring, but I needed a sign, an opening door that would suggest a line of action.

It came during a short holiday in Melbourne towards the end of my teaching period. There I met a man, coincidentally it seemed, who invited me to partner him in launching a suburban newspaper in one of the Melbourne suburbs that was not already served in this way. The idea appealed to me, so just as soon as possible, I ended my teaching career and set sail from my island home towards pastures new. It was the beginning of the long road that wound through the maze of the years towards my promised star of meaning.

3. Destiny's Moving Finger

There's a divinity that shapes our ends,
Rough-hew them how we will.

WILLIAM SHAKESPEARE

WHEN I MADE contact with my friend in Melbourne, he told me that he had changed his mind about risking his capital in launching a suburban newspaper. He was an English pensioner from World War I and I sensed that he did not have much capital to risk anyway. This was fate's first obstacle in the long obstacle-course that lay hidden before me. I remembered my father's warning not to leave a safe job and jump into the great unknown, especially at this time in the middle of the Great Depression. The very thought of stepping out of safety and facing the hazards of life had stimulated me and I was not about to be beaten at this first setback. On investigation, I found that the venture would not take much capital anyway, so I decided to go it alone.

It was to be a four-page paper distributed freely to the residents of the suburb, so I had to sell enough advertising space to cover the costs of printing and distributing and leave me a reasonable margin of profit. I sold the advertising space to the local business people and filled the rest of the paper with news stories of local interest. I gathered and wrote these stories myself. For distribution I employed my British army pensioner friend. He was glad to warm up his 'cold feet' by walking along the streets of the suburb and delivering a copy to each house. He was also glad of the extra money it brought him to supplement his small pension. I was working hard but enjoying it and my weekly profit was more than I could have earned in wages as a newspaper reporter, so the venture was a success. But there was a fatal flaw that would prevent its continued success over a long period. The bulk of the potential advertisers were large retail furnishing stores and these drew their customers from all parts of Melbourne. Therefore their most appropriate advertising media were the large metropolitan newspapers and journals. So I was glad when another opportunity offered and I was able to close my paper down before it became unprofitable.

The new opening was employment with an evening metropolitan newspaper that had not long started its life in bold competition with the long established Melbourne evening paper, *The Herald.* The press pundits predicted that its life would not be long, but that did not trouble me. I would be in the meantime earning a living and gaining experience in the craft of writing and the profession of journalism. By this time I had made the firm decision to become an author. I knew from the lives of well-known authors that it was well-nigh impossible to make an adequate living from freelance writing early in the would-be author's career. A few had started off with the benefit of a private income, or support from a wealthy patron. A number had worked as journalists or advertising copywriters while perfecting their craft and learning some of the ropes of the writing profession. This was the road that I would attempt to take. So my time with the paper was only part of my apprenticeship for a serious authorship that I envisaged some time in the future.

Perhaps it was more than a coincidence that I happened to read the notice of an evening course in advertising copywriting. It was a three-months course conducted by a well-known advertising manager. I enrolled, and fortunately had completed the course with good marks and an encouraging testimonial from the tutor, before the evening paper on which I worked closed down. I found myself without a job. But my experience as a reporter had taught me the valuable knack of discerning a story in almost every event in life. This is simply to find the unusual, the unexpected facet or something amusing, something that reveals a quirk of human nature. So instead of looking for another job in Melbourne, I set off into the great Australian outback.

There I met and moved with the armies of young and middle-aged men who, having lost their regular jobs through the Depression, were wandering through the countryside in the hope of seasonal or occasional work. With them I picked grapes in the vineyards along the Murray River and did other work that came to hand. Of these the most memorable, because the hardest, was cutting swamp gum trees to a length suitable for feeding as fuel to an engine that was driving some irrigation machinery. The trees had fallen some years earlier and were now as hard as the axe I was using to cut them. Swinging the axe, with my torso bare from the waist up, in the burning Australian sun, I was, within a few weeks, almost as black as the Aborigines camped nearby. They spent their time more sensibly lying in the shade or fishing in the nearby river. By the time I saw my employer riding his horse through the trees to measure up the tonnage I had cut, I was physically fitter than I had ever been before but very glad that the job was over. I had cut sufficient, he said, and paid me my wages.

During this period my income was from two sources. One was the payment for the short, factual stories, anecdotes and sketches I wrote for various journals in Sydney and Melbourne, who were glad to have such material. My subject was life on the road or on the 'track', as my nomadic companions preferred to call it, and amusing facets of the picturesque characters I met along the way. This freelance work did not bring much monetary return, nor did the occasional manual jobs that came my way, but then the cost of living was low. Like my brothers of the road, I slept rolled in a blanket on the soft breast of Mother Earth. She charged me no rent, nor did the starry sky that was my only roof above. This is the road to the sweetest sleep. Sometimes we awoke with our faces wet with dew but always refreshed and renewed. If heavy rain was threatening we always found a position under a bridge or in some deserted hut. If the latter, I always felt stifled after my nights under the open sky and my sleep was only second best.

Generally the 'bagmen' seemed to think that the community owed them their food and were not averse to begging. But they never used the word 'beg'. It was always 'bite'. Perhaps they thought that this word made the act seem less demeaning. Though some great spiritual masters, such as Gautama the Buddha and Shirdi Sai Baba, carried their begging bowls as a religious ritual to give their fellow men the spiritual merit of giving, I myself had not reached this status with its accompanying humility to beg for food, even if it was called 'bite'. I always carried a small amount of money to buy the food I needed, though I was ashamed to let my fellow 'bagmen' know this.

Once this led me into a trap. I had gone with a fellow traveller known as Bill the Bagman into the shopping area of a small town to 'bite' some food for breakfast and the rest of the day. He had unconcernedly gone into several shops and in each case came out laden with supplies. Announcing that we had all that we needed except butter, Bill said to me pointedly, "It's your turn now to 'bite' the butter." We were standing in front of a very modern-looking shop that would today be called a mini-supermarket. I went in and bought half a pound of butter. When I came out, Bill looked at me with approval and some admiration. "That was a very good bite," he said, "in a shop like this." I was ashamed to tell him that I had actually bought it. After that I always did my shopping alone, instead of in the company of an experienced 'beggar' or 'biter'.

These nomads of the outback, born of the Great Depression and coming from many different walks of life, were like a sub-community within the general community. They had their own set of principles, ethics and loyalties. Though many were not averse to stealing where the opportunity offered, they would never steal from one another. Among them were a few men wanted by the police but they knew they were quite safe because their brothers of the road would never betray them. It seemed quite natural to them to share what they had with anyone who was in need and where help was required it was always forthcoming from naturally compassionate hearts. This spontaneous but sure brotherhood was warming to the soul. It seemed to give the lie to that mean state which is the usual image of the world. Perhaps in some distant day, I thought, the whole of mankind will be knit in such a staunch brotherhood.

After a few short months of the rugged wandering life, I felt qualified to attempt the test for the 'bagmen's' certificate of approval. This was to jump the Sydney Limited, the well-guarded express train that roared each night from Melbourne to Sydney like an iron monster with its plume of smoke trailing behind it. We had several times seen it from around our camp-fires on moonlit nights as it careered northward along its shining tracks, seeming proud, defiant and unapproachable.

With a friend of the road I made the attempt at Albury on the border of Victoria and New South Wales. Just before she left, the locomotive gave out a great cloud of steam and under cover of that we ran from our hiding place by a signal box and jumped onto a ledge around the tender where the steam locomotive carried its coal for the journey. There, or in the open concertina at the front of the leading carriage, we romped through the moonlit countryside on the great iron horse. Despite a few near shaves, such as when the engine was uncoupled at Junee to renew its supply of water, and we had to leap off quickly and jump on again just as the train was leaving, we finally managed to reach Sydney. There this phase of my life ended and I never went back on the road to claim the 'award of approval' for my success in jumping the Sydney Limited.

In Sydney I felt that I had come home, at least for the time being. In those far-off days, the city seemed to have a carefree, devil-may-care atmosphere about it. It seemed to say, "Any day you may walk down one of my sunlit streets, turn a corner and find something unexpected, wonderful and life-changing."

For the first few weeks in Sydney I continued freelance writing for various journals, using, in the main, material I had gathered on the outback trail. But this provided a very meagre living, hardly sufficient to pay my rent for the room in Paddington near Kings Cross plus my meals in cheap restaurants. So if I wanted to stay in Sydney, which I did, something had to be done fast. One day as I sauntered aimlessly along lower George Street, I turned a corner and was confronted with a large notice on the side of a building which brought me out of my reverie. The notice simply said 'School of Applied Advertising.' I went inside, met the Principal, obtained particulars of the school's curriculum and fees and told the Principal that I would enrol as soon as I had the money to spare. He seemed interested in my present situation. I revealed it to him honestly, told him about my newspaper experience and about the course in copywriting I had done in Melbourne. Looking at me thoughtfully, he said, "If you are interested in a job as a copywriter, I know where there is an opening right now. It is in one of the biggest and best advertising agencies in Sydney. No doubt they are looking for an experienced copywriter, but there would be no harm in your trying." Then he gave me the name and address of the agency together with the name of the Managing Director, whom I would have to see.

This was certainly a challenge. Feeling exhilarated at the prospect, I went back to my room and wrote several advertisements on imaginary products. One of the products was a beer with a name I had invented. These were the only samples of my skill as a copywriter that I had to show a prospective employer. The very next afternoon found me sitting in an office with the Managing Director of the advertising agency on the other side of an impressive polished desk. He was a pleasant, ruddy-faced Scotsman who, I learned later, was one of Sydney's champion beer-drinkers. He read my samples of advertising copy and seemed to be favourably impressed, especially with the one on beer. "But," he said, "I need someone who can write advertisements for two of our technical products. The man who is doing it now will be returning to our head office in London shortly and I need a suitable replacement." He suggested that I spend the next day in this copywriter's office trying my hand at writing an advertisement for one of the technical products.

So the next day I met the English copywriter, sat at a spare desk in his office and, after some necessary instructions and information from him, attempted the advertisement. This, if successful, could open the door to a new world. I kept to the copywriting formula learned from my teacher in the Melbourne course, namely capturing attention, creating interest, stirring desire for the product, establishing conviction about the product's quality and finally leading to action. The action is, of course, a delayed one, the reader not being expected to rush out to the nearest retail outlet and buy the product. After polishing the prose and cutting it to the required length, I handed it to the English copywriter, whose name was Peter. He read it through without comment, then, saying, "I will take it in and show the boss," he went through the door.

I was alone in the office, which was on the third floor of a big city building. While waiting for the important verdict, I stood by a window looking absently out onto a street scene below. It was then that I had an odd precognitive experience, one of the few that has broken through the clouds of my prophetic vision. The scene directly before my disinterested gaze was a corner block of several buildings. I had never looked on these buildings before. They were completely unfamiliar. Suddenly the buildings seemed to go into a spin, so fast that they became a blur. Then the spinning stopped and I found myself looking at the same buildings wearing the cloak of familiarity. Instead of a new scene, it was an old scene, something that I had looked on for months, or even years. Then, with a quick spin, the scene threw off its cloak of familiarity and I was again looking at something seen for the first time that day. It was as if after a swift dive into future time, I had come back to the present. Whatever can that mean, I thought, shaking my head. Then the interpretation came to me. In the future I would often look out of this window and look on the façades of these buildings until they took on the familiar look that I had seen in the vision. Surely this must mean that I would get the job. Soon after that, Peter came back into the office and told me that the boss wanted to see me. I went again into that plush executive office and found I had my first copywriting job on a starting salary much better than I could have expected.

This was the beginning of the year 1936 and I was to spend three-and-a-half years in that same office writing advertisements for the large range of products that the agency handled. And it was true that in moments of leisure, or perhaps in deep thought, I often stood by that same precognitive window looking on the street scene that had spun its message for me, donning a cloak of familiarity while it was still a stranger. I was very grateful to the Principal of the School of Applied Advertising for pointing the way, and almost immediately started attending his evening classes. These covered not only copywriting but all the other departments of the advertising business. At the end of the course I passed the examination with the Advertising Association of Australia and was given a certificate of membership.

At the Agency it did not take me long to discover that most of those who held the key positions on the staff were from the head office in London. I enjoyed the work greatly, not only for the creativity involved, but also as a training ground for the future important work I knew that I would one day do. Nevertheless, it was somewhat irksome to know deep in one's bones that to be from England, or to have had experience there, gave a label of superiority. Though Australia had Dominion status then, some English minds were still back in the colonial days. This was doubtless one of the factors that made me decide to make the journey to England just as soon as I had saved enough money for the fare. I decided not to ask for a transfer to the head office in London. This, no doubt, could have been arranged in time, but there would have been a good deal of patronage involved and I did not want to arrive there with the image of the colonial boy from the bush. No, I would resign and then in London seek a position with one of the other big advertising agencies. The thought of this challenge buoyed me up. Success as an advertising man in the wider arena was the first objective, but the longer term objective was world travel in search of experience that might give a clue to that meaning of life and the betterment of mankind that I hoped to express in the books I would write.

I was busy planning and saving for this great journey when destiny unexpectedly played another of its cards. Moving along the bohemian street of Sydney among the interesting creative people who were my companions, I turned a corner and unexpectedly met a blonde. I had met many blondes before, without any life-shaking consequences, but this one had an inexplicable effect on me. It was not the smile that played over the round blue eyes and the red curve of the full lips but some mysterious quality that made me feel a brief affair with her would not be enough. I would like to have her as part of my life for who knew how many years ahead. It turned out that the blonde, whose name was Gwen, was working in the advertising world as a commercial artist. She had the talent and temperament of a pure artist but, like me, she had to earn a living.

I had always vowed solemnly and fervently to myself and to anyone else who would bother listening that I would never get married. Gwen, who had the true artist's unconventional outlook, would have been content for us to live together without the benefit of the marriage certificate for which she had little respect. But then there were the families to consider. My father, whose health had failed, had on the advice of his medical doctors come to the warmer climate of Sydney.

With my mother and two sisters, he had arrived soon after I started work in the advertising agency and was now living in Sydney, in the leafy suburb of Lane Cove. My mother had the strict Victorian morality that prohibited sex, let alone living with a woman, before marriage. Gwen's mother was dead but her father was a product of the strict, puritanical morality of Wales, where he had lived. Now he was running a business in Canberra and was a cousin of the famous Australian Prime Minister, William Hughes. So we bowed to family wishes and were married, even having the regular church wedding, which we derided as being empty and hypocritical.

The bright spot was that Gwen agreed heartily with my plan to go to England. Although she had come from there only a few years earlier, she liked the idea of gaining experience as a commercial artist in the advertising world of London. So we rented an apartment in Kirribilli near the Harbour Bridge and both went daily to our work. Now there were two of us planning and saving for the great exciting London adventure. But the well-laid plans of mice and men seldom go smoothly. One spring morning as I was walking towards the ferry that would take me to the city, the blue sunny sky suddenly turned black. The black shroud engulfed me and the Harbour Bridge, the Harbour and the city line of buildings. At the same time an icy wind seemed to blow through me. But by the time I reached the ferry, the depressing blackness had vanished and the world came back to its blue spring skies and sunshine. What could such a strange and terrible vision mean, I wondered. I found out soon after I reached my office when a phone call told me that my father had died that morning. The news was unexpected and devastating. His health seemed to be improving when I had last seen him a few days earlier. It was hard to realise that the dear, understanding companion of my youth had gone forever and the family circle which I had valued so much was irretrievably broken.

After the funeral I sat alone under a big tree in the family garden and wept unrestrainedly for as long as it took to wash out the dark pot-holes of sorrow in my subconscious. After that I grieved no more. My father's death did not abort our travel plans but delayed them until the year 1939. By then the wise and knowing English members of my advertising Company began to warn me. "You will get there just when the bombs start to fall," they said. But I, who had imbibed the anti-war literature of the 1930s, could not believe that mankind would be mad enough to become involved in another world war. It would be prevented somehow.

So the day came when Gwen and I were standing on the deck of a huge P & O white liner. Bright coloured streamers led from the hands of those on deck to the hands of the big farewelling crowd on the wharf, among them my two sisters and mother. When, as the ship edged away, the streamers broke and my family merged into the crowd, I wondered if I would ever see my dear old mother alive again. But blue days at sea, five whole weeks of them before reaching England, washed this worrying query from my mind. It was on a day in August, 1939, under a leaden sky that I first walked along Piccadilly and Leicester Square. Everything seemed disappointingly drab and cramped but I told myself that I was in the setting of the English History that I had always loved.

We had scarcely had time to enjoy all the historic London sites before the voice of Neville Chamberlain, crackling from a radio, told us that we were at war with Germany. The blow to our advertising world and with it our bright ambitions was fatal. Newspapers and periodicals shrank to a fraction of their former size and the volume of advertising shrank by the same proportion. The advertising agencies were cutting down on the number of their employees and certainly not putting on new ones. There was no hope for the eager talents that had just arrived from down under. So there we were, high and dry, on the gloomy streets of London without jobs or the hope of jobs. Why had fate dealt us such a terrible, merciless blow, we wondered. What had we done to deserve it? And whatever would we do now?

Author's Postscript: I did not know then, as now I do, the doctrine of rebirth and the karma of individuals, groups and nations, all inextricably intertwined and interdependent. Properly understood, these doctrines explain many things that otherwise seem blind, unreasonable, unjust and without mercy.

4. Some Highlights In Dark Days

Life is a bridge, cross over it but do not build a house on it.

SATYA SAI BABA

I KNEW FROM the stern, sombre faces that moved along the streets of London under black homburgs and bowler hats, and from soap-box orators in the small parks off Fleet Street, that this was not a war foisted on the people by the Government, as many in the past have been. This was a people's war. They hated it, they waved no flags, but they knew that it had to be. Hitler had been bullying and threatening the free world too long. Now he had to be stopped in his tracks. And Britain, the mother of democracy and freedom, had to play a leading part. I, a pacifist, began to think that they might be right. The great Bertrand Russell, a leading pacifist of World War I, stated that some wars are justified and that this was one of them. I felt deep in my bones that he was right and that the people of England were right. In that case I had better get into the main current of the action. It would be good to get away from the sombre autumn streets of London. Being an Australian, I was not eligible for the call-up, even when my age group was reached. So I volunteered in each of the three services but I was told by each that the call-up was providing all the men they wanted and they were not accepting volunteers. There were openings in the civil defence forces of London and Gwen volunteered for that — in the ambulance service. But I felt the need to get away from London into wider fields where there was some life and action. So I volunteered to go to France with the British Red Cross.

This brought me the movement and interest I needed. At first my job was to drive van-loads of welfare aids and equipment from our headquarters in Dieppe to British army hospitals just behind the front line. But the highlight of my Red Cross experience was when I drove General Sir Sidney Clive of the Coldstream Guards from our headquarters to Paris. The General was an interesting figure to me for various reasons, the main one being that he was a direct descendant of the famous Robert Clive of India. He had retired from his regiment and with the outbreak of the war had volunteered to be the Commissioner for the Red Cross in France. Above all he was the perfect archetype of the British gentleman and treated me more as a friend than a driver and aide. I had never been to Paris before but

Sir Sidney guided me through its streets to the little hotel that he always patronised. There he booked me into a fine room near his own and I found myself treated with almost the same respect and consideration accorded to the General.

Sir Sidney used taxis to go where he needed to in Paris and left me free to explore the city on my own. The hotel was near the heart of the city, just off the Place de la Concorde, and from there I spent several days and nights wandering aimlessly through the exciting streets and great boulevards of the beautiful city. I was pleased to discover that it was not blacked out at night as London was and somewhat surprised to see no army uniforms in the streets. In fact, the General and I seemed to be almost the only khaki figures in the whole of Paris. I say almost because on the evening that I went to a big theatre to see Maurice Chevalier and Josephine Baker, I did see one army officer in khaki. He stood out like a sore toe in the huge audience clad in civilian clothes. I must have looked like the other proverbial toe.

In brief, I fell in love with Paris at first sight and it has remained my favourite city of the world ever since.

After the visit to Paris I drove the General to several other places of interest, including British Army Headquarters to talk to the Commander-in-Chief, General Gort. But soon came the blitzkrieg through the Maginot Line and the fall of Paris was imminent. So I returned to London, which city was stirring from its lethargy from the months of the phoney war and awakening to the fact that it would itself soon be in the front-line of action. Knowing that now, after Dunkirk, the army was looking for more men, I volunteered. Because of the fact that I had done a little military service back in Australia in my student days and through the influence of a Major of the Horse Guards (the friend of a friend of ours), I was accepted on the officer's reserve and informed that I would be sent to an officers' cadet training unit in a few months.

Meanwhile the Battle of Britain was on and the bombing raids were imminent. With nothing else to do for a few months, I joined the ambulance service of the civil defence and found myself on the same ambulance station as Gwen in Bloomsbury. This was conveniently near to our residence in a street of attractive Georgian terraces near the house where Charles Dickens had lived. The German bombing began in the east end of London and moved quickly up to the Bloomsbury area where we lived. I spent the quiet days in trying to learn the intricate network of streets in our area and the location of the nearest hospitals. I felt that it would be a formidable task to find my way in the blackout if the raids came at night, as was most likely.

In fact, they did just that. The first night I was called out, the director of the station gave me an address some distance away where a big building had been badly hit and there were casualties. I hoped that I would be able to find it in the blackout. But when I emerged from the underground station, the blackout seemed to have vanished. Huge fires were leaping up to the sky in many parts of the city of London, providing a light strong enough for me to read my street map. The big building that was my objective was half-destroyed by a bomb or bombs and was itself on fire. My attendant, a young English pacifist, was looking somewhat worried in the light from the fires but he was brave enough.

They were loading two casualties aboard our ambulance when I saw another ambulance from our Bloomsbury station drive up. The driver and attendants alighted from the ambulance and, being told that there were no more casualties at the moment, for some were expected soon out of the rubble, they said they would wait. These two young English ladies, whom I knew reasonably well, were as beautiful as they were brave. I thought of them as typical of the great army of courageous, self-sacrificing English women who were serving in the defence forces. "Don't forget to lie flat on the ground if any more bombs fall here," I told them, then realised that this was rather a foolish remark as the road and pavement were covered with broken glass. The girls smiled unconcernedly and said, "You should get your casualties to hospital as soon as you can." I knew they were right but did not like leaving them in this dangerous Dante's Inferno.

As I left, I heard another bomber growling overhead as if looking for a suitable target. I was not more than a block away when I heard another rain of bombs come crashing down. I felt that they had hit the burning building behind us. In fact they had, and reduced it to a pile of rubble. My two young friends did not return to the ambulance station that night. The Director tried to be optimistic, saying they may have taken some casualties to a far-away hospital, but when daylight came they were still not back. The only thing we ever found of them and their ambulance was the badly twisted number plate of the ambulance buried in the pile of rubble. The wanton blow from the sky that had wiped them off the earth without a trace sent a wave of anger through me. The war is crazy, I thought, and would have stopped it then and there if it had been in my power to do so. But we were caught up in the machinery of it and before its end I would become immune to the sight of its senseless slaughter — well, almost. Mars, the war god, under whose planetary influence I was born, after giving a body blow to my personal dreams, now decided to fulfil at least some of them. He decided to give me a generous measure of the world travel I desired.

After some months of strenuous training as a cadet in the mountains of Wales, I received the King's commission and as an officer was sent on regimental duties to the north of England. Then I went to Northern Ireland, with two trips on leave to the dazzling lights of Dublin, where blackout was unknown and there were features of peacetime life that I had almost forgotten.

After Ireland came a long trip in a troop ship, part of a slow convoy down the coast of Africa and around the Cape of Good Hope to the Port of Durban. Following a few days there, I joined another troop ship that travelled swiftly, without convoy, to Port Suez in Egypt. Then came some training in the hot sun of the Canal zone. I was hoping and expecting to be sent to a battalion of my regiment serving in the Western Desert. But the battalion had been transferred to another theatre of war and I found myself instead posted to Palestine, to the headquarters of the Palestine Buffs, which, at a point between Tel Aviv and Jerusalem were busy training units of Jews and Palestinian troops in the great art of infantry warfare. The plan was to use them later in the Allied Forces. My first reaction was depression and doom. I would probably have to spend the rest of the war in this backwater, I thought, while the current of action went on somewhere else. But, in fact, my three months sojourn in Palestine proved to be one of the highlights of the war and after it there were many other countries on my travel agenda.

Looking back on that period through the perspective of the years, I see why it was one of the soul-nourishing highlights of the war. This was not because it gave me the leisure that provided many pleasant hours of horse-riding in the company of a brother officer through the soft, gentle landscapes of the Holy Land, nor was it because I could experience 'swimming' in the Dead Sea and bathing in the Mediterranean on the beach of the Officers' Club at Jaffa. It certainly was not the fleshpots of Tel Aviv — or any similar worldly things. It was, in fact, through my visits to holy places and their deep effects on my mind: Bethlehem, the Valley of the Shepherds, Calvary, the Mount of Olives, Bethany, the Garden of Gethsemane, the road to Jericho, the Mount of Temptation — these were all names written indelibly into the fabric of my childhood culture. Now that I could really see them on the earth, they did not seem to belong to the world but rather to the stage setting of mankind's greatest drama. Such places belonged not to the present but to past time or, rather, to eternity beyond time. While walking in places where the feet of Jesus had trodden, I seemed to move, myself, out of time into the eternal. Part of me felt like staying in this timeless setting for the rest of the war and perhaps beyond, but another part of me said otherwise.

While sitting one afternoon in the Garden of Gethsemane near a battered olive tree that was old enough to have witnessed the agony of Jesus in this very garden before the day of his crucifixion, I realized that the way of life for which we were fighting had begun here. Democratic freedom with its justice and liberty for the individual may have flashed forth for a short period in ancient Greece but it had its permanent beginning here in the Garden of Gethsemane and in the city of Jerusalem now bathed in afternoon sunshine on yonder hill.

It was for this way of life that my brothers, the modern Crusaders, though they may not be aware of it, were fighting and dying right now in the Western Desert. Rommel had pushed them back to a place called Alamein. The Australian Ninth Division had been rushed from this peaceful backwater to help hold the line. People were fleeing from Alexandria and Cairo to fill the King David Hotel in Jerusalem and other places of accommodation. The critical moment of truth had arrived. I must find some way of getting out there where the young Crusaders were giving their lives for a way of life that was dearer than life itself. I knew that now, at the age of thirty-six, I had no chance of being accepted as a platoon or company commander in action, especially as my own regiment was no longer there. So how could I possibly make the transition from dreamy Palestine to the sharp clamour of the 'real thing' in the Western Desert of Egypt? Then the hand of destiny again opened an unexpected door for me. A brother officer of my regiment who was in charge of *The Palestine Post*, the newspaper issued in Jerusalem, introduced me to a Colonel Astley of the Lifeguards, who happened to be passing through Palestine on his way to Syria. Colonel Philip Astley was in charge of army public relations for the Middle East. At an interview he agreed to accept me as one of his conducting officers in the Western Desert. He would request the Military Secretary in Cairo to have me transferred as soon as possible.

I got stuck in Cairo for about three weeks doing a job I disliked on army administration, but then Philip Astley took pity on me and sent me up to the Desert, arriving in the Eighth Army lines shortly after General Montgomery had taken command. I was part of a small team of army public relations conducting officers. Each of us had a group of war correspondents, usually three, in our charge. Our job was to take them wherever good news stories were available. At the same time we had to keep an eye on their conduct and their safety. Each conducting officer had a staff car with a driver, together with a small truck and driver for carrying supplies of food, water and so on. So while we were nominally attached to Montgomery's Tactical Headquarters, we were free to roam the line from the Australian Division on the sea coast to the Free French Forces in the Qattara Depression. At times we had to locate formations such as armoured divisions by compass, somewhere in the vast featureless sands of the desert. At night we tried, if possible, to get back to the cool sea shore. We slept under the stars, which always seemed to hang very low like great lamps over the sands.

It was a free-moving job where I was able to use my own initiative and I was grateful not to be tethered to one spot by being part of a battalion. As the Battle of Alamein raged, I took my party of war correspondents to whichever part of the line promised the most interesting action. I gleaned this knowledge through frequent interviews with staff officers at the various Divisional and Corps Headquarters. On occasions we met General Montgomery somewhere along the line. He would always stop and talk to us so that we could feel and realise his utter confidence in handling every situation.

All the correspondents, together with a few people from Cairo, gathered at the Army Commander's big press conference, at his Tactical Headquarters by the sea, when the long, hard battle was nearing its end. In fact it was at its end though few but the General himself knew it. Our armoured cars and tanks had broken the line, he told us, and Rommel's forces would soon be in full retreat. They were, indeed, and the big chase was on.

Now the war god was on Rommel's side. Heavy rains fell, turning the sands into a bog so that we were unable to attack the retreating army's flanks, but in the main chased him along the narrow ribbon of the road that led along the coast to Benghazi. This route the retreating German forces mined heavily and efficiently. At one point my truck was blown up on a mine and the driver badly injured. Later, after we reached Benghazi, my staff car was blown up too. A brother officer, who was using it at the time, had both his legs blown off. I felt that some hidden power was taking care of me and felt even more sure of this on many occasions throughout the many battles in which I took part in the desert and to the end of the war. I found myself loving the desert campaign in company with the many different correspondents who came under my care, mainly British but sometimes Americans.

At the end of the long desert campaign was Tunisia, a country with a special natural beauty somehow enhanced by the sprinkling of some remains of the ancient Roman civilization. Above all in natural beauty and association with the ancient world, was the Gulf of Carthage. On its shore the ruins of the ancient city remained, broken walls just a few feet above the ground. Here, where history and myth seemed to merge, came the end for the Eighth Army in Africa and the end for me too. My next war experience was in a country which, like Tunisia, I would probably never have visited except for the intervention of my patron god, Mars.

I was one of three army conducting officers chosen to go on the invasion of Sicily. Each of us was allotted one war correspondent for the landing. An army jeep with driver would arrive for our use about a week later. The correspondent allotted to me was one destined to become one of my best friends both during the war and afterwards. This was Larry Solon of *The London News Chronicle*. I can see him now as we waded onto a beach from a small landing craft, his typewriter held high above his head, while bullets from a German aircraft whistled around our ears. Fortunately both Larry and his typewriter survived the ordeal and as soon as we had reached dry land, he sat in the shade of a tree and typed a colourful dispatch for his newspaper in London.

Each of the conducting officers with his war correspondent was allotted to a Division. Ours was the Fifth Division. We moved in the campaign along the coast through centres such as Syracuse, with echoes from ancient Greek history. This was in the hot month of July 1943 and after three months of sleeping in vineyards or sometimes on soft straw stacks, our campaign ended somewhere north of Empedocles, a city of Catania. The German forces had just pulled out as I entered that city with Larry, our jeep and British driver from Newcastle-on-Tyne. In a wine cellar there, a candle lit by the Germans was still burning on top of a cask. There seemed to be something symbolic in this. This city of long and ancient history had changed hands during the burning of a candle.

Taking a share of the good red wine that the retreating army had left behind, we moved up the coast to a town called Acireali. Here, on the edge of the Mediterranean, we found a pleasant villa overlooking the sea. The owners having fled to the mountains to escape the war, the villa was empty save for a caretaker. The caretaker, a middle-aged, wrinkled Sicilian named Maria, seemed quite happy for us to move in and to become our housekeeper. Our Geordie driver was suspicious that she might attempt to poison us and kept a close eye on her cooking.

The waves of the Mediterranean sang a lullaby just below our garden gate, and beyond within swimming distance, was a line of rocks like three black fingers pointing out of the sea. These were known as the Pillars of Ulysses. Legend says that they were thrown at the departing boat of Ulysses by the giant Cyclops, his one eye in the middle of his forehead blinded and red by the burning stake of Ulysses. It was pleasant to think that we were in the legendary setting of the old story. But we had to face the geological fact that the one-eyed giant was Mount Etna, from whose fiery red crater came the molten lava that had spread over the coastline here and into the sea, leaving these three projections of black basalt.

We had only a short period of this pleasant seaside respite before Montgomery launched his invasion of Italy across the Straits of Messina. Now my friend Larry and I had to part company. For the campaign through southern Italy I was given a party of three important war correspondents. One was Alan Moorehead of *The Daily Express*, London; another, Alexander Clifford of *The Daily Mail*, and the third Christopher Buckley of *The Daily Telegraph*, London. These were generally known as the three stars among the British war correspondents at that time. They were all good companions, but my favourite was Alexander Clifford. This was not only because he seemed to like the feature articles I wrote along the way and gave me some good advice about marketing them. Others too had been useful companions in this way, notably Larry Solon and the American correspondent of International News Service, George Lait. Alex Clifford also had a gift for languages and, learning Italian within a very short time, he became our interpreter among the civilian population. Not long after the war, when travelling around the world as a foreign correspondent, he died of some incurable disease. Christopher Buckley, long, lean and rugged like one of the Pillars of Ulysses, could not keep away from war fronts. He went as a correspondent to the Korean War and was killed by a mine there. Australian-born Alan Moorehead, brilliant writer and entertaining talker, became quite famous as an author of non-fiction books after the war years. His end, coming many years after the war, was also tragic — in fact, one author called it a Greek tragedy. A cruel sardonic stroke left him bereft of the power to speak or write for seventeen long years, though he was healthy in other respects. One can imagine the unutterable frustration for somebody whose only ambition was to write and talk, never to be able to ejaculate more than one word. This was, I am told, often a rude one, which dimly expressed his tragic frustration. Finally, after seventeen years, a kinder stroke released this brilliant writer and good companion from his merciless prison of enforced silence.

After the Eighth Army seemed to have reached a dead end for that winter at the Sangro River, we crossed the mountains to Naples and there secured a large apartment on the edge of the Bay of Naples. With us was Ted Ardazoni, the official war artist, and a Major Geoffrey Keating, in charge of the Army Film and Photo Unit. Later on, we were joined there by Colonel Astley himself. On several occasions I was able to cross the blue bay to the saddle-shaped island of Capri. On this dreamy lotus island I would fain have rested from my travels for a time but the war god moved me onward. I was given a transfer to England to join the forces there preparing for the Second Front.

My great Commander-in-Chief, General Montgomery, had gone on ahead and I felt with his departure the glorious odyssey of the Eighth Army had come to an end. So I was not sorry to be heading for pastures new, the green pastures of England. But in wartime things are never as easy as they seem. Before reaching British shores I would have to run the gauntlet of enemy ships, submarines and aircraft, aboard a foreign cruiser without the teeth to defend herself.

5. Hazards And Highlights

And all is well, tho' faith and form
Be sunder'd in the night of fear.

TENNYSON

THE FIRST PART of my transfer back to England was by army plane from Naples to Casablanca in Morocco. I was delighted with this unexpected visit to the sunny Moroccan city but a group of British military and paramilitary personnel I found in the hotel where I was billeted, were morose and dejected. I soon discovered the reason for this. Casablanca was an American transport centre and, while planes were flying daily to America, none were going to Britain. So, feeling forgotten and frustrated, they were drowning their sorrows in the plentiful alcoholic beverages that were available. The irony of the situation struck me forcibly. Here we were in a city where in peace time the rich came for expensive vacations and were wasting our time in unhappy complaining. So soon I decided to enjoy my free, luxurious vacation and set off to enjoy all the city had to offer, especially its golden beaches. But after some days of this, I myself began to feel alarmed. Neither Colonel Astley back in Naples, nor the authorities expecting my arrival in England, knew of my whereabouts. They must have thought that I had vanished off the face of the earth. So I sought out the American naval headquarters with the object of sending a signal in one direction or the other.

There, by a completely unexpected set of circumstances, I found myself lunching with two American admirals. I told them about my situation and problem. Towards the end of lunch, after some inscrutable remarks between them, one of them said to me, "We can get you to England, but it will be a matter of absolute security. You must say nothing to anyone about the way you are going." The result was on that same evening I heard myself being piped up the gangplank of the French cruiser, the *Duquesne*. Fortunately, before I reached the top of the gangplank, I realised that the piping was for me as it is apparently given to all officers of any of the fighting services. So just in time I was able to make the right response.

What a lucky break, I thought to myself, as I stepped aboard the cruiser. While my companions drown their sorrows in the bar of the hotel, I am going to England and by a very interesting and exciting method. But when I heard the news from a British naval liaison officer aboard, I began to wonder. In fact, I felt like beating a retreat to my frustrated companions in the hotel bar. I learned that the French cruiser was acting as a cargo ship. Her decks were laden with special ammunition, none of which fitted her guns. The special ammunition was for the Second Front. Furthermore, having been out of commission for so long in Alexandria Harbour, the *Duquesne* was not fitted with any modern technological equipment such as radar and asdic for detecting the approach of enemy U-boats or aeroplanes. In short, she was a sitting duck for the enemy guns. But the last straw was that, just before I had come aboard, it was announced over the Berlin radio that the French cruiser, the *Duquesne*, was sitting in Casablanca Harbour laden with special ammunition, none of which fitted her guns, and due to sail immediately for Britain. This spoke well for the efficiency of the German spy service in Casablanca but seemed to give the death-blow to our immediate plans. "We were due to sail this evening," the liaison officer told me, "but now we certainly will not. I don't know what we will do. Perhaps we will not go at all."

I had aroused the envy of my friends at the hotel by telling them that I was going to England tonight, but could tell them nothing about my means of travel. How could I now go back to them with my tail between my legs? Better to wait aboard the cruiser while there was a slim hope that we might sail.

A couple of days later I learned that a new course had been plotted taking us away out into the Atlantic around the Azores. It would be about four days' hard, fast sailing before we reached a British port. "That is," said my pessimistic liaison officer, "if we ever reach a port." I knew full well the danger of this French adventure. It would require only one hit from a torpedo or bomb to send us all to kingdom come in one great burst of flame. But there was something in this running the gauntlet through the enemy guns that appealed to me and deep down I felt that my unseen guardian would still take care of me. Even so, on the night when we slipped out of Casablanca Harbour under the stars, I more than half expected a German U-boat to be waiting for us. But only the silvery ocean seemed to be watching as we set course towards the Azores.

As we raced on under sunny skies through the blue seas that seemed to be empty, I spent a good part of my time on the bridge, where frequently signals were picked up that gave us information about the movement of enemy planes and ships, but very little, of course, about U-boats. After we had rounded the Azores and were heading back towards Europe, a signal that was picked up showed that several German destroyers were heading, it seemed, in our direction. I prayed that they would not cross our path and discover our whereabouts. I wondered if the French officers who learned about such hazards were making the same prayer. But as we gathered regularly in the wardroom for the tasty French meals, I could see no signs of apprehension on their faces. Their only concern seemed to be that I as their guest would say the right thing at the end of dinner. This was, "Mr President, the coffee is getting cold." They were not able to leave the table and go for coffee until any guest present had made this statement. This custom, I learned, was connected with exorcism or absolution of a *faux pas* made by a guest on the ship in the early years of the *Duquesne*'s life. Such things, no doubt, helped to take our minds off lurking death below and above the innocent blue seas.

The cruiser seemed to bear a charmed life as she carved her way at top speed through blue days and starlit nights. Then suddenly we came out of the sunshine into a thick fog that surrounded the coast of Britain. Though the French sailors were looking quite unhappy at the change of climate, I myself breathed a sigh of relief as we sailed through mist and rain into the harbour of Greenock on the coast of Scotland. It was April 1, 1944.

On arrival in London, I found that Gwen had achieved for herself the first part of the dream that had taken us from the shores of Australia five years before. She had a job as art director and assistant production manager on a well-known Fleet Street magazine. I was glad for her sake but felt no envy. That life seemed now unimportant, stale, and such a long time ago. I was due for some homecoming leave and, perhaps because some of the glamour of the Eighth Army still hung about my name, Gwen found no difficulty in obtaining the time off to spend a couple of weeks holiday with me. We spent these days of respite and reunion on the coast of Cornwall, where the surf was good but not to be compared with the pounding breakers we had known on the beach at Bondi. Back in the sands of the Western Desert, I had oft times dreamed of coming together with my wife again in the green, kindly landscapes of England. But, though on the surface our days together were very happy indeed, underneath I felt that she, I and the pattern of our lives had changed so much. Would the pieces of the pattern ever come together again? I hoped that they could.

After the leave, I joined my unit of the Second British Army, waiting in the green, pleasant pastures a few miles west of London. The wait had been so long that the men seemed to have gone half asleep in the spring sunshine. But there was a tension behind their eyes. They knew that each tomorrow might bring the awaited order. Then the Allied forces, strung out across southern England, would move to the Channel ports and embark for the northern coast of France. It was well-known that the efficient German war machine had turned this coast into a veritable fortress. Many lives would be lost in its taking. But take it we must, whatever the cost.

The order came, as all the world knows, early in June. Then the greatest invasion fleet of all history left the coast of England and crossed to breach the impregnable wall of steel and concrete. With grim courage and considerable loss of life, the Allied soldiers fought their way in and gained a toehold on French soil, precarious though that toehold seemed at first.

I crossed with the public relations unit of the Second British Army, which was commanded by General Montgomery. Our headquarters was in Normandy not far from the city of Bayeux. As an officers' mess, we were using the old castle from which William the Conqueror had crossed the Channel in the other direction some nine centuries earlier. I hoped that our invasion would prove as successful as his. But I found that my free-booting life as a conducting officer had ended back in Naples. Now I had other jobs to do, some pleasant, some quite the opposite, but all revealing.

After setting up a press communication centre in Normandy, my first job of interest was to liaise with the American Third Army which, under the command of the famous George Patton, was racing across France from the west like a steel arrow aimed straight for the Paris defences. I felt that, whatever those defences may be, George Patton would break through. And it was a fascinating thought that I would be there to witness the liberation of the beautiful city.

I joined a column of tanks, armoured cars and other vehicles as it careered along the straight French roads between silvery trees and the occasional French family that had come to the roadside to wave and cheer. But our forward thrust halted suddenly at the city of Chartres some miles from Paris, and we were told to pitch camp. I, like many others, wondered why the impetuous General George Patton had stopped dead on the very edge of the promised land. This man, who could sometimes turn a deaf ear to restraining commands from higher up, was unlikely to be held up by German defences around the city, so what was it? Later I learned that orders from the Allied Governments had made him pause. A column of the Free French Army, under the command of General de Gaulle, was marching towards the city and must be allowed to enter first. This, I thought, was a fine diplomatic gesture, revealing a sensitive understanding by the Allies of the French psychology. At least they would be pleased that French forces had played some part in their liberation.

It was during the days of waiting, with some impatience, for the arrival of the French column that I experienced an unexpected highlight or mandorla in the Chartres Cathedral. The mandorla was not on the stained glass windows of the great cathedral, magnificent though they are. It came suddenly to me while I stood in the dim religious light within the cathedral itself. It felt as if I were breaking through the bonds of my body and being lifted upward — beyond the upward pointing arches and spires, beyond the confines of earth, into a realm of bliss. Like all such experiences, it was outside of time and space, a journey between the moments of earthly time to refresh me and reassure me of the reality of the world of spirit, beyond yet very close to the dark world of war all around me. I wondered afterwards if it was the cathedral itself that had brought me this superphysical experience. But later on I learned that this was one of the magnetic spots of earth where the Druids, the religious leaders of the Celtic people, had long centuries before built a temple. With the coming of Christianity, welcomed by the Celtic people, Saint Peter himself had preached a Christian sermon in that ancient Druid temple. During the Christian centuries, a series of religious edifices had stood on this sacred spot, culminating in the present magnificent cathedral. So many people must have felt the overlapping of the spiritual circle here.

Soon after that, I found myself in a column of the American Army moving into Paris. How would the shining city of my memory be, I wondered, after four years of enemy occupation? Probably dull and drab and partly ruined. But I was in for a pleasant surprise. Welcoming crowds lined the route of our progress from the very outskirts of the city. I was in an open jeep moving slowly with the column of tanks, armoured cars and army vehicles. As we moved through the avenue of people, they smiled, waved and shouted words of welcome and joy. They seemed completely unperturbed by the occasional sound of gunfire, showing that final clean-up operations were going on not far away. Whenever the column stopped, which was frequently, people from the side dashed forward to touch us and give us the embrace of welcome. By the time we reached the centre of the city near the opera house, all faces in the jeep were completely covered with lipstick, women being in the ascendancy among the crowd.

When the jeep finally stopped at the end of our journey, I could see that our destination, a big hotel, was on the other side of a square crowded with welcoming Parisians. There was no possibility of my driver taking the jeep through that crowd. We would have to walk. It was a formidable prospect, with thousands of outstretched arms waiting to squeeze us all to a Parisian purée in their enthusiastic joy. Such a welcome, though it fills the heart with happiness, can be quite overpowering. Finally, it was a relief to get through the doorway of the big hotel, where I was not only to reside but assist the American public relations officers in setting up a Paris communications centre for war correspondents. But it was difficult to get much work done. Parisians poured into the hotel and for most of that night champagne parties of delirious celebration went on. No doubt in other centres where the Parisians were mixed with members of the army, the same abandoned, spontaneous liberation madness was in progress. All normal conventions were swept aside. Everybody was the close friend of everybody else.

Next day in the streets I found this same atmosphere of happy brotherhood. The normal barriers between individuals had been dissolved in the loving joy of their welcome. I found myself wishing that mankind could always be like this — always in a state of happy oneness through the loving joy that flows spontaneously from human hearts. Driving my jeep through the great boulevards, empty and spacious through the lack of any civilian vehicles, I saw what appeared to be a large flock of colourful butterflies coming towards me. The butterflies were young Parisian women on bicycles, smiling and waving to me as they rode past. I had expected the women to look drab, but here they were brightening the city in their gay frocks of many colours. Later I learned that they had stored the material for years in trunks and boxes waiting for the day of their liberation. When they heard of our landing on French soil, they made up the frocks ready. What a rewarding sight they were for weary soldiers' eyes!

As I drove on through the beautiful city, I found that none of it had been destroyed, as Hitler had ordered it to be. The German soldiers had loved Paris too. I spent about a week in the city on that occasion and the euphoria had not abated when I left to go to Brussels. The front line had moved eastward beyond that city, but our Army public relations headquarters had been established in the Avenue Louise there. Near to our headquarters and officers' mess was a large solid house belonging to an old Belgian baron. He had offered to billet one of our officers and I happened to be the fortunate one sent there.

Living with the old Baron was his nephew and heir, the Baron de Rotsartt with the Baroness. Both were approximately my age. Like Brussels itself, in these days of extended liberation euphoria, the baronial family was warm-hearted and friendly. As well as sleeping there, I had many meals in their great dining room with portraits of ancestors on the walls. This family was descended directly from one of the seven nobles who had founded Brussels. They drew me into their social life, which was mainly in the private clubs established especially to isolate them from the occupying German forces. They all seemed to have a strong hatred of the Germans. Now they felt they had the freedom of their own city again and sometimes took me with them to house parties and to nightclubs.

When I first started on my travels, one of my ambitions was to meet and mix with all men and know their ways of life. But I doubt if without the help of my war god patron, I would ever have been able to rub shoulders with the Belgian nobility and made to feel like a member of their family. They were natural, unpretentious and very pleasant companions. The old Baron, who was himself the most friendly and natural of all, still was old-fashioned enough to think it was infra dig to work, and he was not altogether happy that his nephew owned a factory in one of the provincial towns. But it had become an economic necessity, the young Baron told me, part of the march of history.

One of my PR jobs during that winter of 1944–45 was to fly over to London and bring back parties of provincial newspaper editors, taking them up to the front in Holland, though there was not much for them to witness there, the armies being bogged down in mud and slush.

This travelling to the War Office in London to pick up the parties of editors enabled me to spend some nights at home in our flat at Hampstead. It seemed like a soft peace-time cop-out, but one morning I got a rude shock. I had arrived at the Brussels airport just after sunrise and was walking with a few other official travellers towards our waiting aircraft. Suddenly there was a crackle of gunfire above us as German aircraft came in out of the eye of the morning sun. Bullets whistled close to us as we dodged quickly back into the airport building. But their target was really the aeroplanes sitting on the ground. We watched from the window as they flew low, systematically shooting up every aeroplane, some of them fighter planes, that sat on the Brussels airfield. Soon every plane was burning. Then the attacking planes turned their attention on the building. Bullets and cannonballs shattered the glass of the windows and ricocheted off the solid brick walls around us. Miraculously, none of us were hit. Then the German planes left as suddenly as they had arrived and all was quiet. A pall of black smoke hung over the ground where not a single plane had escaped the swift attack. My journey to London was successfully ruled out for that day. The attack was not isolated. It coincided with a big German counter-offensive in the Ardennes. Back in Brussels I found my Belgian friends very alarmed, though I tried to assure them that the Germans would never get back to Brussels.

Just before I left on a later trip to London, I received a signal in code from a friend in the War Office. The signal read: "One commando arrived." I knew just what that meant. Later on, the same day, I found Gwen in a London hospital and saw the 'commando' lying in a cot fast asleep. He looked as if he had just come through a hard battle against heavy odds and was resting. I decided that this warrior must be named Richard of the Lionheart, one of my favourite characters in English History. Gwen was very proud and happy to have a son.

The trip after that was my last to London, as the winter was merging into spring and the armies in Holland were on the move. When my headquarters moved with Montgomery into Germany, I, of course, had to go too. After the life in Brussels, I did not look forward to the prospect of operating in enemy country, especially as some dire warnings had come from the War Office. The service chiefs in their great wisdom decided that the German civilians would not give up the struggle and that we must guard against all kinds of stab-in-the-back tactics behind the lines.

6. *Into The Horror Pit*

Look up and swear by the green of the spring
That you will never forget.

SIEGFRIED SASSOON

IT WAS WITH a heavy feeling that I drove from Holland across the border onto enemy soil. My heavy-heartedness was not decreased when I saw around me nothing but wrecked buildings. After a while I saw people moving among the ruins. They were mainly old men and flaxen-haired women of varying ages. Without looking in my direction, they kept their heads down, busy about their tasks. Then the strange feeling came to me. These are not enemies, they're my cousins. I have known them before, at some time long ago. How inexplicable, I thought. Is it a racial memory, lingering deep in my blood? For, of course, our Anglo-Saxon ancestors came from Germany. Some say that race ties and race memories are written in our blood. Others say that we live many lives on earth, so perhaps I have lived one or more of those lives in Germany. Whatever the explanation, I immediately felt akin to the Germans and to Germany and felt at home in that land from the first day. So it was that when I came to our headquarters and saw the high barbedwire fence around it, I felt how unnecessary and silly it was. For the first week or two, my work took me around parts of Germany and the feeling continued that I had come back after a long time to a place I knew, to the cousins who had stayed at home while I had wandered far.

One day my colonel, who was also an old friend from Eighth Army days, said to me, "Belsen concentration camp has just been liberated by our forces. Several war correspondents have seen it and written stories that are making headlines in the British press. The stories tell of such horrors that our service chiefs think they may be exaggerated. They want a Public Relations Officer to go there and make a factual report to be sent to the War Office. I have chosen you because you are a professional writer, but you will have two officers of the Division of Psychological Warfare to help you compile the report." I had never heard of Belsen concentration camp before, so was not unduly alarmed at the prospect. But the colonel went on: "Reports say that typhus is rampant in the camp, but as I want you to go without delay, there will not be time for you to have anti-typhus injections, which would not be effective for some days anyhow. A unit of the Army Medical Corps has arrived near the camp, so you and the other two officers will stay there and you will not need to take anything with you except your personal belongings, your car and driver. Leave just as soon as you are ready." He gave me directions on how to get to Belsen, which was hidden away in a pine forest some miles north of the city of Celle. The war was still going on and the front line not many miles east of this point. My old friend continued, "Take as long as you need on the job, and don't worry, the Belsen lice will not bite an old desert rat like you." He gave me a pat of encouragement and farewell.

The sunny spring weather of April was at its best as I set off along the great empty autobahn towards Hanover. From near Hanover I turned north through Celle and continued to a town called Bergen. There I turned onto a lesser road that led through the pine forest to my destination. The sun was westering over the pine tops when I reached my new quarters with the Royal Army Medical Corps. My two assistants had not yet arrived and, as it was late in the day, I decided to leave my entry into Belsen until the next morning.

They had not arrived the next morning either, so along I left the pleasant park, where we were quartered in fine buildings that had once housed a German armoured division. The air was crisp and sweet in the early morning as I walked along a road to the gate of Belsen. What would I find beyond the tall guard house at the gate, I wondered.

First, I was taken to a room in the guardhouse and sprayed under my clothes, all over my body, with anti-louse powder. This was carried out by an army medical sergeant and was to be a morning ritual for the whole ten days that I laboured at the camp. Not far beyond the guardhouse, on the long straight road that led through a line of wooden huts on either side, I met my first horror. It was a pile of human corpses. It was impossible to know the number because they had been thrown together carelessly like logs of wood, but there may have been about fifty in the pile. The thing that struck me first about the bodies was their twisted, contorted shape. Like old gnarled roots they were. It was as if death had frozen them in the writhing agony of their passing. Open dead eyes stared at me from many of the corpses. Bones protruded through the skin and there was not much smell of decomposition because there was very little flesh left to decompose. Did they die of starvation, or were they very near to starvation when they died of some disease, I wondered. I felt sure that they had been lying there for a long time.

At intervals along this nightmare road I found similar piles with as many or more corpses, their gnarled bodies and faces telling the same story of a frightful, agonising death. Towards the end of the road, the piles seemed more recent, less dried up, and the putrid smell of decomposition pervaded the air. Along this street of death I saw a few of the living moving. They seemed scarcely alive, more like automatons, or sleepwalkers in a deep trance, indifferent to or unaware of their surroundings. Belsen had not only killed bodies but something inside those still alive. I saw one of these living dead sitting on a pile of corpses as if they were wood, while he ate his bowl of apparently some sort of soup. It would be no use talking to these sort of people, so how, I wondered, could I get an adequate picture of the tragedy of Belsen? How could I even stay here in the horror that surrounded me? The only way, I thought, was to detach myself by building a psychic wall of resistance between me and my surroundings.

I was helped in this psychological operation by one of my two assistants, both of whom arrived during that day. Before the war he had been a University lecturer in Philosophy and History. During the first few evenings in the mess, this philosophical officer talked about parallel cases where man's inhumanity to man had reached incredible proportions on a number of occasions throughout the centuries. These, being remote in time, seemed somehow to make Belsen more remote, pushing it away into an historical perspective. These talks made it possible for me to bear my days in Belsen without overpowering emotions of horror and repulsion. We decided that we would interview as many as were still alive and able and willing to communicate. My two assistants worked on this job together. I worked alone and at the same time made notes for a detailed description of the camp as we found it.

There were several compounds at Belsen, each of them divided off by high barbed-wire fences. Practically all the inmates had been Jews but there had been a small compound of gypsies and reports spoke of a few German political prisoners, some habitual criminals and a few Russian prisoners-of-war. All of them were housed in long, narrow wooden huts, which stood in rows with muddy evil-smelling roads between the rows. Inside the huts, I was to meet with more incredible horrors. When I entered the first hut, the stench almost drove me straight out again, but I forced myself to walk some distance along the aisle between the two rows of bunks that reached from floor to ceiling, one above the other. Each was about wide enough for one person to sleep in comfortably but I could see that there were several people in each bunk. All seemed ill and only half alive. None would be in a fit condition to help me with my enquiries.

Coming out and taking a few deep breaths of the fresh morning air, I saw an army ambulance standing outside one hut. I made towards it and in the hut found two British medical orderlies taking very sick patients from the bunks to the ambulance. On enquiry, I found that these were being taken to a British army hospital improvised in the tree-studded park where our billets stood. The orderlies were appalled at the conditions they found in the huts. Often as many as four people crowded into the same bunk, many of them sick and sometimes, indeed, they found dead people lying under the sick.

The next day I paid a visit to the British army hospital and with the Medical Corps colonel stood watching a scene that brought some appeasement to my outraged feelings. A team of German female nurses were washing the bodies delivered by the ambulance before putting them to bed. The pathetic figures being washed on the tables were mainly loose skin over skeletons, but the German nurses never paused in their work and seemed to me to be doing the job with an air of intense dedication. Picking up my thoughts, the colonel said, "They are trying to make some atonement for the crimes of their countrymen."

"The crimes of the Nazi gang," I replied.

"But Germans, even so," he pointed out. Learning about my official work in the camp and realising its difficulties, the colonel said, "You must meet Madeleine. She was an inmate at Belsen and is now helping us in the hospital canteen. I think she will be able to help you." But Madeleine was not available just then and, in fact, it was several days before I met her.

In the meantime, a new activity had begun in the camp. The piles of dead that littered the roadways were being loaded onto British army trucks. The men doing the loading were the ex-SS guards. They were not doing this job willingly. In fact, they were obviously loathing the contact with the Jewish corpses. But British soldiers stood by, urging them on with fixed bayonets. I had never seen hatred and anger on the faces of British soldiers before, even when they were grimly attacking enemy lines. But now I saw those emotions written large on their faces and if any SS guards showed rebellion, a prick of the British bayonet helped him on. It was as if the common soldier knew now, if never before, what he was fighting for.

I followed one of the trucks, loaded high with corpses, to its destination in the sandy soil just outside the camp. Mass graves had been bulldozed there, each of them looking like an average-sized public swimming pool drained of water. The truck drove down the slope onto the floor of one of these graves and, while other British soldiers watched with their bayonets ready, other SS guards unloaded the bodies and lay them side by side on the floor of the grave. When at last the great yawning graves were carpeted with corpses and the pathetic heaps of gnarled and twisted bodies had been cleared from the roadways, bulldozers filled in the mass graves with the sandy soil, leaving flat mounds a few feet high to mark the spot where the thousands of the Belsen dead had been buried.

Unearthed official documents at the camp revealed a strange thing. Belsen was not officially listed as a death camp like a number of other Nazi concentration camps where Jews by the million had perished in the gas ovens. It was, in fact, with an incredible irony, listed as a convalescent and rest camp. How was it, then, that all this mass killing had come about? No light was shed on this by the interviews turned in by my two assistants, nor was I able to solve the mystery myself until I met Madeleine.

She looked to be in her mid-twenties, very thin with slightly stooped shoulders. But the surprising thing was that she did not look like any Jewess I had ever met. In fact, with her very blonde hair, short and curly, her sky-blue eyes and pale skin and anything but aquiline nose, she looked more like one of Hitler's favourite Aryan types. She spoke English very well and, over a cup of tea at a canteen table, Madeleine began to tell me her story.

She was a Hungarian Jewess living in Budapest. Her husband there was a young medical doctor and she herself was a trained nurse. Her Jewish parents lived in the same city. When the Nazis came, they took her parents and her husband but left her. Perhaps they thought she was not Jewish. But she let them know that she was and asked them to take her to the same camp as her husband was in. They did so but she was put in a different compound from him. However, she said, it was good to be near him and they were able to exchange letters now and then. Both her parents were in the same camp. This was a death camp located in the east of Germany. She saw her parents being taken to the gas chamber. Soon after that, her husband was taken too. But she did not know whether he went to a gas chamber or to a forced labour camp, where life would probably be worse than death.

When the advancing Russian armies began to draw near to her camp, and to others in the area, rather than let the Russians discover them and liberate the prisoners, the German authorities loaded them onto railway cattle trucks to be transported across Germany to the west. It was a terrible journey, Madeleine told me, taking about three weeks. Sometimes when their trucks were shunted onto a line near a railway station and left there for a night, or longer, they would hear the Allied bombers overhead. They knew that if the railway station was bombed, they would most certainly be badly hurt or killed, but such a prospect did not worry Madeleine at all, she said. Death would be a release from the misery of living. "So," she said, "we prayed for the success of the bombers, knowing that an Allied victory was our only hope of salvation." But her train got through untouched and finally reached its destination.

All half-starved and some very sick, they found themselves bundled out of their cattle trucks at a place called Celle. Without being given any food at all, they were forced to set off in the snow for the long walk of many miles to Belsen concentration camp. Some of the sick and weak, she said, just laid down and died by the roadside. Eventually they found themselves waiting outside the guardhouse at the main gate of Belsen. "We were so hungry and thirsty," she said, "that we ate the snow off each other's shoulders as it fell and drank the dirty water from the puddles on the roadside."

Finally they were taken into the camp. Now, perhaps, we'll have some food and shelter and rest at last, thought Madeleine, but first they all had to go naked through a cold bath in a concrete pool where SS women guards, with whips in their hands, stood around the edges. Then at last Madeleine and a girlfriend she had made on the journey were taken to their allotted hut. "But," said Madeleine, "not only were the bunks full but the floor was covered with sleeping people. There was not even room to lie down, so we knelt up all that night and tried to sleep in that position."

Next morning came food at last, a bowl of soup made from bad turnips. "It was difficult to keep down," Madeleine said, "but I forced myself to do so." In the days that followed, the food they had, which was very scarce, consisted of nothing but this soup made from turnips that had gone bad. Meantime more and more people were being crowded into the already overcrowded camp and as there was, apparently, no increase in the food ration, there were days when they had nothing to eat at all.

This outline of the beginning of Madeleine's story was sufficient to reveal to me how conditions in the sub-human world of Belsen had come about. Inhuman overcrowding with prisoners from the eastern camps, with no official increase in rations for the prisoners (though the SS guards, both men and women, looked well-fed and fat), had brought about mass death from starvation and typhus. One of the inmates told me that the possession of a food parcel received from outside was sufficient motive for murder and the price for prostitution was a raw potato.

Another day, in the canteen over a cup of army tea, Madeleine, who made me think of a jewel discovered in a dung-heap, continued her story. Lice were plentiful in all the huts, she said, and though she found a bunk to sleep in, it was not long before she caught the dread disease of typhus. "Now," she thought gladly, "I will die and escape from all this." But miraculously she did not die. After her recovery, an SS woman, who had known her at the other camp and knew that she was a medical nurse, arranged for her to become an official nurse in the camp. This meant, she said, that she was given a small amount of rice each day to supplement the soup. And so it was that Madeleine managed to stay alive until that wonderful spring morning when she heard the sounds of the British army outside the gate and knew that liberation was at hand. Though calendar time was no part of the life in Belsen, where one dreadful day seemed the same as the one before it, where in Shakespeare's words "Tomorrow, and tomorrow, and tomorrow / Creeps in this petty pace from day to day," Madeleine knew she had come to Belsen in the biting cold of winter, probably the winter before the spring of her liberation and the beginning of her useful days with the Army Medical Corps.

"Well, now you are free to go wherever you wish, Madeleine," I said to her at our farewell meeting.

"Yes," she replied, smiling wanly, "but where do I go? My mother and father are dead. My husband has vanished. The Russian communists have taken over Budapest, so it's no place for me to go back to." The Parsifal in me wanted to help this lonely damsel in distress, but what could I do? I belonged to the army and had to return to my headquarters to write a report for the War Office and then move on to wherever duty took me. I never saw Madeleine again but often wondered what had happened to her, one of the millions whose lives had been turned upside down through the evil plans of a little man called Hitler. I did, however, see the SS guards again in the dock at the Luneburg trials. Some were hanged, some sent to prison for long terms, but the fiendish Nazi system was as much to blame as the guards for the holocaust, the crime against humanity, of which Belsen was just a small corner.

Some inner urge called me back to Belsen again, but this was about five years later, before my final departure from Germany. Driving alone through the soft pine forest, I came to the spot where the entrance gate had once stood. But the horror pit, as we always called it, had completely vanished. Every building had been burnt to the ground some years before. Yet, as I walked across the site, towards the mass graves beyond, I felt that Belsen was not yet completely cleansed and freed from its terrible past. Psychic cobwebs of depression seemed to hang in the air and reached down to me as I walked. The appalling atmosphere of depression seemed almost to cast a shadow over the bright sun. I found the graves without any difficulties. The wide, flat mounds marked the spot where so many thousands lay buried. Lettering on a large polished gravestone told the story and announced to all who passed and cared to read that six million Jews had been slaughtered in the Nazi holocaust. But who would come to read the terrible message in this lonely, desolate spot? Would future generations forget this greatest of all atrocities, committed against the body of humanity? Some might say that we should forget. But, standing there while the wind sighed in the pine trees and the unseen fingers of the Belsen dead seemed to reach out and touch me, I felt it was a good and necessary thing that we should remember, lest if we fall asleep for a moment at our watchtowers along the frontier of human freedom and dignity, the same thing should happen again. I thought of the line by Siegfried Sassoon, the young poet of World War I, who wrote against the lesser horrors of that war: "Look up and swear by the green of the spring / That you will never forget.". This is a message to all lovers of freedom and justice who must remain always aware and watchful.

Adolf Hitler seems to have been born with a strong virus of anti-Semitism in his blood. Of course, he was not alone in this. His two main living gurus, the philosopher Friedrich Nietzsche and the great composer Richard Wagner, were both violently anti-Semitic. Nietzsche, who hated Christianity and the Jewish race from the bottom of his soul, was undoubtedly the philosopher and prophet of the Anti-Christ. Although Richard Wagner came to accept Christianity, as revealed in his opera *Parsifal*, he could not accept that Christ came out of the Jewish race. He worshipped a Christ born of the Aryan people. Hitler could not accept Christianity and Christian values even on Wagner's terms. Although Wagnerian music moved him to the depths of his soul, philosophically Hitler remained faithful to Nietzsche's teachings. Like the mad philosopher, he turned all Christian values upside down. All that Christianity said was good was to him bad and all that Christianity said was bad was to Hilter's philosophy good.

Thus he became the Anti-Christ in action, determined to carry out on the world stage what Nietzsche propounded in philosophy. And there were dark forces on the astral planes willing and eager to use him as an instrument to carry out the anti-God work on a world scale. According to a deeply perceptive observer* who knew him in the years just before World War I, when Hitler was a drop-out living in a flophouse in Vienna, the young Hitler laid himself open to such dark forces by his use of drugs and black magic practices.

There were two main planks in the evilly-inspired Hitler plan for human engineering. One was his 'final solution', the complete annihilation of what he believed was the scum, the pollution of humanity known as the Jewish race. On this, he with his lieutenants made a substantial beginning until the defeat in 1945 stopped them. The other plank in his plan was the building of a new super-race. The Teutonic Germans who, in his eyes, were mainly Aryan, he regarded as the Master Race or the *Herrenvolk* and from this he would create the super race of men prophesied by Nietzsche: blond, super-Aryan giants, intrepid, ruthless, cruel and loveless. This race would dominate and rule mankind for a thousand years. No wonder a great living Indian sage and seer said that if Hitler won the war the Divine Plan would be set back by a thousand years. Hitler had, in fact, made a start on this world-changing scheme by the creation of human stud farms. I will describe my contact with one of these in the next chapter.

* The great Austrian scientist and occultist Walter Johannes Stein.

7. Nemesis At Nuremberg

Though with patience He stands waiting,
with exactness grinds He all.

LONGFELLOW

I, LIKE MOST people, had heard about the Nazi plan to establish human stud farms for the purpose of breeding a Master Race but I had no idea that Hitler had already begun to put his plan into action before the end of the war. In May 1945 I learned, on good authority, that such a place had actually existed and that its bombed-out remains could be seen deep in a dark forest a few hours drive south of our headquarters. It was, my informant said, in a district called Vogelsang, which means 'birdsong'. If true, this would be a very interesting find, I thought. Belsen was one end of the Nazi human engineering story and here perhaps I would find the other end of it.

My informant had given me directions on how to get to this place, so as soon as possible I drove off alone in my staff car. After some hours I found myself west of the Rhine, driving through a dense forest of black trees and black rocks. It was a silent, gloomy place with not a note of the birdsong that might have been expected from its name. Eventually I came to what must be my destination. I had been told something of the story of Vogelsang before the Allied bombers had destroyed it. But it was not easy to set the story in the pile of rubble that confronted me. Apart from an intact brick building at some distance, there seemed to be no wall left standing anywhere. But then I discovered a piece of wall sticking up like a broken tooth. On the wall I found, almost as if left by the design of Fate, a lifelike profile of Hitler, standing out in bas-relief. Some distance away I could see what looked like a sports ground and gymnasium and, down in a valley beyond, a steely lake seemed to be trying to hide itself behind the dark trees of the forest. Around the shores of the lake, as far as I could see, was a string of bombed-out chalets. They must have been the honeymoon chalets of the story, I thought. Not a soul was moving in the silent ruins around me, so I decided to walk across to the one unbombed building.

On the outside was a small notice in English which said 'Transit Officers' Mess'. Inside I found one officer and a small staff. He was about to start his lunch and cheerily invited me to join him. Over lunch I learned that he had spent some days in this area, though I did not learn what his business was in the dark forest. He belonged to the British forces occupying this zone of Germany and, from enquiries he had made around the area, he had learned enough to confirm and fill out the story of Vogelsang that I had learned earlier.

In outline the story is this. A selected number of SS troops were given leave from their duties at the front to come here and become the fathers of Hitler's new super race. They were, of course, the types considered by the Nazis to be true Aryan stock. Having seen some of these big, soulless, blond animals I had no doubt that none would refuse this opportunity to enjoy a honeymoon at Vogelsang with the Führer's approval. The mothers-to-be were selected from different parts of Germany on the same racial line. If any disliked the idea of serving the Führer in this unconventional way, they probably remembered the looming threat of concentration camps and accepted the invitation of the Nazi recruiting officers.

Males and females, paired off either by choice or by direction, were given a pagan marriage in the Hitler temple. That was, of course, the building where his profile had been left on the wall. It seemed odd that the Nazis bothered about a wedding ceremony but perhaps, with Hitler as the reigning deity, it was a ritual of fertility and fruitfulness. After the wedding, each pair was given a chalet for a happy honeymoon on the edge of the lake. Perhaps the sports ground and gymnasium were meant to keep them in good fettle for their breeding activities. When the woman was pregnant beyond all doubt, the male partner was sent back to his SS unit at the front.

The pregnant bride stayed on at Vogelsang until her baby was born. It was born here in the Transit Officers' Mess, which was then a maternity hospital. Much of the equipment for a maternity hospital was still here. Soon after the birth of the baby, the mother was returned to her family. She was never to see again the child of her Nazi honeymoon by the dark lake. No dubious maternal or paternal influences were to be allowed to shape the child. The children born here would be brought up in groups by specially trained teachers and guardians, who would inculcate the Nazi philosophy and condition the young minds from the beginning for the role they were destined to play. They would be developed into the arrogant, ruthless members of the Master Race which would dominate and a master/slave relationship would come into existence with the German super race as the masters. A nice arrangement, I thought — that is, for the masters. But, of course, it flies in the face of God's law of spiritual existence of all peoples and could not be allowed to come into existence.

What happened to the children born here I never could find out. Nor did I hear of any other German stud farm of human breeding until, decades later in Australia, I met a German who had lived during his youth in the Harz Mountains, a place I loved to remember for its witchery pine forests and its easy snow slopes for skiing. Not many miles from his home in Bad Harzburg, my German friend said, there had existed for some years such a human stud farm, but, of course, it ended with the defeat of the Nazis.

The unconditional surrender of the Nazi leaders brought the whole German nation to its knees among its smoking ruins, but what about the leaders themselves? Those who had laboured to put the evil Pan-Germanic dream of Hitler into practice and came very near to enslaving the world? I saw their nemesis at Nuremberg.

In the spring of 1946, some three months before I was due to leave the army, I was sent to the Nuremberg trials as a Public Relations officer in charge of the British Press section there. I was replacing another British officer who had reached the date for his demobilisation and was due to return to England. I was not pleased with this assignment but I know now that it was a good thing for me to witness the international trial of the Nazi leaders.

On first seeing the gigantic, imposing, almost threatening Palace of Justice where the trials were being held, I felt a depression of my spirit. This was enhanced by the sight of the acres of flat ruins not far away. Broken piles of rubble were all that were left of the ancient city of Nuremberg, said to be one of the finest examples of Medieval architecture in Europe. I thank God that my billets, in the rural village of Stein, were some distance away from these two depressing pictures. I slept here in a pleasant country cottage but each morning, after an American breakfast in an incongruous modern castle (requisitioned as an American Officers' Mess), I drove to the Palace of Justice, where I found myself in charge of a press copyroom staffed by German clerks and a British army lieutenant.

It was to this room that the British war correspondents, now perhaps better called foreign correspondents, brought their dispatches about the daily progress of the trial. In this way I renewed my acquaintance with a few old friends from the war fronts and met a good number of new ones. Looking back through the perspective of time, I think that my best companion, and the foreign correspondent I admired most, was the bald-headed, Dickensian figure, Robert Cooper of *The Times*, but I will say a bit more about him later. Another place where I had more informal and convivial meetings with the press corps was a large recreational room where, with pots of powerful German beer in their hands, drawn freely from a large keg in the room, they would sit and gossip and grumble and give their true opinions about the trials.

Robert Cooper was one of the very few I ever heard express a positive approval of this trial of the vanquished by the victors. Most of the correspondents seemed to regard it more as a farce than a trial. I began to ask myself, was it really a good thing for the judges and lawyers of the victorious Allies to be sitting here in judgement over the beaten leaders of gang that had tried to wade through slaughter, bloodshed, cruelty and horror to a throne of power over the world? Or was it, after all, only a farce? The German ex-service men, whom I was fortunate enough to meet in the countryside around Nuremberg, thought that the trials were quite an unnecessary farce. "Why try them?" they said. "Just kill them if you think they deserve it, or let them go into obscurity. None of them will amount to anything any more." In the past, the leaders of defeated nations were not tried by their conquerors. They were either killed by their own people, let live in obscurity, like Kaiser Wilhelm of Germany, or exiled to some remote place, like Napoleon. But the world had now begun to think differently. A new chapter in international affairs had opened.

The thing I wanted to do most at Nuremberg was to see face to face the men whose names had assaulted my ears and eyes through the radio and newspaper headlines of the world and changed the pattern of my life. So on the first or second day there, I found my way through the maze of corridors to the door that led into the courtroom where the trial was in progress. Pushing through the door, I found myself at what could have been the back of the dress circle in a theatre. A few people were sitting in this dress circle but there were many empty seats. I found a seat near the front and looked down on the courtroom below me, where the slow relentless drama of the trial was in progress. My eyes went first to the left, to the dock. And there they were, row behind row of the world-shaking leaders who had led the plot and the war against humanity. Individual faces and expressions could be seen very clearly because each row was raised higher than the one in front of it. In the very back row stood American military police in their snowy white helmets and white gloves.

My first emotion was that of disappointment. This bunch of men, some twenty of them in the dock, looked so ordinary, so insignificant.

Some of them even looked pathetic. Of course, none of them had the glittering badges of rank and status to bolster their importance. Most wore civilian clothes and even the few permitted to wear their former uniforms looked, without badges, as if they were wearing ordinary civilian suits. Ribbentrop, stripped of his ego of importance, wore a pitiful expression of haunted agony. Hess, who had been mad enough to fly to England, hoping to bring the British Government onto the German side against Russia, still looked half mad. The big chiefs of the services who sat there were no longer big. They were little, unhappy, worried men. Only Hermann Goering, sitting on the right of a front row, still had some charisma. His expression was one of indifference, nonchalance, even slight amusement at the whole proceedings. It was as if he was nursing some secret not yet revealed, as indeed he was.

I turned my attention to the court proceedings. Doctor Schacht, the renowned German financier, was in the witness box. However humble his attire, his intelligent face would have made this man impressive. Furthermore, he seemed to be doing quite well under the brilliant cross-examination of the star of the Allied prosecution, Sir David Maxwell Fyfe. I could follow the proceedings by wearing the earphones provided and switching the small lever on the arm of my chair to the word 'English'. Then whichever of the four languages in the court was being spoken, I would hear it almost instantaneously in English. Those who wished to hear things in French or German or Russian could do so comfortably by a similar procedure. Some of the best translators in the world must have been brought into service here at the trials.

The court was conducted on Anglo-American lines, but there was a panel of judges drawn from the four main Allied countries. Also there were two prosecuting lawyers from each of the four countries. The counsel for defence consisted of a number of German lawyers chosen in the main by the accused themselves. But the most impressive figure in the court was its president, Lord Chief Justice Geoffrey Lawrence. This mild-mannered British judge won the respect and admiration of everybody in the court, including the accused. He seemed to be the linchpin that held the unwieldy proceedings together and allowed the trial to proceed with dignity and an air of impartiality.

The four charges laid against the men in the dock were:

(1) crimes against peace

(2) war crimes

(3) crimes against humanity, which, of course, included genocide as carried out in the concentration camps, and

(4) the common plan and conspiracy of the Nazi party.

The launching of an agressive war, which Germany did by the invasion of Poland in 1939, had been recognised as an international crime by the leading nations of Europe, Germany among them, before this time. The purpose of the trial was to determine to what extent, if any, each of the accused was guilty of one or more of these indictments. A good deal of time had been spent before the opening of the trial in gathering, from German archives and other places, thousands of documents relating to these charges. Counsel for prosecution and defence had access to these relevant documents for the preparation of their cases.

The presentation of the case for the prosecution took about three months. The case for the defence was allowed five months, which indicates that the defence was given a good hearing. The long speeches of the defending German lawyers were only curtailed by the President of the court, Sir Geoffrey Lawrence, when they went off into airy flights of metaphysics and Nazi propaganda. Often they presented opinion as evidence and seemed to vie with each other in quotations from the philosophers, mainly German ones. I noted that, when in the witness box under cross-examination, many of the accused hid behind the authority of their Führer, Adolf Hitler, who had committed suicide in Berlin at the end of the war. Very few of his henchmen on trial were brave enough to speak up boldly in defence of the Nazi principles which they had served. They were, with the exception of Goering, a sorry lot, more like cringing hounds than heroes who had sought to bestride the world.

During the three months I spent at Nuremberg, my Public Relations duties were not time-demanding, and I was able to enjoy the grim drama of the courtroom for many hours. I gained the impression that the trial was by no means a front for wreaking vengeance on the conquered people, as some thought. It was, as far as possible under the circumstances, a fair and just trial. I noted, however, with some disgust, that the law representatives of Stalin's Communist Russia were more interested in airing their Communist propaganda than in the facts of the situation. As I had had some brushes with the Russian Army in their zone of Germany after the war, I was not altogether surprised to find this domination of propaganda in their thinking and speaking.

The historic trials were still going on when I was demobilised from the army and returned to England in June, 1946. So I had to learn about the conclusion of the trial from other sources. My main and most reliable source was the book written by Robert Cooper, entitled *The Nuremberg Trials* and published by Penguin. This book was made up from his dispatches, recognised by the press corps as the best out of Nuremberg. Sadly, however, this historic document now seems to be out of print and I had to search the libraries of Australia to find one battered copy.

I was back in Germany in the press division of the Control Commission when the Nuremberg trials ended in October, but I was stationed far away in Westphalia when news of the end and of the verdicts became known. Before hearing what had actually happened, I was surprised to see smiles on the faces of old men driving elevators, waiters in the clubs and other German men. It was as if a sudden shaft of sunshine had come into their lives and I wondered why. Robert Cooper gives a good description of that last day of the trial when verdicts were announced that wrote the end of Hitler's little day. The court was crowded and loud speakers had been fitted in the corridors so that all in the Palace of Justice could hear the judgements of the court. Through a sliding doorway at the back of the court, the accused came in one by one, stood in the empty dock alone and, with headphones attached, heard in their own language their sentence pronounced in the dispassionate voice of Lord Chief Justice Lawrence.

The first to come was Hermann Goering; he heard his sentence of death and strode, without word or any show of emotion, back through the sliding door. The next to come was Hess, retaining his air of abnormality. Waving aside the proffered headphones, he looked idly around the court as if not listening to his sentence of life imprisonment, then walked jauntily from the dock. Five sentences were passed in fifteen minutes. Altogether twelve sentences of death by hanging were passed. Seven others were given terms of imprisonment from life to ten years. To the surprise of many, some were acquitted. One of these was the financier Dr Schacht, but it was some time before he could leave his prison cell because it was known that many Germans were waiting to recapture and re-try him. He knew that from his fellow countrymen he would probably receive the sentence of death.

The setting of the final scene of the monstrous Nazi plan against humanity was, appropriately enough, the grimy gymnasium of the prison where American GI's played their ball games. Three scaffolds stood in this gymnasium on October 16, 1946 and at dead of night, under the glaring lights, those adjudged the chief leaders of the Nazi crimes met their nemesis at the end of a rope. That is, eleven of the twelve condemned men were hanged here. The twelfth, Hermann Goering, had died by his own hand on the night before the executions. He had swallowed a phial of potassium cyanide which, a board of enquiry decided, he had carried on his person right through the trials, thus making a mockery of American military security. Now I knew the reason for his little mocking smile, worn throughout the trials. I understood, too, the reason for the little wintry smiles on the faces of a few old Germans in Westphalia. For, whatever they may now have thought of their Nazi leaders, Hermann Goering, second in power only to Hitler and the commander-in-chief of the German airforce, had laughed at the security of his gaolers and beaten the Allied hangman's rope. To them, death by suicide was more dignified and honourable for a commander than death by hanging, like a common criminal.

But whether by suicide, the hangman's rope or the prison cell, the end of the Nazi evil was not dignified. I believe that at Nuremberg we had witnessed a trial that was just, fair and as impartial as humanly possible. It was, no doubt, the hope of many who laboured there in the name of Justice and of freedom-loving men everywhere that the trials would become a landmark in human history. It is more than likely that the future will see the rise of other anti-Christs, godless men who would crucify humanity and wade through blood to the throne of world power. But it is hoped that the precedent of Nuremberg will stand as a grim warning to such men.

But by the time the trials were over, or perhaps even before that, I had arrived at a not so happy conclusion. We had used a demon to eliminate a demon. Now at some time, and in some way, we would have to deal with this second demon: Stalinist totalitarian Russia. And though the Western world paused breathless for a time, soon came the Cold War with the growing threat of a nuclear holocaust bringing about the destruction of the world and of humanity. The thorn we had used to extract a thorn from the flesh was now festering in the flesh of mankind itself.

This century saw not one but two gigantic threatening tides of darkness. To me now, in hindsight, it seems significant that Satya Sai Baba was born in 1926 when both tides were rising and gathering their strength. Does this not mean that the Avatar of God Himself had come to spearhead the unseen forces of Light against the Satanic powers that were threatening to overturn His Divine Plan for humanity? It was a timely arrival for a world-changing, epoch-making Avatar.

8. *Life Transcends The Ruins*

I sometimes think that never blows so red
The Rose as where some buried Caesar bled.
OMAR KHAYYAM

THE WAR THAT had shattered cities, wrecked national economies, and changed the pattern of many lives, also brought the final ruin of my marriage with Gwen. Yet I cannot blame the war entirely. The seeds of incompatibility were in our personalities from the beginning and there was no deeper spiritual tie to hold us together. We faced the situation during my demobilisation leave of several months between leaving the army in Germany and returning there as an official of the Control Commission in September, 1946. The scarcities of the war-time years had made Gwen very tired of life in England. She longed to go back to Australia, the land of plenty, the land where her only blood relations, her father and two brothers, were waiting to welcome her. I, for my part, had not finished with Europe and especially with Germany. Apart from having agreed to return there officially, something deep within me called me back to what I felt had once been my own Fatherland. I needed to spend more time among my Teutonic cousins. I needed to observe and, in a sense, share their life among the ruins. So my wife and I decided to part. She would sail back to Australia on the first available ship and I would answer my heart's call and go back to Germany. "We must cut clean and have a divorce," Gwen announced. The idea of this shocked and appalled me. For in myself, as in my dear old mother, there was a streak of conventional puritanism. But after some years it went the way that she had said and we were, in fact, divorced. Young Richard 'of the Lionheart' went, of course, with his mother and I did not see him again for a number of years.

By the end of the year, my dull routine work with the Control Commission was left behind and I had accepted a promising opening with the paramilitary organisation known as the Navy, Army and Airforce Institutes, or NAAFI, for short. It was a plum job. I was the organisation's director of public relations and advertising for Western Europe. This meant that, with the equivalent army rank of lieutenant colonel, I had a staff car in which I could drive myself all over western Germany, into Austria and Trieste, with occasional pleasant returns to Paris and Brussels. My headquarters were in Westphalia, not far from the headquarters of the British Army of the Rhine.

The author in uniform during World War II.

After a year or two in this job, as the scope of work was expanding, I established a branch public relations office in Hamburg and made a number of friends in that fascinating, virile city. Though, in one terrible night, acres of the city had been reduced by Allied bombing to flat fields of scattered bricks, in the rest of the city the pulse of life still throbbed with persistent strength. I felt very much at home there. The bulk of my travels were, naturally, in the British zone of occupation in Germany and Austria, but this suited me well enough.

The unbelievable acres of ruin in the Ruhr and other war-shattered cities such as Hanover were, of course, depressing, but to make up for that were the rolling rich farmlands with their shining rivers, the great gentle pine forests, the architectural gems left standing in villages and small towns and even one or two beautiful old cities that had escaped destruction, such as Lubeck. But most appealing of all was life among my German cousins. I felt that I could spend a long time, though not the rest of my life, among them. It was like going back to what was folksy and homespun in myself. But I, of Anglo-Saxon blood, had moved too far away from the Teutonic blood to remain for too long a span in the Fatherland.

Yet it was somehow hard to tear myself away. From the time I first crossed the Rhine with the army till the day I finally left Germany, almost six years had slipped by. General Helmuth von Moltke of the German High Command in World War I had prophesied, from beyond the grave, the rise of Hitler and Nazism, saying that the resulting holocaust would bring Germany to a state of moral degradation among her smoking ruins. There is no doubt about the ruins, though the smoke had long subsided, but I did not see the life of the people as that of a state of moral degradation. The situation was simply that thousands of Allied troops had been brought together with thousands of German women. The wives and sweethearts of the men had been left behind, the husbands and lovers of the women were either dead or away in prisoner-of-war camps, so when masses of womanless men and menless women meet the result is not difficult to foretell, especially when both sides had been through years, harsh years of wartime discipline, and now hoped to enjoy what *Alice in Wonderland* called 'jam today'. Inevitably many unmarried daughters of respectable families were soon pushing perambulators. I salute the normally conventional German parents for accepting this situation. Perhaps this acceptance was the beginning of the change of the old, rigid, cruel attitude of convention towards unmarried mothers in the Western world. In Germany, it was interesting that Mother Nature was playing her wise part too. The majority of babies were male, so that a reasonable balance of the sexes would again be established.

It is true that for a period the black market became the normal market, but this was not moral degradation; it was a necessity for living. The old reichsmark had become valueless and the ancient method of barter had returned. The main items used in this were cigarettes, chocolates, coffee, alcohol and such luxury items coming from the army of occupation. From the German side came articles such as cameras, binoculars and jewellery. If I wanted to hire a horse to ride, I paid the owner not in valueless reichsmarks but in cigarettes. If I wanted to have a suit of clothes made, I paid the tailor in cigarettes, coffee or bottles of alcohol, whichever he desired. I can still see streams of German women trekking along the roadways to a farm where they could buy the food they needed. But the farmers would not take reichsmark currencies for their products. The joke current among the Germans was that on the farms the pigs were wearing gold earrings and the cows were walking on Persian carpets.

Whenever possible, I used to treat some of my German friends to sumptuous meals at one of the British clubs where such fraternisation was permitted. This would be in a club of the British Control Commission, never in a British Army Officers' Club. I noted too with some surprise that the Christian churches were always full for Sunday services. Was this, I wondered, a reaction to the anti-Christian Nazi rule. Then, the services over, the Germans would go for the recreation they loved, long walks in the country. On the whole, the German people, humbled, repentant with nothing beyond the bare necessities for living, seemed more spiritually alive and happier than they had been when in a state of material plenty, but living under the stern, repressive heel of the Nazi bosses.

Before I left Germany, I saw the beginnings of a great economic change. The Marshall plan had begun. The valuable deutschemark had replaced the old reichsmark so that now the money was worth working for. More and more men were returning from faraway prisoner-of-war camps. So, with these factors, came the rebirth of worldly ambitions for wealth and position. More and more goods began to appear in the shops and day and night I could hear the hammer of reconstruction. The deathless German energy and industriousness were resurrected and a beaten people were beginning to rebuild the broken country. Perhaps, I felt, given the right leaders, a high spiritual destiny lay ahead for these people and this land of my heart.

But what of my own search for the Grail of meaning? It seemed to have gone into abeyance during these years in Germany. Parsifal had forgotten about his search. The Prodigal Son had gone off on a detour and become immersed in the sensuous life again. Odysseus' long, hazardous journey to the true home had been interrupted by years spent with the nymph Calypso and the reformed witch Circe. There had been many Circes and Calypsos in post-war Germany and Austria. In the whole of that six-year period, I can remember only one small peephole in the curtain of *Maya*. That was when in Vienna I looked on the

The author in Germany in 1948 broadcasting over British Forces Network (BBC) for the Navy, Army & Airforce Institutes (NAAFI).

Cathedral of St Stefans. I don't know the reason why, but at that moment I once more experienced the uplift and expansion of consciousness that reminded me of something beyond the pleasures of the flesh, and the voice of the wise hermit within told me that my search must continue. Perhaps, however, as the myths and legends seemed to show, a period of rest, of respite with a taste of jam on the bread, is a necessary recuperation, a necessary tax paid to Caesar during this long, long odyssey to the spiritual home.

The time came around when I felt I must leave the prehistoric home deep in my subconscious and return to my present home in Australia. After twelve years away, it was high time I saw my mother again. Now in her mid-seventies, she would, maybe, not have much longer to live, and I must see her once more before the beloved form vanished into the great unknown. I would return to my Australian roots, not to settle down there, but to see my old mother and young son again, before setting forth once more to search through the cloud of worldly stars for my own promised star of meaning.

Airline travel to Australia had not yet begun in the late German spring of 1951 and berths on passenger ships were hard to come by. But through the influence of what was known then as 'the old boy net', I managed to get a sea passage more quickly than I had hoped. I was reluctant to leave but the wave of other people's well-meaning efforts engulfed me. I found myself, once again, on a white P&O liner, her sharp bows carving the seas southward towards Sydney.

9. *Hidden Steps Towards The Goal*

I am not of this world, for it does not suffice
to explain myself to me. I do not come from earth
and I am going elsewhere. But where?
This is the mystery of Psyche which includes all others.

PYTHAGORAS

I STOOD ON deck as my ship drew into the wharf in Sydney Harbour, my eyes searching through the waiting crowd, hoping to see a face that I knew. But I could find no recognisable face. I knew that my sister Leone would not be there because she had married an American during my twelve years' absence and was now far away in America. But I had hoped that my mother and sister Rita would come to meet me. Finally, I caught sight of my mother, now grown stouter and more wrinkled. But who was the thin bent woman beside her, and the three lively children? Unbelievably, I discovered when I disembarked that it was my sister Rita. But what had happened to my old playmate of the Westwood meadows? Now only in her mid-forties, she looked close to sixty. It was as if her three children had taken over her vitality and now ruled the world that was once my home. A chronic lung disease had established itself and was ruling the life of my old companion. What had happened in her life to cause such a devastation, I wondered. Some years later, after my sister died, I gained a clue to the mystery. While I was on a visit to Leone in America, she told me that Rita's husband, a naval man whom I had known before the war, was a compulsive gambler and had caused Rita a great deal of trouble and misery. This was most probably a factor in my old playmate's tragedy. Always humble, always unselfish and self-effacing, my dear sister Rita died a few years after my return.

My first feeling about Australia was that I did not belong here. It was not yet time for me to take my rest by the home fires. My search had not been completed and, until I found my star of meaning, I must continue to wander the earth. I felt a strong urge to take the next outward-bound ship, but there was my mother. I had been away from her for a long time and I felt that she would not have many more years on earth. I should try to spend them with her. So, reluctantly, I turned a deaf ear to the call of foreign places and decided to stay, at least for a few years.

The first necessity was to find a job. My last job in Germany had included most of the facets of modern Public Relations: writing for editorial publicity and commercial advertising, managing a staff of artists, photographers and office workers, regular radio broadcasting over the British Forces Network — a branch of the British Broadcasting Commission (BBC) — press relations and entertaining. I wrote about a dozen letters to the managing directors of Sydney's largest companies. Most of them brought me an interview. But I was a little downcast to find that in almost every case I had to give a lecture to the managing director explaining to him the meaning and function of public relations. Perhaps I should not have been surprised because before the war when I tried to find out the meaning of the term, the only one who could tell me anything was my friend the Principal of the School of Applied Advertising. He loaned me a textbook on Public Relations, saying he thought it was the only one in Sydney.

Eventually, in the middle of 1951, about a month after I landed from the ship, I was somehow led to the right place. This was a newly established chemical manufacturing company, a subsidiary of one of Australia's oldest commercial organizations. As Public Relations and Advertising Director, I did much of the same kind of work as I had in Europe, except that there was no radio broadcasting. Another difference was that I now had to write articles on scientific subjects for the understanding of the general reader. The old love in my student days of Chemistry and Physics stood me in good stead here and I gained good experience in giving simple, clear explanations of abstruse subjects.

Another advantage of the job was that it took me at times to Canberra to make contact with government circles. In this way I was able to spend more time with Gwen and Richard. I had first gone to see them in Canberra soon after my arrival in Australia. Gwen had put aside her beloved art work and taken a job teaching small boys at Canberra Grammar School. In this way she was Richard's teacher for his first year at school and was able to keep a motherly eye on him during the subsequent years. She seemed to be a born teacher and loved her new profession. Not until many years later, after her retirement as a teacher, did she go back to her art work. Although divorced, we remained very good friends and I was able to stay with Gwen and Richard in her school house during my visits to Canberra.

But although I was beginning to enjoy the social and business life of Australia, it was all within the thick walls of Maya, through which no light came until 1954. Then my sister Leone arrived from America with two small children, and a few grey hairs above her intelligent forehead, to spend a holiday in Sydney. Ever my good companion, she told me about a spiritual illumination she had had working with a friend and teacher in America. She also brought me several spiritual books that seemed to open a door for me and rekindle the slumbering fire of my Grail search. The royal visit of the Queen of England that same year was of very secondary importance to the visit of my twin-soul sister.

About a year after Leone's return to America, I took another preliminary step towards my goal. This was very hidden and I had no idea of its significance at the time. One day I walked into a large bookshop, looking for more spiritual books, for which my sister had whetted my appetite. On the wall above a line of books was a very small poster advertising yoga classes. I knew from the illustration, a fine specimen of a man in a yoga posture, that this was the body culture type of practice called Hatha Yoga. Many years earlier, when I was a student, I had read a book on Raja Yoga. Somehow the word yoga had a strong appeal to me, but I knew then that I was not ready for the way of life that it demanded. As I stood in the bookshop in Sydney in 1955, I felt that I was ready now for Hatha Yoga. I regarded it as a kind of physical culture and felt sure that, after the years of social life demanded by public relations work, it would give me the health and harmony I needed. So I decided to enrol in the classes.

I found that the classes were conducted several evenings each week in the large upper room of a building in Lower George Street. The teacher was the fine physical specimen I had seen on the poster. His name was Michael Volin. I subsequently learned that he had come to Sydney from Shanghai where he had worked in a yoga school with a Russian-born lady known as Indra Devi. She later became famous in America as a teacher of some of the film stars and the author of a number of books on westernised yoga.

When I began going to Volin's classes twice a week, I told myself that I was only interested in the physical culture side, not in yoga philosophy. Others, I knew, came to the classes with the same pure physical get-fit motive, but all of them, like myself, gradually became interested in the deeper side of the subject. We learned the postures from simple ones to the headstand, the mudras, the breath control, the yoga breathing and the control of *prana* (subtle cosmic energy), These practices certainly brought a sense of well-being to the body, but they also had a subtle effect on the mind. I began to feel that I wanted to have a deeper understanding of the meaning and purpose of yoga. The word yoga, I knew, meant 'union', but union with what? Did it simply mean the union of the forces within your own body and mind, so that you reached a state of harmony? Or, did it mean union with the higher being we call God? There seemed to be differences of opinion about this and I could see that there was much to learn.

As we Hatha Yoga students advanced in body control, yoga breathing and conscious relaxation of the nervous system, we began to learn two Raja Yoga practices: mental concentration and meditation. During the decade of the fifties, the famous yoga teacher, Sir Paul Dukes, came to Sydney and conducted classes for several months. I attended his classes which were on much the same lines as those of Michael Volin. Sir Paul was advanced in years and it was an inspiration to see how, through Yoga, he had retained a supple, vital, youthful body.

During these years, life on the surface was becoming more satisfying, but underneath there was always the persistent urge to be off on my travels again. Then, in the latter part of 1957, the emotional tie that had been holding me in Australia was broken. My mother, who had always wanted to end her life suddenly while attending her rose bushes in her garden, was fated to spend a whole year in bed with cancer. I went to see her as often as possible, but my conscience nagged me that it was not often enough. It was, I feel, by the grace of God, that I happened to be sitting beside her bed, holding her hand, when the rattle in her throat told me that, at the age of eighty-one, my first spiritual guru had left her body. The cliché 'death is a happy release' certainly applied in her case, but I could not help feeling sorrow at the passing of the form I had known and loved so long. I felt reasonably sure that there is a life hereafter but, to make sure that she was all right, I began a search for her through spiritist mediums and clairvoyants. When I eventually found her, I learned that this search, born of my love for my mother, had helped her. Love from the living is always a help to those who have passed on. I tell about this search in another book* so will not repeat the details here.

I was now free, with my mother's passing, to set off on my odyssey again, so I began to plan it. This time I would go first to the isles of Greece where my friend Alan Moorehead had stayed to write one of his books and two other Australians I knew were in the same, quiet, remote setting for their writing. I might, I thought, somewhere in those magical isles, find the right spot to settle and

---

* *Beyond Death The Undiscover'd Country* by Howard Murphet (Quest Books, 1990).

write my own serious books, when I had finally imbibed and assimilated the right authentic material for them. In the meantime, my wanderings must go on. And I must say, world-wandering was something I enjoyed for its own sake.

A few months after my mother's death, something of great karmic importance happened to me. I had no idea at the time, within the limits of my human vision, that it was in fact a significant step towards my ultimate goal. One day in January, 1958, I was standing on the pavement in Lower George Street outside the entrance to Michael Volin's yoga school. I was waiting there because I thought I had arrived a little too early for the school. As I watched the traffic, I saw a car pass slowly near me in which there was a woman. Suddenly I had the feeling that I had known this woman before and that I would like very much to know her again. But she had gone on in her car and there was little chance that I would ever see her again. I felt sorry, even a little frustrated, at the thought. But about five minutes later, I saw her walking along the pavement towards me. What could I do to detain her, I wondered. But before I had decided on any plan of action, she turned suddenly and went through the door that led to the stairway up to the yoga school. I decided it was now time for me to go in, too, so I followed her up the stairs.

On the landing at the top of the long flight, she was knocking on the door of the school. There was no response, so, after a moment, I knocked too. After further alternate knocking, we both realised that we had come a week too early after the Christmas vacation and that the school had not yet begun for 1958. This led easily to some conversation between us. During this, she asked me if I were Indian. It seemed to me an odd question, even though the light on the landing was not very bright. When I assured her that I had never even been to India, she said simply, "There seemed to be something Indian about you." It was odd, we thought, that as we had both been going to the yoga school for several years, we had never seen each other before. Perhaps we had never gone on the same evening. It seemed as if we both had to make the same error in order to meet at this particular moment. We had dinner together at a restaurant that evening and so our romance began.

Her name was Iris Godfrey. Born in England, she went through the full training there as a medical nurse. After qualifying, she came to Australia with her mother and sister, arriving at Sydney in the same year that I returned from my wanderings. Now she was in charge of a nursing clinic at a large industrial complex. Curiously, we thought, she had been attracted to the yoga school by the same notice in the bookshop that had led me there. I was pleased to find that she had had a good deal of experience in the psychic world and, like me, was keenly interested in the deeper search for the spiritual meaning of life.

About a year later, we were planning to get married. But where? It must be where the marriage ceremony imparted some sacramental, spiritual meaning. Eventually, through hearing a broadcast sermon from the Liberal Catholic Church of St Alban's, we decided to attend one of their services there. I shall never forget the day I first came into that church and walked down the aisle towards the altar. There seemed to be a large number of ministers busy performing the rituals. From memory, I think there were two bishops, two priests, several deacons and an acolyte. Great power seemed to emanate from the altar and, for the first time in my life, I felt that church ritual had a meaning and an impact on Man's deeper mind or soul. It certainly had an impact on me. It seemed almost as if I was lifted off my feet and floated into my pew. Afterwards we were invited to a room at the back of the church, where the members of the priesthood had tea. Over tea and biscuits, we met them all and were not sure whether they were wise men or angels. In fact, they were ordinary businessmen during the week and gave their Sundays to the service of the church without payment.

We began attending the services at St Alban's Church (now, alas, no more) regularly every Sunday. All the ministers were members of the Theosophical Society and, through their influence, we eventually joined the Society too. We planned to have the full marriage ceremony at St Alban's Liberal Catholic Church, which had, among its other spiritual assets, a fine organ and a talented organist. But before the blessed event that was to make us partners in the great search, I had a memorable yogic experience.

It came unexpectedly, like all the chinks that appear in the wall that holds us prisoners in the world of the senses. Iris and I had independently read the inspiring book *The Autobiography of a Yogi* by Paramahansa Yogananda and had begun taking lessons by correspondence from the Self Realisation Fellowship, which Yogananda had founded in America. Then, a member of the Fellowship, known at that time as Brother Kriyananda, appeared in Sydney and began giving lectures. Iris and I attended the lectures. He followed the lectures with lessons, which I attended alone because Iris was unable to go. During one lesson — I think it was the second — Brother Kriyananda was sitting on the stage dressed in shining white robes, beneath his black beard, and playing the harmonium to accompany the Yogananda chants.

I think it was during the chant 'Oh God Beautiful', which appealed to me greatly, that I was flooded with bliss. So much so, my consciousness disappeared. Nothing existed anywhere but the unutterable bliss of being. I came out of it, back to consciousness, as my body fell sideways, almost hitting the floor.

This out-of-time experience of the Ananda that is part of our inner nature, taught me a number of things. A practical one was the reason for having a firm seat, preferably cross-legged on the floor, for meditation practice. The aim of meditation is to reach that state of *samadhi* of which I had tasted a little. With its coming, awareness of the world vanishes and, unless firmly seated in a stable position, the meditator is liable to fall to the floor, as I almost did. More importantly, however, the experience was a reaffirmation of the Reality I sought. Brief tastes of it, such as this, whet the appetite for the bottomless chalice of ambrosia, and to find it the pilgrim moves onward, ever onward.

We were married in St Alban's Church in May, 1959. One unexpected, unhappy result of this happy event was a letter from Gwen telling me that, now I was married again, I would not be welcome in Canberra to see Richard any more, nor would she permit him to come to Sydney to see me, as he had often done in the past. I was stunned. How strange, how inexplicable are women, I thought! But then I remembered that women do not have the monopoly of inexplicability. Men also seem curiously planned. As a woman sighed when the caravan left for the golden road to Samarkand, "They have their dreams and do not think of us."* Anyway, I consoled myself, the ban did not make such a difference as I would be leaving Australia in a few months. Some day in the future, when God willed it, I would see my son again.

One of our preparations for the journey to Europe was to buy a Volkswagen from the manufacturers in Germany at about half the price it would have cost us in Sydney. It would be ready to be picked up in Munich soon after our arrival in Europe. With the car we planned to tour all countries of Western Europe. "But what will you do for money?" our friends asked. "We will live on the smell of an oily rag, especially if it's motor oil," we laughed. The great thing, we told each other seriously, was to live a free, unshackled life and not worry about anything. When our nest-egg of savings began to run low, I could earn money by my pen from short stories and articles;

---

* From *Hassan* by James Elroy Flecker.

and while we were in England, which was on our travel itinerary, Iris would have no difficulty in finding employment as a nurse. We knew that all this was really in the kindly hands of the great One who sits above.

We booked passages to Athens on the Greek passenger ship *Patris*, leaving Sydney in May, 1960. So it was just a year after our marriage that we drove towards Circular Quay, where our ship waited. Our driver was our friend, Nancy Phelan, whom we had met at the yoga school, and in the car was Iris's mother, Eve Godfrey. She was coming to join our many friends who would be waving farewell from the wharf.

It was a sunny autumn day as we came near the ship that would take us on the most enjoyable sea voyage into the most wonderful years of my life.

10. New Lamps For Old

We are Thy Light, by mortal lamps enshrouded ...
Shatter the lamps, the Light, the Light remains.

FROM A HYMN TO SIVA

THE GREEK SHIP, the *Patris*, had just begun the business of running immigrants from Greece to Sydney and was striving to build up a passenger trade for the return journey. This was not easy because the powerful shipping ring was doing its utmost to squeeze the Greek intruder out of any profitable business. This was to prove a boon for us, though we did not at first realise it. In fact, when we arrived on the wharf, we had to push our way through a dense crowd to get aboard the ship and then we found all decks absolutely crowded with people. The whole Greek community of Sydney seemed to be there to shout their excited farewells to the ship as she began her journey to their fair home. Some could not resist the temptation to sail on her as far as Melbourne, there to disembark and come back to Sydney by train. After all this excited activity was behind us, we found that the ship was little more than half full. This is, of course, good for the passengers, though bad for the shipping line.

On board we met an Australian married couple, who proved to be both good shipboard companions and a help to us in our search for new Lamps in the dark world. Their names were George and Helen Sandwith. They had previously travelled a large part of the world in search of miracles and, in fact, had had a book published called *The Miracle Hunters*. But the only miracle they seemed to have unearthed was the fire-walking in the Pacific islands. Now they were off again on another miracle hunt. Their real value to us was that they told us about a new spiritual movement that had started in Indonesia, spread to America and England and other places, and had recently touched Australia, just before we set sail on the *Patris*. The new movement was known as Subud. It had been introduced to Australia by the English author of spiritual books, John Bennet. George and Helen had met John personally when he visited their home in Australia. They themselves had become followers of the Subud way and told us something about it as we sat on deck, enjoying the sunshine and the great blue spread of the Indian Ocean around us. They gave us a book on the subject, written by John Bennet himself, an appealing writer, and as we showed interest they wrote a letter of introduction to John for us, suggesting that we use it when we finally reached England.

The ship's master, Captain Z. Xenios, seemed to us to be a worthy modern representative of the ancient great ones. In short, he was a thorough gentleman and doing his best to create the goodwill that his owners needed to survive in this lucrative run. He gave two free cocktail parties to all the passengers aboard and as we left the Suez Canal and came into the Mediterranean, he announced that instead of going straight to Piraeus, the port of Athens, he would take us on a tour through the islands. This news seemed to gladden the hearts of everybody aboard, particularly those of Iris and myself.

The islands, floating in the opalescent light of sea and sky, seemed more like a dream than a piece of earth. The beauty was such that I felt I could not only see it but taste its refreshing flavour on my tongue. One of our fellow passengers, a professor of Classics from one of the Australian universities, was so overcome that when he finally went down the gangplank onto the mainland, he went on his knees and kissed the sacred earth.

The end of the voyage brought two more public relations favours from the shipowners. One was that we could stay aboard and use the ship as an hotel for three days and nights while being conducted on sightseeing tours around Athens by professional tour guides. The second was that the shipping company would pay half our fares from Athens to any part of Europe. These onward journeys were arranged through their travel agent. One of our tour guides was a young Greek Master of Arts from Cambridge University, England. He wore a white peaked cap and spoke perfect English. He took us to a number of spots that remain a joy in my memory. But the two that etched themselves indelibly into my soul were the Parthenon and Eleusis.

On the Acropolis the guide took us around and told us all that he could, but I gained something there that no guide could give. As I sat quietly alone, looking at the great skeleton of the Parthenon against the sky, I had another expansion and elevation of consciousness. I seemed to be lifted out of my body and carried above the ruins of the grand structure that crowns the Acropolis. As always, it was an indescribable out-of-time experience. Afterwards I wondered what beauty there was left in this ancient stone skeleton to have such an effect on me. Somehow I thought the beauty must lie in its proportions. Somewhere I had read of the lost Egyptian canon of proportion. This lost canon was used by the architects and artists of ancient Greece. It certainly would have been used, I think, in the construction of the

Parthenon. So perhaps it was this edifice of proportional perfection against the sky that had brought me the wonderful inner experience, yet it might also have been caused by the lingering psychic vibrations from all that had happened through the centuries in this mighty temple to the virgin goddess, Athena. The word Parthenon itself means virgin and on this sacred spot the ancient Greeks worshipped the virgin Mother who watched over the welfare and glories of the ancient city of Athens.

Another place of deep spiritual interest to me, probably not visited by the average tourist, lies a little distance outside the city of Athens. This is Eleusis. There was not actually much to see here on the ground, just some low walls and remains of a Greek temple. Our scholarly guide told us something about the dramas that took place here but did not touch on the inner significance of the place. I had learned a little of this already from Theosophical literature and learned much more later on. Eleusis had, in fact, been one of the most famous centres of the Mystery religion of the ancient world. As a lamp of the divine Light it had existed for about two thousand years, coming to an end in the early centuries of the Christian era. But it was a Lamp for the few, not for the many. The masses had the gods and goddesses of the myths to worship, but the few who were deemed worthy and ready were taught the deeper meanings that lie behind some of the myths. A moral, upright character seems to have been the main criterion by which candidates were accepted. Worldly power could not make you a member here. In fact, of all the mighty Roman emperors who applied for membership, only one was accepted. Most of them were evil men at heart and the Mystery religion at Eleusis seemed to have worked on Christ's principle, 'Cast not your pearls before swine or wild dogs lest they turn and rend you.' A vow that new members had to take indicates the high spiritual level of this Mystery school: "I swear to give up my life for the salvation of my brothers who constitute the whole of mankind and, if called upon to do so, to die in the defence of Truth."

The main myth used for deeper teachings here at Eleusis was the well-known myth of Persephone. To the average Greek of that time, this was simply a myth of the seasons, a story explaining how the seasons came about. At the same time, it showed them the power of Zeus, the Father of gods and men, and the slightly lesser power of the evil one, called Hades. But, to the candidates at Eleusis, the esoteric meaning of the myth was revealed through drama, ceremony, the ritual and actual visions of the Divine Light and the Gods.

Persephone, the beautiful maiden who, while playing in the pleasant meadows, was kidnapped by Hades and taken to the Underworld, symbolises the human soul going into incarnation. The Underworld of the myth represents our earth. Persephone's mother, Demeter, was the Goddess of the cornfields and all vegetation. Her sorrow at the disappearance of her daughter caused the crops to fail and famine to come to the earth. Greatly alarmed at the prospect for mankind, the Father god, Zeus, ordered Hades to release his captive. Hades needs must obey but, cunningly, he first gave her seven pomegranate seeds from the world of the dead to eat before he would release her. Her release symbolises the death of the human being and return of the soul to the heaven worlds. In the myth the heavens are symbolised by the sunny meadows and fields of ancient Greece. With great rejoicing, the divine Mother, Demeter, met her daughter, Persephone, the released soul, at the spot where Eleusis now stands. The joy of the Mother set the vegetation growing again and the life of mankind was saved. But Persephone had eaten the food of the dead, the pomegranate seeds, and these perforce called her back to the Underworld. Finally, Zeus, or the chief of the forces of good, came to an agreement with Hades, the chief of the forces of darkness, which would safeguard the life of humanity on earth. This was that Persephone would return to Hades in the Underworld for part of the year and for the rest of the year be with her mother in the worlds above. This meant alternating winter and summer to the common man of Greece, but to the initiates of Eleusis it meant the cycle of the soul's births and deaths, which we call human reincarnation. The pomegranate seeds that drew Persephone back symbolise mankind's karma, his desires, sins and attachments that call him back again and again to earth. He can, of course, escape the rebirths by refusing to partake of the pomegranate seeds, that is, by living a virtuous, blameless, wise life while on earth. These were the kind of spiritual and moral truths revealed to the fortunate initiates of this Mystery school.

On pain of death, members were forbidden to reveal what actually went on in the Mystery school. But through the two thousand years of the life of Eleusis, enough was leaked to indicate what took place. Much of this can be read in the works of Rudolph Steiner and Edouard Schure, particularly the latter's profoundly revealing book called *The Great Initiates*. Some of the great men of ancient Greece and Rome, while keeping their vow of secrecy, spoke of the effects of the Mystery revelations on them in terms of glowing praise. Plato, for example, wrote in his *Phaedrus*: "A man in the Mysteries alone becomes truly perfect," and, "Being initiated in those Mysteries, he is freed from the molestations and evils, which otherwise await us in a future period of time." Likewise, "in consequence of this divine initiation, we become spectators of entire, immovable, blessed visions resident in the pure Light." Proclus, another initiate of the Mysteries and a neoplatonic writer, speaks also of the pure divine Light witnessed in the ceremonies at Eleusis. He says: "In all the initiations and Mysteries, the gods exhibit many forms of themselves and appear in a variety of shapes." Here, at Eleusis, evidently one of the great insights was that God can take any shape or form and can also appear as formless, manifesting as Divine joy bringing Light. This is in accordance with one of the divine truths that Sai Baba taught me later.

So insights into the great eternal Reality that lies beyond appearances were given to the chosen few here at Eleusis. In consequence, such men lived lives that were inspirational to their fellow men. And many of them, such as Plato, wrote immortal words of wisdom that are still a guide to mankind. But here at Eleusis I was looking at a broken Lamp. Jesus Christ, himself 'rent by the wild dogs' of ignorance, told his apostles to preach the gospel to every person, not just to the few. Doing this, the apostles were themselves martyred by men of darkness, but the Lamp of Christianity was lighted for all and the Light that had shone only for the elite of character was finally extinguished.

Driving back from Eleusis to begin our tour of the Greek islands, I thought about how the carefully guarded Lamp of the Mystery religions, that had borne the Light of divine wisdom for some two thousand years, had been replaced by the Lamp of Christianity. This too had shone for about two thousand years. Was it also, stained by the dirt of human fingers, beginning to grow dim? The empty churches of many Western countries were beginning to say so. Had the time come, therefore, for a new major Lamp to arise and shine its beacon across the world? If so, would my search for Divine Light and wisdom reveal its beginning?

Our tour of the islands was a feast of shimmering light and colour. On the rocky, treeless island of Hydra we heard the sound of a typewriter and met the novelist Charmian Clift. She seemed strangely tense in the relaxed, sleeping tranquillity of the island. Seeing her, and remembering something Alan Moorehead had said to me about his experience on the Greek islands, I wondered if Iris and I could be happy in such a remote, lonely setting. Well, there was a motoring tour of Europe to come before we had to make that decision.

From Athens we went by a small ship through the narrow Corinth Canal to Brindisi in Italy then, travelling by train through Italy and Switzerland, we came to Munich where our car awaited us. On entering Germany, I felt that I had come to my old home again. Iris had this same inexplicable feeling, as if she had lived in Germany before. We decided to tour Austria first, spending some time in Vienna and in the Vienna woods at Baden-Bei-Wien. Then we returned to Southern Germany and rented a flat in Garmisch. From there we were able to do a good tour of Bavaria while waiting for the Passion Play to open at Oberammergau. We had booked seats for the theatre and hotel accommodation while still in Australia.

Driving into Oberammergau, we were struck by the shining new look of the buildings, each with its bright pictorial mural. It was as if the town had just the day before been lowered from some astral world above. This impression was enhanced by the fact that all the men and boys walking in the streets had long hair. The famous Passion Play is produced here once every ten years, and we learned that all the men and boys start to let their hair grow long some time before, hoping to have a part in the play, even if it's only in a crowd scene. We found that the accommodation booked for us from Australia was in the hotel owned and run by the man who played the High Priest, Caiphas, in the play. Watching him as the villain in the drama, we found it hard to respond suitably when he greeted us cheerily and warmly every time we met in the hotel. The best hotel in the town was run by Jesus, but that had been full up at the time we booked. However, Caiphas, the villain, proved to be a better actor than Jesus, whose whining, sorrowful performance seemed somehow out of character. Surely, I thought, Jesus the messenger of God, must be a man of joy, not sorrow. On the whole, we were both disappointed in this historic Passion Play. The only scene that impressed me enough to linger in my memory was when some followers of Jesus took his body from the cross and carried it towards the tomb. They handled the body that had borne their Messiah with such reverence and love that I myself felt a flow of love towards the body of the Lord.

After Oberammergau, there was a special house we wanted to visit in a village near Munich. As soon as we had taken the flat in Garmisch as a firm address for a while, we had sent the letter of introduction from George and Helen Sandwith to John Bennet in England. John had responded promptly, saying that we would be very welcome to stay at the Subud colony in Coombe Springs when we came to England, but in the meantime, he said, why not visit some

Subud places in Europe? And he gave us some addresses in Germany and France. The nearest address to us was this one in the village of Planegg-Bei-München, a few miles outside Munich.

In the middle of one sunny afternoon, we arrived outside a gate that led into a big garden. In the garden was a typical two-storey German house with pointed roof. A woman was busy tending the plants in the garden. Our plan had been to locate the address and then to drive off and find some suitable accommodation before returning and announcing our arrival. But as soon as the woman saw us in the car outside her gate, she dropped her garden tool and walked down the path towards us. She greeted us warmly with the surprising words, "I was expecting you this afternoon. A letter from John Bennet told me you were in this part of the country." But we had not informed her that we were coming to her house this day or any day. Were all the Subud people psychic, we wondered. She told us that there would be a Subud meeting in her house that very evening. She would telephone several of the Helpers and ask them to come before the meeting to decide if we were ready to be initiated that night. This rather carried us off our feet because we had only wanted to investigate, but the manner of the woman, whose name was Ruth Gruesen, was so friendly that we agreed. She recommended that we stay at a small hotel in the village and gave us the address.

The little hotel was clean and homely so, as suggested by Ruth, we booked in for a couple of nights. As if drawn by a force outside ourselves, we found we were back at Ruth's home in good time to meet the Helpers. Leaving us in one room, they went off into another to test if we were ready to be 'opened'. We knew that the word 'Helper' meant a senior member who had been in Subud for some time. We were not sure what 'testing' meant, but guessed that it probably had a psychic basis.

After some time the group of Helpers returned and happily told us that we were both ready for initiation. Soon after that, the main meeting began. Iris went off with a group of ladies and I found myself in a large room with some twenty or thirty German men. We had left our shoes outside the room and now removed watches, jewellery and anything hard from our pockets, putting these articles on a side table. Then we stood on the carpeted floor, silently waiting.

When the Helper, who was the leader of the group, said, "Begin", the whole scene changed suddenly. Standing near me, a tall blonde fellow, who reminded me of the SS guards, gave a moan and fell flat on his back. He fell unbendingly as a tree falls. But nobody took any notice of this. They were all busy doing their own thing. I was supposed to keep my eyes shut, but I was too interested to do so. I found that each man seemed engrossed in his own activities, as if nobody else was present. One was standing on his head, another was standing upright on his feet, with hands clasped in front, singing a Christian hymn fervently, several were crawling on hands and knees about the floor making noises like different animals. The gentlest were swaying about doing whatever physical exercises came to them. The quietest of all was lying on the floor, as if asleep.

After a while, I found myself swaying too and performing a few yoga warming-up exercises. Whether this was brought about by the divine current that was supposed to come into me, or whether it was just an urge brought about by the activities around me, I do not know. After half an hour of this, the leader stopped the *latihan*, as this exercise was called, and we all came back to our normal everyday selves. I asked the leader how this was supposed to open me. "It's like this," he replied. "A heap of dry grass among burning heaps catches fire from them. In the same way, you are open to the divine current by the power of those exercising around you." We had been warned by Ruth that we might, after opening, feel the symptoms of all of our old diseases. It was true that traces of the symptoms from many of our old complaints came back to us that night. Another unexpected effect was that we felt so happy that evening that we could not stop laughing. Back in our hotel room we continued to laugh. The noise was so uproarious that the manageress knocked on our door and looked in with a startled face.

After that, our tour of Germany was punctuated with visits to Subud centres. The latihan was much the same wherever we performed it, but we seemed to learn something new at each place. We were building up to a true understanding of this spiritual movement, which we felt would come when we spent some time at Coombe Springs, the headquarters in England. Meantime, it brought us ready-made friends in each country of Europe and made our tour twice as interesting and fulfilling than it might otherwise have been.

I was happy to see that my hard-working 'cousins' in the Fatherland had rebuilt all their ruined cities. But we preferred to stay, whenever possible, in small villages or in the countryside. As afternoons drew towards evenings, we kept a look-out for a *frendenheim gasthof*, or small hotel, and always found one. These were clean, homely and economical. At Wolksberg near the border of the forbidden Russian zone, we stayed a night or two at a Subud home. Here many people, most of them young, gathered for Subud latihans. Their leader was an ex-cavalry officer of the German army, who had sought for a spiritual centre in many places before he had found Subud. In Holland we were guests at the home of a Dutch Subud lady in the Hague. Our final Subud association was at Nice in the South of France.

Then, as winter was fast approaching, we motored through Spain to the Costa-del-Sol in the South. Here, in a quiet fishing village by the sea, but not far from the city of Malaga, we found a Moorish house right by the beach. The rent was incredibly low. So, warmed by the balmy airs from North Africa, I settled down to do some steady freelance writing while awaiting the coming of spring and England.

11. The Subud Way

Let different faiths exist. Let them flourish. Let the glory of God be sung in all the languages in a variety of tunes. Respect the differences between the faiths and recognise them as valid as far as they do not extinguish the flame of unity.

SAI BABA

IT WAS A glorious spring morning in the year 1961 when we drove through the English countryside towards Coombe Springs. On a quiet, tree-lined road, near the town of Kingston-on-Thames, about eight miles from London, we finally found the gateway. Just inside the gate was an attractive stone cottage called 'The Lodge'. We knew that John Bennet, with his wife Elizabeth and young family, lived here. Shown in by his wife, we found John at his desk. He was a big man with shaggy hair, a very wide forehead and intelligent eyes. He left his desk to walk with us up the short drive to the main house. This was an impressive two-storey building with extensions and outhouses. In front of it was a rose garden and all around there seemed to be extensive grounds, with many trees, shrubberies and lawns. Some of the Subud colony seemed busy in the gardens and inside the house, while others just sat and sunned themselves. John introduced us to several and then left while we were being shown to the room that had been allotted to us. This was a large upstairs room with a view across the Sussex downs. It gave us a feeling of promise.

Before taking our belongings from the car, we decided to explore the grounds. Seven acres of them, we were told, with high surrounding walls. In one secluded spot, we found an unusual-looking nine-sided building with stained-glass windows. This turned out to be a kind of Subud temple where the latihans were held. In another place we found a natural swimming pool and in a far corner was a stone pump house. One of the members opened the door and showed us inside. The pump was there but not really needed because the water, bubbling like champagne, came right up to the surface and could easily be dipped out with a jug. It tasted like the champagne of all waters.

This sparkling spring had, we learned later, played a little-known role in English history. Cardinal Wolsey, when Chief Minister of Henry VIII, had liked it so well that he had it piped from Coombe

Springs to his palace, Hampton Court. His water pipe had to cross the Thames, but was set down deeply enough to be safe from the shipping at his time. Sometime in later years, a ship with a deeper keel had broken the Cardinal's pipe and the precious Coombe water did not reach the other side of the Thames. Wolsey had died and the pipe was never repaired. But we enjoyed the water daily at the tables in the Coombe Springs dining room.

Members of the Subud colony could work part-time for their keep, full-time for their keep and a small wage, or pay their board and live a life of leisure. The majority worked while the rich few loafed. Iris, who had done a course in catering, was given the full-time job of catering officer, this position being vacant. Because I wanted to make some money by writing, Bennet agreed that I should do a part-time job at Coombe Springs for my keep. This was to take charge of the publications department, where there was a small printing machine, a printer who was not in Subud and a secretary who was. The main work here was the printing and preparation of a book on Subud, which was published later under the title *Subud and the Active Life*.

My open door to Fleet Street was my old friend, Larry Solon, who shared my happy memories of the Sicilian campaign. He was editor of a weekly journal in Fleet Street and introduced me to several other editors as well as to two literary agents, one for fiction and one for non-fiction. So, when not supervising the Coombe Springs publishing department, I kept busy writing articles and short stories for the London journals. The pay for these was good and we were able to store up a nest egg for our next winter in the sunshine. We decided it would be the south of Spain again with visits to Morocco.

There were a little over twenty residential members of the Subud centre at Coombe Springs. These were in the main from various parts of England, with several from European countries and one Australian apart from ourselves. The Australian, small in stature with the movements of a ballet dancer, was a graduate of Sydney University. At Coombe Springs she was the cook, and a very good one too. As cook and caterer, she and Iris worked in a happy partnership.

From discussions with our friends at Subud and weekly talks given by John Bennet, we began to learn a little more about Subud. Its birthplace was Indonesia and its founder, an Indonesian Muslim by the name of Mohammed Subuh, often called Pak Subuh which means 'Father Sunrise'. The story of its foundation is this. When Pak Subuh was a little over thirty years of age, he witnessed one day a great light coming towards him. The light was round in shape and brighter than the sun itself. Pak Subuh felt it come into his being and from that moment his outlook and life changed. A small group of Indonesians gathered around him and he knew that he was able to open them to the divine force that had come into him. And so his followers received the divine current or Light from him. He was aware that they too, in due course, would be able to open or initiate others who were ready to receive the power of Almighty God in this way.

The *latihan*, which is an Indonesian word meaning spiritual exercise, began to be practised regularly at the centre in Indonesia. Briefly explained, the latihan consists of surrendering yourself completely to the divine current or spirit and allowing It to do what It will to your body and mind. The personal will must be kept in the background or submitted entirely to the divine will. I knew from my opening night in Germany and my many practices of the latihan in different countries that the power did strange things to the bodies and minds of the people practising the latihan. The effects witnessed in oneself and others were considered to be purifying, balancing, harmonising work brought about in the person's physical, emotional and mental vehicles. It was evidently so powerful that Pak Subuh made the edict that no individual should practise the latihan more often than once a week and for a period of no more than half an hour. If the practice was overdone, I was told, it could lead to mental unbalance or even death. Two other strict rules were that men and women should never practise together and no person should practise alone until he had been in Subud for a considerable time. Helpers, or people of considerable experience, were appointed by Pak Subuh and it was considered desirable that there should be at least one Helper present at a latihan to begin and end the spiritual practice. When the door was open for the divine spirit to flood into one's being, there was no danger, we were told, of a low, unprogressed spirit taking advantage of the opening and slipping in. Some people thought otherwise and so, of course, they did not become members. One safeguard against possession or partial possession by an unwanted entity was that Helpers, when testing a candidate, would know if there was a history of mental unbalance or insanity in his family. We later saw a young Spanish friend of ours refused for this very reason.

Many people from London and other surrounding areas used to come to Coombe Springs, especially in the weekends, to practise the latihan with the residents. Among the people from London were two journalists I knew from Fleet Street. The latihans were nearly always held in the nine-sided temple, which was known as the *djami*, a shortened version of its real Indonesian name, the *djamichunatra*. I often practised here with sometimes scores of men at the same time. As soft light filtered in through the stained-glass windows and men were doing strange things under the influence of the inner force, I witnessed all that I had seen in Germany and France: bodily movements, violent or gentle, men crawling on their knees making noises like animals, others singing spiritual songs and hymns, some sitting quietly in yoga postures or standing on their heads, some lying quietly on the bench that ran around the walls of the building — they appeared to be asleep and perhaps they were. Several times I saw one man making the sign of the cross in front of his friend who seemed to be lost in some manifestation of his animal nature. Sometimes there was a great noise, yet I always felt isolated from that noise, as if I was in the quiet centre of a cyclone. At the end of half an hour, which seemed timeless, the helper would call "stop", and we would go downstairs to the lower exit room to put on our shoes, collect our watches, rings and any other hardware. Then, in silence, we would go out into the beautiful gardens. I always felt completely relaxed, cleansed and somehow renewed. That was all I ever felt consciously from the Subud latihan, though to some it reportedly brought hidden lifts of consciousness.

Subud was a practice rather than a philosophy. In fact, very little was written about its philosophy and such writing was not encouraged. Pak Subuh had visited and given talks in various countries to which Subud had spread. He had given a series of talks in England, not long before we went there, and it was those talks that we were putting together in book form in the small publishing department at Coombe. All members of Subud referred to the leader as Bapak, which meant 'little father', so I will use this title of affection for the rest of the chapter.

Bapak had put three Sanskrit words together to compose the title of his spiritual movement. These were *susila*, meaning surrender to God, *budhi*, which can be translated as the intuitional faculty for acquiring direct knowledge of truth without the use of the reasoning mind — it might also be called Truth-consciousness. The third word, *dharma*, may be translated simply as right living, or living a righteous life. These three words give the key to Subud teaching. By surrendering to the will of God, the student will learn to reach beyond the mind to the deepest truth of being and thus come to live his life rightly. Those three aspects, surrender, Truth-seeing and right living, come together to create the Subud life. In the latihan help towards these three major aims was given by the divine spirit. I felt there could be some parallel here with the visitation of the Holy Spirit in early Christian times when people spoke in tongues and later with the Shakers and Quakers, whose very names come from the fact that in their early years they shook and quaked when the spirit of God entered and drenched their bodies and minds.

Another interesting and valuable practice in Subud is known as 'receiving'. This is an individual, not a group, practice. You simply sit quietly, preferably with eyes closed, move your attention as much as possible beyond your thoughts and consciously open yourself to receive the Holy Spirit. There is not such an onrush or inrush of spirit as in the latihan but simply a gentler flow that can bring bliss and peace with sometimes glimpses into the *akasha*.

Bapak instructed the women to quietly practise 'receiving' when preparing food. He always knew when eating the food if this had been done or not. Once he sent congratulations to a woman who had prepared his meal, saying that she had 'received' except when preparing the carrots. In that, she had allowed anger to come in and he had tasted it. Of course, conscious awareness of the divine spirit may be practised during many other activities besides food preparation.

One interesting thing that Bapak taught was that the vibration of your name can have a definite effect in the development of your character. Some of the names, he said, given by parents were certainly not conducive to spiritual growth and development. He had changed the names of a number of people at Coombe for this reason. They persuaded Iris and me to write to Bapak, who was then in Indonesia, and ask if we had the right names for our spiritual growth. We did so. Iris felt she would like to change from her name. I had, since my life in the army began, been going under my second name David. This being the name of my great-uncle who was a father to my father, I liked well enough and did not want to change it. My first name, Kelvin, I had always disliked. This dislike would have been alleviated somewhat if I had found that my father had named me after the great scientist, Lord Kelvin. But, no, he had named me after a character in a novel that he was reading at the time. So I was glad when my Kelvin days came to an end. Bapak disappointed Iris by telling her her name was quite suitable, then he disappointed me by ditching the name David and calling me Howard. At the same time he said that writing was my dharma and that on no account should I change from that occupation. Immediately, everybody at Coombe Springs addressed me as Howard and I began writing my press articles and stories under that name. If anybody were to call me David or Kelvin or Kel now, I would look behind to see who was approaching.

With Bapak's name of Howard, I have continued writing successfully, moving into psychic and then deeper spiritual subjects, and finally prose-writing has become part of my surrender to God, my service to God and my own spiritual evolution towards the Light. It could well be that the Indonesian master played an important part in this. Thank you Bapak.

When the first browning leaf appeared in the Coombe Springs gardens, we knew it was time to begin our migration southwards. Senior members of Subud at Coombe Springs told us that neither of us was yet ready to do the latihan alone but they said, if we let them know our new address in Spain, they would make it known to Subud members in England so that anyone going to our remote area might be happy to call and do the latihan with us. We did not expect anything so unlikely to happen but, in fact, we were to meet two important friends this way.

Our new address seemed far off and unimportant as we drove towards the Channel port, pulling our newly acquired small caravan behind us. We would first visit a monastery in Normandy where John Bennet had taught the latihan to two of the monks, then we would visit the spiritual centre at Lourdes. After that we would cross the interior of Spain, visiting a few historic cities on the way. Our plan was then to have a look at parts of Portugal before heading south to the palm trees of Andalusia and the sunshine of the Costa-del-Sol. In our little car and home-made caravan, with the name 'Digger' written large on its side, it seemed like an exciting, adventurous prospect. "Too adventurous," declared one British mechanic, shaking his head as he did a minor repair to the tow bar of our caravan. But our faith remained bright and undaunted.

12. A Door To The East

You will know your next step from this step. You will never find it any other way. Your intellect does not know it.

EMMANUEL'S BOOK

THE SCOURGE OF mass tourism had not yet begun in Spain when we went through its heart in the autumn of 1961. It seemed as empty and remote as it had a year earlier, when we had crossed it by the southern route along the Mediterranean coast. Now, as we drove past the olive groves and the grand historic cities, the people as well as the places seemed to be living in the past. Perhaps they were still in the proud dream of long ago when Spain had been master of the New World, the Spanish Main and much of Europe. Perhaps they had not quite recovered from their Civil War and were feeling the national discipline of their dictator, Generalissimo Franco. Whatever it was, we never felt quite at home in this old Spain, though we liked and admired it.

Sometimes the remnants of old world courtesy could be surprising and slightly embarrassing. I remember on one occasion in the quiet, remote countryside, our car engine conked out and refused to budge. Though I had had considerable experience with engines, I could not locate the cause of the trouble. So there we were, on a country road in an empty landscape dreaming in the sunshine, but with not a building in view. What could we do? Before ten minutes had passed, several people appeared from nowhere. We knew a modicum of Spanish by now and were able to understand that not far away, hidden in some trees around the corner of the road, was a small town. They volunteered to push the car to a garage there. So we left our caravan by the side of the road and sat in the front seat steering while we came to the edge of the town where there was a garage and workshop. The kind-hearted Spaniards pushed us into this and then vanished before we could say a word of thanks.

When the workshop owner learned that we were from Australia, he left the job he was on and started working on our car. It took him over an hour to find the problem and put it right. When I asked him how much we owed him, his reply was, "Nothing. You are guests in this country. I can't charge a guest." He was quite adamant in this. On the other side of the street was an open-air bar and, as it was a very hot day, I said, "Well, will you come over and have a drink with us?" He agreed and I felt pleased that I could at least make this small gesture in appreciation of the Spaniard's generosity. So the three of us stood at the bar and ordered long, cool drinks. When they came, I took out my wallet and asked the bartender how much, but the garage owner beat me to the draw. He knew the price of the drinks and had the money on the counter before I was told the price. I felt floored but determined to have the right money ready for the second round of drinks. Yet here again, the old-world Spanish courtesy won the day. He excused himself from having another round of drinks, saying that he must get back to his garage. It was an experience that neither Iris nor I would ever forget.

Soon after that, we drove across the border into a rural area of Portugal. We stopped in a quiet spot for a picnic lunch. A small boy appeared, spurred on by curiosity but held back by fear. I had learned to say "Good day" in Portuguese and decided to encourage the boy by saying "Good day" in his own language. But as soon as I spoke, he disappeared into the undergrowth like a streak. Did he think we were dangerous space people or was my Portuguese pronunciation so bad?

As part of our tour of Portugal, we visited Fatima, where in 1917, three peasant children had seen a vision of the Virgin Mary. Now a great cathedral was built on the spot. We could not go into it because Iris was wearing slacks, but we did not need to go inside. As we stood looking at the beautiful building, I had another expansion of consciousness, another indescribable but unmistakable mandorla, where the spiritual overlapped the material. Why did this experience come in some places and not others, I wondered. Why had I experienced it at Fatima and not at Lourdes in France where I had half-expected such an experience? Lourdes had been beautiful, peaceful, with a vibration of holiness but it had not brought me the mandorla experience. Feeling that we would not find anything in Portugal to surpass Fatima, we did not linger very long in the country. Returning to Spain, we headed in a general way towards the arc of road that ran around the sunshine coast. Somewhere along that road, we would find our home for the winter.

Andalucia, with its echoes of the old Moorish civilization, was the part of Spain we loved best. It was always a delight to visit the remains of an old Moorish castle. The most famous of these was the Alhambra in Granada but there was also an interesting one at Seville, the city which itself had the elegant beauty of a Spanish lady. A third but smaller Moorish castle beckoned to us from the hill above whenever we visited Malaga. Several times we responded to the beckoning. The Moors had gone away a good many centuries ago. But it felt as if they had left only a few minutes before, were not far away and would soon be back. Nothing would I have liked better than to see them walk in and greet me as a brother.

We found our second home on the Costa-del-Sol in the fishing village of Fuengirola, a few miles from Malaga on the Gibraltar side. This time it was not a sparsely furnished Moorish house, but a sparsely furnished apartment. But, like the house, it had an open fireplace where we could burn the driftwood found on the beach to create warm, crackling fires on the winter evenings.

Among the friends we found in Fuengirola were a Subud couple from Calcutta, holidaying in a cottage in the village. He was an English businessman working in Calcutta and she was a Bengali woman. So now Iris and I each had a partner of latihans.

Then, one day, another couple arrived at our apartment. They were doing a motor tour around the south of Spain and, having obtained our address from Coombe Springs, they had called hoping to do a latihan with us. While doing their tour of Andalucia, they returned several times to practise them with us. He was a Dutchman who had lived many years in England. His wife was a lovely person with corn-coloured hair, soft eyes and pink cheeks. She seemed to embody all that was sweet, gentle and friendly in England. Their names were Leo and Gwen Giebels. We became so friendly that they invited us to spend a holiday in their home, a manor house in rural Berkshire. We had planned, of course, to spend the next summer at Coombe Springs, but accepted their invitation to pay them a visit. We had no idea, then, that they were to rank among our best friends.

British Indian Subud friends believed that all symptoms of a disease are a purification that is working in the body. Perhaps in a sense they are, but one has to use one's commonsense. Through his influence, I disregarded some symptoms so long that I finished up in a Malaga hospital having an operation for my ethmoid. I would like to have delayed this delicate operation until I was back in England. But the specialist warned me against this, saying that a sneeze could cause meningitis and kill me. The operation and some convalescence delayed our departure from the south of Spain that year. Then we decided to continue the convalescence by a visit to Andorra, a little country between Spain and France, followed by a camping tour through parts of France that we had not seen before.

It was while we were driving along a French road that a car passed us and a rich female Australian voice called, "Hello, Australia!" The sign 'Digger' on the caravan had done its work. The sound of the Australian voice brought a pang to my heart and reminded me of where my grass roots were. The effect on Iris was to make her terribly homesick. We discussed the idea of returning to Australia and decided that the time was getting near.

Spring had merged into high summer by the time we touched English shores. We decided to pay a quick visit to our friends Leo and Gwen Giebels in Berkshire before going to Coombe Springs. After some intensive map-reading and a few enquiries, we found their home, Sandford Manor, among the delicious meadows and hedgerows a few miles from Reading. Their house was an attractive three-storeyed Edwardian building in red brick trimmed with white. Around it were spacious lawns and gardens with a tree-studded meadow that sloped down to a brook. The contented at-homeness that I have always felt in rural England seeped through me again. Surely England is familiar ground from former lifetimes, as is Germany. Though we had descended on them without warning, Leo and Gwen gave us a warm welcome. They gave us the whole top floor of the manor for our use, though we were only staying a few days. Leo used several rooms of the manor as headquarters for his business, which was mainly concerned with importing machinery from Holland.

After some discussions, I found that I could help him by writing some sales letters and advertisements to go in appropriate trade journals. Leo seemed delighted with this work and the results it brought him. It was finally agreed that we would stay on in the upper floor of the manor, instead of moving to Coombe Springs. For rent, I would take care of Leo's publicity. This arrangement suited us all well. Sandford Manor was close enough to London for us to motor there for a day's business or, if necessary, stay a night or two in the Chelsea flat owned by the Giebels'. I had to renew my Fleet Street editorial contacts and do research for some series of articles they were requiring.

The articles that Larry Solon and one or two other editors wanted from me, were becoming mainly on the subjects of yoga and psychic phenomena. For the latter I had several fertile fields of research. One was the fine Theosophical library in Gloucester House in the West End and visits here were to yield fruits that I never even dreamed of. A second field of research was the Society for Psychic Research (SPR). I became a member of this and spent a good deal of time reading their literature, talking to the leaders of the Society and interviewing several of the clairvoyants and mediums with whom the SPR had experimented. After over eighty years of scientific psychic research (since 1880), there was much fascinating material to be studied in their quiet little rooms in Kensington.

A daughter of the old London mother society was a centre for psychic research in Oxford, recently formed by several graduates of Oxford University. Researching for material to make popular articles, took me several times to this Oxford centre. Their main work at the time seemed to be concerned with out-of-the-body experiences (OBE's).

Being away from Sandford Manor for unpredictable periods, sometimes two or three days at a time, provided us with some unexpected psychic experiments and observations. Gwen's beautiful Persian cat, Mimosa, strawberry blonde in colour, had for some reason taken a fancy to us. She spent most of her time with us in our top-floor apartment. On the first occasion when we returned after being in London for several days, we were surprised to find Mimosa sitting patiently waiting for us just inside the front door. "She has been there for over an hour," Gwen remarked. Though we had not known ourselves for certain just when we would be returning, Mimosa seemed to have got the message at about the time we left Chelsea. But she showed her disapproval of our long absence by turning her back on us as soon as we spoke to her and stalking off silently. We decided to do some experiments in telepathy with Mimosa. She would be sitting on the window ledge in our apartment looking at us with her large, bright, intelligent eyes and we would say mentally, without speaking a word aloud, something such as, "Go down to the garden, Mimosa. We are going down there now." After our repeating this mental message two or three times, she would jump off the ledge and go downstairs into the garden where we would find her shortly afterwards.

On one occasion, I was writhing on my bed and groaning with the agony of a kidney stone. Mimosa watched me for a while with anxious eyes, then she dashed downstairs and spoke in urgent, loud cat-language to Leo; so much so that he came to see what the matter was. When he arrived at the bedside, she still talked to him as if trying to explain what I had been doing. Then Leo brought me a mixture in a jug, saying "Drink this. It is what Bapak takes." It was a solution made from an Indonesian herb and it certainly caused my kidney stone to pass without further pain or trouble.

On another occasion, Mimosa's keen psychic faculty prevented what might otherwise have been a domestic catastrophe. Leo and Gwen had gone off for a week's holiday, leaving us in charge of the manor. One day we were working on our car across a lawn from the house. Suddenly Mimosa appeared behind Iris and started talking to her urgently. Realising that something was wrong, Iris began to walk back across the lawn to the house. Mimosa went in front of her, looking back occasionally and talking as if to encourage Iris to hurry. Mimosa took her to the kitchen, where Iris found that she had left some food cooking in a large saucepan, forgetting to turn off the heat from the gas jet before she went out. A catastrophe would have happened in the kitchen in another minute or two. Our little four-legged, but almost human, friend had exercised what psychic science calls precognitive vision. She seemed to me to be superior to the average human being in her extrasensory perceptions. Will she be a beautiful blonde lady in her next incarnation, we asked each other, or is she already a human in cat form?

Life with our friends in rural Berkshire, with occasional visits to London, was so happy that we were not fully aware of the changing season until winter was almost upon us. We debated about whether we should return to the south of Spain that year or not. Then, snow began to fall heavily and the decision was made for us. A thick white blanket of snow covered the whole of southern England and we heard that the blanket extended over into France and Spain. So we concluded that it would not be pleasant and perhaps not safe to make the long journey by car to the southern sunshine. Sometimes it was not even possible to drive up to London. But I had plenty of commissioned work from the London editors and agents to keep me busy. On many days I would just sit typing in my small office, with the window in front of me, looking out on the snow-clad landscape, the trees in the Sandford Manor garden covered with ice and looking like glass. Mimosa sat on the desk near the typewriter, looking with me out of the window. Whenever a little bird came near the window on the outside, Mimosa would make a strange, deep growling noise in her throat. Once I tried to imitate the noise, at which she gave me a strange look, as if to say, "You feel that way too."

Eventually the snows melted away and the fields of England were green with spring again. Iris kept well occupied in her profession. A nursing agency provided her with a number of private nursing jobs. These were among the well-to-do people in the stately homes of Berkshire and nearby counties. The work brought some interesting contacts for her and sometimes for me also. These contacts included the daughters of General Booth, the founder of the Salvation Army.

My writing work that spring and summer included a book on yoga, commissioned by a London publisher. The yoga treated was, of course, the westernized Hatha Yoga that I had learned in Sydney, for I had not at that time been near the land of the deeper yogas, India. I called the book *Yoga for Busy People*. It met with success in the West and surprised me by being accepted by a large publisher in India some years later. In addition, the demand among the magazines for articles on psychic subjects continued, requiring occasional visits to my main centres of research.

Visits to the library at Gloucester House in London brought me friendship with some members of the Theosophical Society who had their offices in the same building. Most of these were officials who ran the British section of the International Society. One of them, though he did not know it, was due to be the mouthpiece of that 'divinity that shapes our ends'. In the course of a conversation over a morning cup of tea, I let him know that we would probably be returning to Australia after we left England in the autumn of that year, 1963. He knew that we were members of the Australian section of the Theosophical Society. "Why not stop over in India on the way back," he said casually. "You could stay at the headquarters in Adyar and do the School of the Wisdom there."

The name 'School of the Wisdom' intrigued me. "Is there a school where one can learn wisdom?" I asked him.

"It's really a study of the ancient wisdom of the East, he explained. "There are two terms of three months each," he said, "beginning in September. You could attend one or both of the terms."

"It sounds appealing," I said, "but what does one do for money while studying?"

He told me that it was quite cheap to live at Adyar and that it might be possible to work there part-time while doing the School of the Wisdom. "I believe that they are hoping for a new Superintendent for Leadbeater Chambers to show up. That's the big hostel where people from overseas stay. Maybe your wife could do that job and you, as a writer, could help them with their magazine, *The Theosophist*."

I had no idea then that this suggestion, given casually over a cup of tea in an office in London, was the opening of a door to the East that would change our lives.

Soon after that fateful conversation, we found a buyer for our little caravan, piled our belongings into the faithful Volkswagen and paid a fond farewell to our friends at Sandford Manor. The four-legged friend responded by turning her back abruptly and walking off in disgust. We were ourselves loath to leave this lovely place but it was October and we wanted to be well south before the chills of another winter began. This time we had an address to go to. Leo, who loved Spain, had bought a flat in a newly-built block of flats at Algeciras on the Bay of Gibraltar. He invited us to live there while we furnished the place as a holiday flat for him and Gwen. We were very glad of this offer because it enabled us to write to the Theosophical Society headquarters at Adyar in India, giving a firm address in Spain for their reply. In the letter we requested acceptance for the School of the Wisdom beginning in September the next year, that is, in 1964. At the same time, we requested part-time work and gave our qualifications. Iris' experience as catering officer at Coombe Springs would, we hoped, secure her the position of Superintendent at Leadbeater Chambers, if there should be such an opening.

Our new winter home on the Costa-del-Sol was in a delightful position. From the ninth floor in the new block of flats, its windows looked across the bay, dominated by the high rock of Gibraltar on the other side and busy day and night with the movement of small boats. At night, the many lights at the foot of the fortress and up its steep sides gave a spectacular display. We never tired of looking at it from the window, with the lighted ships moving about its feet in the bay. Eventually, after weeks of waiting, the reply came from India.

Opening the envelope with trembling fingers, we both gave a whoop of delight. We were accepted as students in the School of the Wisdom and they would be very happy for Iris to take over the position of Superintendent of Leadbeater Chambers. So the door to the East was open. I remembered the long-ago prophecy about my star in the East. Was it a true prophecy, I asked myself. Would I find my star of meaning there in India?

So we began to think about the best way of getting to India at the right time. Would we have to return to England in order to get a passage to India? We hoped not. Perhaps there was some other way. But how could we find out down there in the quiet, little, old-fashioned town of Algeciras? But we had always found that if one makes a big decision, the right decision, then help will come from somewhere. This time it came in a very odd way. One of our regular winter friends in the south of Spain was a Dutchwoman named Tilly Heil Zurr. Tilly was a migratory bird like ourselves. Each autumn she would drive from her home in Holland in a little French car with her large, beautiful Spanish hound sitting beside her and find herself a winter home in the Costa-del-Sol. Always her home seemed to be not far from ours. In the autumn of 1963, she appeared again. This time a Dutch lady friend was sitting beside her and the Spanish hound, named Pietur, occupied the rear seat. Pietur, incidentally, seemed to us to be another human being who like Mimosa, the cat, had managed to incarnate with four legs. Our association with this courteous Spanish 'gentleman' is one of our fond memories of our winters in Spain.

Well, to keep this story short, Tilly's friend had a son who had a travel agency in Paris. The upshot was that she wrote to him on our behalf and we managed to get passages on a Dutch cargo ship sailing from the Italian port of Genoa for Colombo in Sri Lanka in time for us to go by train and ferry to Madras, on the outskirts of which was Adyar, our destination. But, before sailing, there was ample time for us to camp our way along the Mediterranean coasts of Spain and France, then tour Italy as far south as Rome. After this we sold our little car and went aboard our ship.

It was one of those cargo ships permitted to carry twelve passengers. Yet there were only two besides ourselves and they disembarked at Aden. After that, through the Gulf of Aqaba and across the Indian Ocean, we had the passenger accommodation to ourselves and it was certainly luxurious accommodation.

Colombo seemed like a depleted, saddened, down-trodden caricature of the bright fairytale port I had encountered in 1939 as my first foreign port. But we were given wonderful hospitality and help there by two Theosophists: one, a Singhalese, the other a Tamil. Then, after about a week of sightseeing, we caught a train to the north and a ferry across the bright waters to where Mother India awaited her children.

PART TWO

FINDING THE REAL

Lead me from the unreal to the real, from darkness to light, from death to immortality.

FROM A VEDIC HYMN

Satya Sai Baba

13. The School Of The Wisdom

Spiritual evolution represents the development of consciousness in the individual monads and their efforts to rejoin across the cycle of lives the divine spirit from which they emanate.

PYTHAGORAS

Become what you are.

H.P. BLAVATSKY

THE SOFT, GENTLE green of rice fields among palm trees and temples glided slowly past the open door of the guard's van of the country train as I sat there with the guard. I was there because the ferry from Sri Lanka had been late reaching India and the express train on which we had booked first class tickets had left without us. After a long wait we had boarded a slow country train that had no first class carriages. So we were faced with a slow journey of a day and a night and a day before reaching our destination, Madras. The guard had asked me to sit with him in the van while he did all the paper work necessary for a refund of the balance between first and third class fares. It was a slow process. At every station he had to leave and carry out his duties as guard, then again he would interrupt his writing to tell me about the countryside through which we were passing. He had himself come from this part of southern India, so he was telling me all he could about the villages and the temples as we passed them. It was a very relaxing and restful experience, like a meditation. Gradually the realisation dawned on me that I had seen it all before. Mother India was welcoming back a child who had left her long ago. My heart overflowed with joy as the sights and sounds and smells intensified the feeling of a much loved memory. When after many miles and many stations I returned to my carriage, armed with papers which the guard assured me would get me a refund, I did not care if I never got the refund. In fact, I never did. I found that Iris had the same feeling of familiarity with India and was certain that she had lived here before. Later Sai Baba confirmed that we had indeed lived in India, telling us about one life in which we had both been boys and very close friends.

The train journey, which we had expected to be our first austerity in a country of austerities, turned out to be otherwise. The discomfort of sitting and sleeping on hard benches was alleviated, indeed completely erased, by the happy friendliness of our fellow travellers. They were Buddhist pilgrims on their way to various shrines in India. Being experienced in such pilgrimages, they were well prepared for the journey with large hampers of food. We, not expecting any such journey, were just as unprepared. So our Buddhist, new-found friends insisted on sharing their food with us. That long, slow journey with the gentle, generous Buddhist pilgrims, has become for us one of our happy memories.

Finally, late in the evening of the second day, our steam locomotive puffed, as if reluctantly, into a Madras railway station. Two Theosophists were waiting impatiently for us on the platform and drove us immediately to our destination, the Theosophical estate at Adyar on the Adyar River. In the dark we did not see much of our new surroundings, just a few lighted buildings among trees and gardens. Then came the imposing three-storey pile, Leadbeater Chambers, which was to be our home longer than we then guessed.

Our first desire, next morning, was to obtain a glimpse of our new surroundings. So in the bright sunshine we stepped from our spacious quarters onto a broad balcony that ran completely around the building. There was a similar balcony on the floor above us and on the ground floor below. On the side opposite our window, a lawn sloped down to the Adyar River, flowing slowly between trees to the sea. In fact, it formed the boundary of the estate on that side. Its mouth, about a kilometre away, was hidden by trees. But, through the trees, we had promising glimpses of a sandy beach on the Bay of Bengal. This beach formed another border of the estate. By walking around the balcony, we could see on the other side of the building the third boundary of the estate, which was a wall with some roofs of village houses showing beyond. The fourth boundary was the road by which we had come the night before. This was too far away to be seen and too far for the sounds of traffic noises to reach us. Within this large estate there were roads leading in various directions through unspoiled jungle, palm groves and gardens. Hidden, or half-hidden, by the greenery were fine white houses, some by the sea, a Hindu temple, a Parsee fire temple, a Muslim mosque, a Buddhist shrine and a Christian church of the Liberal Catholic denomination. The truth at the heart of all religions was honoured by the Theosophical Society. In fact, its motto was: 'There is no religion higher than Truth'.

Later in the morning, walking back along the road by which we had come from the main entrance gate, we passed the great banyan tree, said to be the largest in India. Then through a palm grove we walked to the offices of the Headquarters. These were surrounded by gardens of bright flowers. Across a well-kept lawn, we saw a thing of beauty. This was the Headquarters Hall, with a line of white elephant faces looking through a façade of red trimmed with white. I could never look at that building, thereafter, without a little thrill of joy in my heart. It was to bring me, moreover, some uplifting spiritual experiences. The whole Theosophical Headquarters estate had a feeling of sheltered tranquillity, as if one was in a large monastery garden.

The School of the Wisdom was not due to start for a about a week and during that time we explored our surroundings in more detail and Iris was introduced to her new job. It had a facet, a rather troublesome facet, not met with at Coombe Springs. This was that she had to control a large staff of native servants, who did the domestic work, including the cooking and waiting on tables. They belonged to the *harijan* caste, came in daily from the village outside the wall, spoke and understood English sufficiently but required a watchful, supervising eye and stern discipline. Could she, we wondered, do this demanding job while still attending the lectures at the School of the Wisdom? Well, somehow, she managed to do that. My work with *The Theosophist* was more intermittent during the school. Afterwards, I was asked to be its Editor, but that is another story.

About thirty students, of various nationalities and ages, assembled for the School in a large, sunny room of a building called Blavatsky Bungalow. The Principal was the International President of the Society, a dignified, platonic figure named Sri N. Sri Ram. The Director of Studies was Dr Taimni, a retired scientist who had spent years in England and had been a leading Theosophist for many years. Hailing from Allahabad on the Ganges, he was short in stature and seemed filled with a happiness that made him smile a great deal. From time to time, other teachers assisted with the School, most notable of these being the Theosophical clairvoyant, Geoffrey Hodgson. With the assistance and guidance of our teachers, we studied a number of text books on the ancient wisdom of the East, with particular emphasis on the Indian spiritual philosophy. Among these was *The Secret Doctrine*, written in part by the great occultist, Madame H.P. Blavatsky and in part by several Masters of the Wisdom, using H.P.B. as amanuensis. Others were: *The Crest Jewel of Wisdom* by R.D. Sankara, perhaps the best text book on non-dualistic *Vedanta*; a number of *Upanishads* which come from the *Vedas* and enshrine the spiritual insights of the ancient *rishis*; the *Bhagavad Gita*, perhaps

India's greatest scripture for the man in the street, and now becoming known more and more in the Western world.

Dr Taimni seemed to love the yoga philosophy and spent a good deal of time interpreting the yoga *sutras* of *Patanjali*, India's leading text book on Raja Yoga. Later in the term he tried to introduce as to Narada's *Bakti Sutras*, the text book on the yoga of love and devotion but the response from the students was not enthusiastic. Like me, they all seemed firmly centred in the head, with little interest in the heart. Dr Taimni gave up the attempt, yet I felt that his own heart centre had been opened. He emanated a warm affection, which, however, was not strong enough to waken our interest in the great teachings of the ancient rishi Narada. In addition to delving into the ancient wisdom through such text books, we studied the heart of all the main religions, including the teachings of those spiritual giants of the Far East, Confucius and Lao Tzu.

Looking back, I see that my mind was too joyfully occupied with its own expansion to bother about the spiritual heart. That could remain on the shelf, so to speak, for a later time. But I was certainly busy breaking through the boundaries of the mind and reaching out to broader horizons. The sky-walking God of my childhood, the ancient bearded man who made heaven and earth and all that in them is, was swept away. The agnosticism of my later years, the aching hungry void, was filled with something satisfying and yet not quite fulfilling. In place of the bearded man-God, there was Brahma, more a principle than a person yet much more than we generally mean by a principle. None of the pronouns, He, She nor It could be used adequately and in truth to stand for this formless God, this one Existence, one Life, beyond and within the whole cosmos. From this Brahma, this one Divine Existence, came the whole universe and all that is. Rather than creating all, Brahma consciously emanated it from Himself. Behind all that we call creating stands his conscious ideation and his divine desire and will to create. Life, from its lowest form to its present apex in man, began, as Pythagoras said long ago, with monads of consciousness coming from the one Divine Consciousness. We can think of them as sparks from the eternal fire or seeds scattered by the hand of God.

For reasons that only the divine One himself knows, the monads of consciousness must begin a long journey of necessity, an evolutionary journey through the material kingdoms of Nature. Evolving through the mineral, vegetable and animal kingdoms, they reach the human state. Then, I learned, there is a leap forward in evolution. In the transition from animal to human, there is the infusion of an individual soul. Perhaps the myth of the Garden of Eden implies this when it says that, after making all other forms, God made man and breathed into him a spirit in God's own likeness. The journey of necessity does not, however, end with man. Being self-conscious and dimly aware of his destiny, he helps on his own evolution through his search for knowledge and spiritual practices, such as the yogas of India and the practices of the great religions. The word 'religion' itself, from its roots, implies a journey back to God. Perhaps another great leap forward will be necessary for mankind's evolutionary jump from the human to the superhuman and the end of the journey is beyond that, being the state of divine consciousness itself.

So I learned that the great journey of necessity is a circular journey, from God, as monads of consciousness, back to God as self-conscious divine beings. It is what we experience and how we grow and what we become on this hurdy-gurdy of evolution through the aeons that is important. In this great concept, I could see God's purpose for my life, my many lives and for my brothers and sisters in the schoolroom of Earth, but I could not see the divine reason for the divine plan.

One woman at the School of the Wisdom, herself weak and tired with lack of vitality, asked plaintively, "Why did He bother?" The whole School laughed — and what answer can there be to this eternal mystery, other than laugh? One thing that the School of the Wisdom did for me was to put the horse of consciousness firmly in the shafts pulling the cart of matter, rather than being led behind the horseless cart without means of propulsion, as it is in the materialistic philosophy. The material world of Nature came from consciousness rather than vice versa. Divine consciousness created all. As man is heading along his evolutionary path towards divine consciousness, I wondered whether any individual had reached the point where he could command material Nature. Patanjali said that through the practice of yoga this was possible. Were there any living in India, the land of yoga, who had such powers? I had heard stories of such and I hoped fervently to meet one.

This idea of breaking the material walls of our prison by its master builder, the Superconsciousness of Divinity, appealed to me greatly. It would be a demonstration of the principle learned at the School and a confirmation of the reality behind appearances. I knew through reading Theosophical literature that the Masters of the Great White Lodge, a few of whom had been behind the foundation of the Theosophical Society, had supernormal powers, but I felt it was unlikely I should ever meet such remote beings in the flesh. The founders and some of the early Theosophists had met them and witnessed their powers, but that was all long ago, in the final decades of the last century.

Once at the School of the Wisdom, the President N. Sri Ram, gave an interesting talk on this subject of supernormal phenomena and the Masters of the Wisdom. He said that the practice of yoga often brought *siddhis*, as he called these supernormal powers, to the yogi before he had reached the final goal of yoga, which was union with the Divine. People with such limited powers could almost certainly be found in India but the truth was that if they used such powers for selfish, egotistic reasons they would lose them. The attainment of high spiritual status must precede the use of such powers. Speaking about the Masters, he said we should regard them as ideals towards which we should aim, rather than as beings we could meet in the body and talk with. Asked about their supernormal powers, he said that they only used them sparingly in their work. Their siddhis, though powerful, were not unlimited and through overuse such powers could be weakened or lost. Only a great Avatar of God, he concluded, has unlimited miraculous powers which never wane through time or the frequency of their use. Such were the powers of Lord Krishna. Their manifestation and amplitude is the sign of the Avatar. Neither Iris nor I expected to meet a great Avatar, but our search for the sacred through the secret recesses of India was still necessary. "I hope to meet a Master who will guide my footsteps," Iris said. I myself still hoped to meet a perfect yogi who had full command over material Nature and could reveal in clear terms the purpose of my presence on Earth, giving me sure directions and help towards its attainment. He would probably be, I thought, a Raja Yogi. Perhaps he would also be my promised 'Star of the East'.

After the School of the Wisdom, when the weather showed signs of heating up towards mid-summer, Iris would be able to obtain a long summer leave from her job and we would set off on our journey. But where to go? We needed some leads, at least to begin with. Help came from an unexpected quarter. Our main place of recreation during leisure hours was the fine beach on the Bay of Bengal. It was within easy reach along the pleasant river path, either on foot or by bicycle. Occasionally, when Iris was not able to go with me, my companion was a fellow student of the School of the Wisdom. He was a retired business man in my own age bracket. He had, in fact, retired from business early in order to search through India for the right Master of Yoga. Lying on the sands, with the bubbly, broken waves curling about our feet and legs, he talked to me about the ashrams he had visited. Finally, he agreed to give me a list of their names and addresses. They were, in fact, spread all over India but concentrated more in the north. Last on the list was in the interior of southern India. Its name was Puttaparthi. "I have never been there," my companion told me. "It's in a very remote place with no roads. In fact, part of the journey has to be done by bullock cart. The name of the teacher there is Sai Baba. They say he has phenomena." He spoke the last as a throwaway line, but I knew that to Theosophists the word 'phenomena' meant miraculous powers. This made me prick up my ears. The last shall be the first, I decided. We must make this Puttaparthi our first port of call. Never mind about bullock carts. I'm a farmer's boy from Tasmania. Rough bush tracks and bullock carts are within my experience. Playing down the bullock cart angle to Iris, who was city-bred, I was pleased to find that she agreed heartily to targeting Puttaparthi as our first port of call. But it turned out otherwise. Sai Baba has said, in both his incarnations, "Take one step towards me and I will take ten towards you." Our one step towards him was nought, but our firm intention was to go to his ashram just as soon as possible. Then he saved us the uncomfortable journey in the hot season by coming to us in Madras. The details of that momentous event, when we first met him, belongs to another chapter. In hindsight, I see that we had to meet Sai Baba before we made our spiritual journey of search in the north so that through experience we would realise that he was the One. Inferior metal had to be etched away through our safari to leave Sai Baba embossed in gold on our hearts.

Our travel schedule had matured before Sai Baba came to Madras. After the planned visit to Puttaparthi, now no longer necessary, we would go to the north where the promising ashrams were and the climate would be cooler in mid-summer. At least, that is what we thought, visualising the ashrams in the Himalayas. As it turned out, this was not entirely true. However, the first place to visit on our revised list, was certainly in the snows of the mountains. This was the Himalayan residence of the Dalai Lama of Tibet. He had paid a brief visit to the Theosophical estate, some time before we went there for the School of the Wisdom. The T.S. chiefs held him in great respect and readily gave us all details about how to get there, together with a letter of introduction to His Holiness. They suggested that we write, in good time, saying when we would be there, requesting an interview with the Dalai Lama and enclosing the letter from the Theosophical Society. This we did.

A replacement for Iris at Leadbeater Chambers was arranged for the quiet months of high summer and she was free to set off with me on our spiritual safari to the north.

The view of the world is that the seen causes the unseen, the manifest explains the unmanifest, but the rule in the realm of spirit is different. The latent Atma causes the patent world. Being is behind becoming, and, finally, becoming merges in being.

SAI BABA

14. Spiritual Safari To The North

One has to wander through all the outer worlds
to read the innermost shrine at the end.

TAGORE

AFTER A LONG third class train journey northward, followed by two punishing bus trips, better forgotten, we found ourselves on a steep mountain pathway heading towards our appointment with the Dalai Lama. Snowy peaks of the Himalayas reared their heads above us, while sleet and rain seemed determined to hinder our progress. But, at last, we came to a red-roofed building surrounded by high barbed-wire fences with soldiers guarding the entrance. Passing the scrutiny of the guard, we walked along the garden path and knocked on the front door of the house. The door was opened by a youngish, smooth-faced man with close-cropped hair. He gave us a welcoming smile and the little Tibetan dog standing beside him seemed to do the same. We had never seen a photo of the Dalai Lama but somehow we knew intuitively that before us was the great priest-king himself, now exiled from his Tibetan kingdom.

We offered the scarves we had brought, to fulfil the traditional Tibetan custom. The Dalai Lama took them with a little giggle, as if the custom in the hands of foreigners seemed slightly ridiculous. Then he took us into a large, warm, comfortably-furnished room and offered us coffee. This, after the cold climb up the mountainside, was exactly what we needed. The well-mannered little dog had not come into the lounge room, but two Tibetan lamas appeared, one being our host's secretary and the other his interpreter. While, in later years, the Dalai Lama gave public addresses in English, in these early days of his exile, he preferred to talk through an interpreter.

After coffee, he asked us what subject we would like to discuss. We had been warned of this and advised not to choose politics, if we wanted the interview to last the half hour which was the usual time he gave to visitors. So we answered, quite truthfully, that we would like to discuss metaphysics. The Dalai Lama smiled and we found that this was a good choice. He told us that in Tibet this was a subject of higher education and that it was possible to obtain there the University degree of M.M., meaning Master of Metaphysics. He, himself, he said modestly, had not attained that high level before he had to leave his country. But, even though he was an undergraduate, he led us on a fascinating discussion. He was able to answer in a satisfactory manner all the questions we put to him on metaphysics, though once or twice he said honestly, "My master in Tibet could answer that, but I would rather not attempt it."

When we brought up the subject of reincarnation, I was rather disappointed to find that the Dalai Lama did not remember his previous life. He had, he said, remembered it in his childhood and it was on the test of such memories that he was chosen as the present Dalai Lama. But, as he advanced in age, the memories faded as they do with all human beings. Mahayana Buddhism is, of course, the religion of Tibet and, in its philosophy and metaphysics, is very close to Theosophy. The latter is not classed as a religion but as an ongoing search for divine wisdom. Our lesson on Tibetan metaphysics went on for quite a long time and, in the warm lounge room with the rain still beating on the windows, the atmosphere seemed to become quite informal and homely. It was as if we were talking to an intelligent, wise brother.

In the end, we dared to slide away from the subject of metaphysics and ask him if he thought Tibet would ever regain its independence. "Yes," he replied simply and confidently, "there is an old Tibetan prophecy that says that it will." "How soon?" I asked. "Oh, perhaps a thousand years," he replied, as if that was nothing at all. Well, I thought, as he comes back in life after life to lead his people, perhaps he will still be here, though in a different body, in a thousand years. What is time in Tibet! He showed no emotional reaction to what had happened to his country, pointing out that it was, in fact, the inevitable karma of their policy of isolationism. "If we keep ourselves closed off from other countries," he said, "how can we expect them to help us in time of trouble?" He suggested also that much had gone wrong in Tibetan Lamaism. The great yogic powers developed in that religion had often been used for selfish rather than spiritual reasons. Not only must their religion be purified, he explained, but in future they must be more tolerant to other religions and become part of one brotherhood of nations. It seemed to me that this sincere, open-minded, young spiritual leader of his people was saying that in the end his nation would learn and benefit from the karmic suffering they were going through.

Time seemed to be forgotten in that Tibetan lounge room too. The allotted half hour stretched into an hour and then into two hours and finally the whole morning slipped away in friendly discourse.

Hospitably, the Dalai Lama asked us to stay for lunch and afterwards insisted that one of the vehicles from his headquarters should be used to take us down the mountain to the tourist bungalow where we were staying. When, before we left, the Dalai Lama stood at the front door to bid us farewell, his little Tibetan dog again appeared from nowhere to stand beside him. It was as if the shaggy little animal's duty was to help welcome and farewell guests, while keeping out of sight at other times.

I had been somewhat surprised to find that the leading holy man of the land of holy men had so many worldly human graces and was such a pleasant human companion. I wondered, however, if he had any of the yogic and esoteric powers attributed to many Tibetan lamas. I discussed this question soon afterwards with a fellow Theosophist who was doing welfare work among the Tibetan people who had left Tibet at the time of the Dalai Lama's exile and were living in a village on the mountains near him. This Theosophist, a European woman, told me that she had a guru-devotee relationship with the Dalai Lama and knew from experience that he did have such powers. He could, for instance, travel out of his body and did so when he felt the call to help somebody. He had been very grateful for the help given him by the late Prime Minister of India, Pandit Jawaharlal Nehru, and when the latter died in 1964 the Dalai Lama had travelled out of his body to be at the Prime Minister's death-bed. This, I thought, was an act of true compassion, for two reasons: the dying man was said to be an atheist and would need such help, and who better to give it than the spiritual leader of a nation that had produced the wonderful Tibetan Book of the Dead?

At the Dharmasala tourist bungalow, where we spent a couple of nights, we met an Indian who told us that there was a very great yogi somewhere near the mountain resort of Nainital. He could not tell us the great yogi's name but told us we would find him if we made enquiries around Nainital. But, before that search, there were several other places on our list. The first of these was Rishikesh on the Ganges.

What a joy it was to arrive at this shining place, drenched, it seemed, by the uplifting spiritual atmosphere from the great rishis who must at some time have lived here and given the place its name. Although we visited several yogis and ashrams by the racing waters of the great river, we made Sivanandanagar our main centre and place of residence. We had written to them about our proposed visit and were made very welcome. The great Sivananda himself had left his body some years before and the present leader was away on tour somewhere in India. But several swamis were there conducting the life of this busy ashram. Active service seemed to be its keynote. One swami conducted Hatha yoga classes before breakfast each day and also took care of the photographic unit. This swami had spent some years in the high Himalayas in a cave in the area of Ganghotri but had returned to the ashram when called back by its leader to help in the work there. "What is to be gained spiritually by living alone in a cave in such a remote place?" we asked him. His reply was, "It is something that everybody has to do some time, either in this life or another one. Each *sadhak* (searcher) will know when he has to do it." Another swami conducted daily classes in Sanskrit and each evening there was Sankirtan, or devotional singing, conducted by one of the resident swamis.

Iris and I took part in all the useful activities and enjoyed spiritual discussions with several of the swamis. Our quarters were primitive but adequate, while the vegetarian meals were very good. The grey-coated black-faced monkeys, who seemed to be part of the ashram, seemed to ignore our presence but never missed an opportunity to purloin fruit from our room or snatch it from our hands as we passed.

There was a regular ferry service from the foot of the ashram across the broad river to an ashram on the other side. This service was free, being provided by a wealthy Indian industrialist who had also established the big ashram on the other side of the river. Soon after our arrival at Sivanandanagar we met there a young Indian business-man from Delhi, who had been a devotee of Swami Sivananda during his lifetime. He said he would like to take us to see the *sadhus* living in caves on the mountain side on the other side of the river. So we crossed with him on the ferry, walked a distance through pleasant, lightly-wooded country, then climbed a mountain slope that seemed to be riddled with caves. In every cave there was a sadhu, or hermit. On that occasion, we were able to talk to several of them. Then, a few days later, Iris and I went back there ourselves, making the acquain-tance of several others.

The life of the hermits, or anchorites, in the caves seemed to consist mainly of meditation, although some spent time studying the Hindu scriptures. In one cave we saw, for example, a copy of the *Bhagavad Gita*. For lunch, most of them walked down to the ashram on the river opposite Sivanandanagar. There a free meal was provided by the grace of the wealthy industrialist. Otherwise the cave dwellers depended on offerings of food brought to them by visitors. I expect that generally they had to survive on one meal a day. But there was one who seemed to believe in the adage 'God helps those who help themselves'. We found him sitting just inside his cave cooking his evening meal on a kerosene pressure heater. He looked more like a picnicker in the bush in Australia than a cave dweller in the Himalayas of India, especially as his skin was white. He seemed happy for us to sit and talk to him for a while. He was, he told us, from New York and, having heard the Maharishi Mahesh give a lecture in that city, he decided that he must spend some time living in a cave in the Himalayas of India. The Maharishi had agreed and kindly helped to arrange it. So here he was, living a life of solitude far away from the noisy rat-race of New York. How did he like it? He liked it well enough, he told us, and would stay here just as long as he thought that he should for his spiritual well-being. We told him that we planned to visit the ashram of the Maharishi Mahesh on the morrow. "Oh," he said, "will you please say to him, 'Sol is all right'. He will know what you mean." We promised to do so, if possible.

The most striking sadhu in the colony of cave-dwellers, however, was a man by the name of Tat Wallah Baba. He was a tall figure with nut-brown skin and a physique that any Hatha yogi or physical culture teacher would be proud of. His hair was in a roll on top of his head, looking like a crown, and when he let this down it touched the ground at his feet. The other sadhus seemed to regard him as their leader. Wanting to have a discussion with him one day, we went straight to his cave, taking with us some vegetables as an offering. Blessing the vegetables and putting them aside, he told us that there was a special luncheon on that day, further around the mountain side, and invited us to go with him to the lunch. It was some special Hindu holy day and a number of ladies had come from Delhi to prepare a lunch for the sadhus on the mountains. We sat with about twenty sadhus in the sunny glades surrounded by trees. Lunch was served on large banana leaves as plates and the delightful curry was ladled out from a large pail in the sensible Indian way. Sunshine, greenery, birdsong, the spiritual company of the hermits, with a waterfall providing the luncheon music nearby, created for me a setting of eternity the like of which not the finest restaurant in the world could have provided.

But such banquets were rare events in the life of the sadhu. Generally these renunciants lived lives of austerity, not without some dangers. Some of the sadhus to whom we spoke had been for many years in these caves. Several told us that in the early days they had sometimes seen in the darkness of night the burning eyes of some big cat, perhaps a tiger, perhaps a cheetah, looking in at them from the opening of the cave. But the beast always went away without molesting them.

One day we walked along the banks of the sacred river some distance to the ashram of the Maharishi Mahesh Yogi. This was in the very early days of his mission to the world and his ashram was still under construction. On the day of our visit, the Maharishi was taking part in a ceremony of initiation conducted by his own guru, the Shankaracharya of the north. Even so, he kindly made the time to talk to us. He was a man who smiled a great deal and when we gave him the message of Sol, the New Yorker in the cave, his smile became a happy laugh. "Yes," he said, "Sol needed to have that experience for his spiritual progress, so I helped him to have it." The Maharishi was apologetic for not being able to give us as much time as he would have liked to do and kindly invited us to return the following day, but we knew that he, like the other spiritual leaders we had met in the Himalayas, was not the great Master of Yoga we sought, so we did not return. In his later mission of Transcendental Meditation to the world, the Maharishi Mahesh Yogi did, in fact, make a fortune. He was certainly an astute businessman but he had something else besides. Many people we have met around the world in the years since then have told us that it was the Maharishi who led them on the first step from the world of Mammon, or material values, into the world of spiritual values. This is a great thing to have done and whatever criticism may be levelled at the Maharishi, I bow to him for opening the important door for many people.

Some time after leaving the enchanted world of Rishikesh, we decided to pay a visit to an impressive spiritual master named Charan Singh. I had met him earlier in Madras and received a warm invitation for us to spend time at his ashram on the Beas River, not too far from the city of Amritsar. Charan Singh's ashram seemed like an oasis on a hot dry land. Charan Singh's own substantial house stood among lawns and trees, surrounded by a high wall. Among the other buildings around was a guest house, in which we were given a comfortable room. With cornflakes for breakfast and other Western style food, it was hard to believe we were in an ashram. But there were ashram rules that had to be obeyed. We, like the other guests, had, for instance, to be up at three o'clock in the morning to meditate. This, Charan Singh said, was the best time. Every day we were expected to attend an outdoor meeting where Charan Singh addressed his followers. There seemed to be at least a hundred thousand of them sitting on slopes that provided a natural amphitheatre. All the men wore white clothes and white turbans of the Sikh style. Charan Singh sat on the stage facing them, wearing the same style of white clothes with a shining jewel in front of his Sikh turban. With his long, greying, wedge-shaped beard and benevolent countenance, he presented a noble figure. My wife and I, along with several other Westerners, sat on low stools in front of the stage. All the Indians sat, as is customary, on the ground.

As Charan Singh spoke in the Punjabi language, we did not understand a word he said. Immediately after each meeting, he took us English-speaking visitors, with several elegant Indian princesses, into his walled garden. There, on the lawn, he sat in a chair with us sitting on chairs in a semi-circle around him. There, in very good English, he would repeat, in general, the teachings he had given to his Punjabi followers.

This centre on the Beas River was, in fact, a Radha Soami colony. I found that their spiritual philosophy was, in the main, in accord with the eternal verities or the ancient wisdom. There were, however, a few slight variations and some differences of emphasis. They practised what is known as Shabd Yoga, or the yoga of the Anahat sounds. In meditation, they taught, the student should concentrate his awareness deep within, in the attempt to hear these Anahat sounds. The highest of these sounds, they claimed, was not the sacred creative word 'Aum' but the sound 'Radha Soami'. 'Radha' is the name of the human soul, while 'Soami' means lord. So the name of their religion, as well as the highest sound sought in meditation, meant 'lord of my soul.'

'Aum' is one of the other sounds sought inwardly, while several others are difficult to describe in words. The attempts at description by the Radha Soami teachers lead me to think that they are the sounds which, according to Raja Yoga, come from the various chakras when activated. Reaching an awareness of the inner sounds is, according to the Radha Soami faith, a vital step towards achieving liberation or enlightenment by whatever name it is known.

Members of the colony greeted each other with the phrase 'Radha Soami', instead of the 'Aum' to which we had become accustomed at Rishikesh. It is used instead of 'Hello' or 'Good day.' One very keen young American in our group was eager to be initiated by Charan Singh into the Radha Soami faith straightaway, but Charan Singh told him that, as he had recently come from America, he should experience several other spiritual leaders and ashrams in India first. Then, if he still wanted to be initiated at Beas, he could come back in a couple of months when Charan Singh would be having an initiation ceremony for several. He indicated that Iris and I would be welcome to do the same but, though we admired and loved this old leader at Beas, we felt that he was not for us. Intuitively, we felt that we did not belong to this flock. We admired his fair-minded impartiality towards the keen young American. Very different, this was, from another Radha Soami leader whom we met later. This one was so keen to enlarge his flock that on our first arrival he told us he would show us the Light that day. But we had no faith in his instant liberation.

We discovered that there were over twenty Radha Soami colonies at that time in 1965, all of them stemming from the original group founded in 1861 at Agra by a living saint who went by the name of Paramguru Soamiji Maharaj. The split began when he died and continued at the death of each leader. Before leaving his body, the leader would appoint his successor, but some would not accept his decision and appoint another leader whom they preferred and so the one group became two and this process continued through the decades. Each Radha Soami colony believed that its leader was the only representative of God on earth and that all the others were wrong. This did not help my faith in any of their religious leaders, yet some of them had undoubtedly been great men.

One of these was the late Sahibji Maharaj, about whom Paul Brunton wrote so favourably, referring to him as 'His Holiness.' It was some thirty years earlier that Brunton had made contact with Sahibji Maharaj at Dayalbagh near the city of Agra. So we decided to go to Dayalbagh just to see how Sahibji's inspired experiment was progressing. We went there after a visit to the famous Taj Mahal at Agra.

We met the leader, a little, self-effacing, humble man, who did not wear the divine mantle with any charisma, but the old secretary of the colony was very kind and hospitable to us. He told us that Paul Brunton had stayed in the guest house where we were housed, but more importantly he told us many things about the late Sahibji Maharaj and we obtained some books on the latter's spiritual teachings. The great fifteenth-century saint, Kabir, seems to have been his spiritual inspiration, but I had the feeling that Sahibji's Dayalbagh experiment was in a state of decay. Its farms, factories and educational institutions were all continuing as of yore, but where, I wondered, was the spiritual vibration of brotherhood and purpose that Sahibji had created among them? In the days of the great leader, the old secretary told me, the whole colony would gather each evening in the great hall to hear Sahibji give his inspiring addresses.

Two years later I was to meet in Hyderabad a man who had obtained his engineering degree at the tertiary engineering college of Dayalbagh and told me two very interesting things about Sahibji. The man's name was E. Krishnamurti and I considered him a star in the Sai Baba crown and a man of purity and light. He told me that when Sahibji Maharaj had died, he could find no other spiritual guru to replace him. He was without a spiritual leader until he met Satya Sai Baba. Sometime after he had become a Sai devotee, he invited Swami to his house. As is his wont, Sai Baba walked about the rooms of the house, looking at everything. When he came to a photo of Sahibji Maharaj on the wall, he stood looking at it, then pointing, said to E. Krishnamurti, "That man was one hundred percent God." E. Krishnamurti was very pleased with this appraisement of his former guru by his present one.

Among the stories he told me concerning his days at Dayalbagh, was one that I probably would have doubted from the lips of anyone but E. Krishnamurti. Dayalbagh had been suffering from a terrible drought, he told me. Conditions had become very serious when, one evening, during a meeting in the big hall, Sahibji sitting on the stage said words to this effect: "We have had enough of this drought. The crops and the animals are desperate for water. Old people are dying from heat. We must have rain now." Then, pointing to one man in the audience, he said "You (naming the man) have a link with Lord Indra.* Stand up and ask him for rain." The man stood up, put his palms together in the gesture of prayer and said simply, "Lord Indra, please send us some rain." Then he sat down and they all waited in silence. Presently they heard the rain beginning on the galvanised iron roof. It grew in intensity and played a glorious tune, like the drumming of an army on the roof above them, for some half-hour. Sahibji had to raise his voice to shout above the din. "Have we had enough rain?" "Yes, Sahibji," they called in loud unison. Then the leader told the same man to stand up and ask Lord Indra to stop the rain. The man, with the strange esoteric link with Lord Indra, stood up and made the same simple prayer. Within two or three minutes, the rain on the roof had stopped completely. Dayalbagh's farming life had been saved from ruin.

From Dayalbagh, Iris returned straight to her job at Leadbeater Chambers at Adyar. I went to Nainital and searched the neighbourhood

---

* In Hindu mythology Lord Indra is the god of the sky. He is also known as the chief of the demi-gods, in charge of the five elements — ether, air, fire, water, earth.

for the great yogi we had been told about at Dharmasala, but I fell ill there for a time and later could find no leads to the yogi. Then, as the rainy season was beginning, I left the Himalayas and hastened back to Adyar. From information gleaned later, I think the yogi near Nainital was perhaps the fascinating little godman Nimkaroli Baba. I would probably have found him of interest, but whether he could have diverted me from my path towards Sai or not, I do not know. But that 'divinity that shapes our ends' kept the prow of my ship firmly towards my destined star.

15. Star In A Fog

If I call not Thee in my prayers,
if I keep not Thee in my heart,
Thy love for me still waits for my love.

TAGORE

"AND WHO DO you say I am?" Jesus asked his disciples after they had been discussing the reincarnation of the old prophets. Although they had been living close to Jesus for a long time, none of them seemed certain of the answer except Peter, who said, "Thou art the Christ." The divinity that would change the world was shining in this godman, yet only one could perceive it and his was only a temporary vision. Likewise with the great Avatar, Lord Krishna, the earthly veil that clouds men's eyes prevented them seeing the truth before them. Even his close friend, the warrior Arjuna, frequently saw Krishna as no more than a human friend, while the Kauravas, the enemies of the good, saw Krishna as no more than a human king whom they could kill. Today, as in earlier times, we poor mortals can entertain angels unawares, let alone Avatars. So it was that when I first laid eyes on my Avataric guiding star in Madras, a fog covered my spiritual eye. I would like to think that I recognised him as a divine Avatar at first sight, as some rare individuals do, but, in truth, I did not. If my wife and I had seen him then in the same deep dimension as we see him now, undoubtedly we would have cancelled our safari to the north. Even so, that journey in itself was, no doubt, part of the process that eventually opened our spiritual sight and led to the concept that Sai Baba is a shining star from the highest spiritual realms that has come to earth to guide man's footsteps on the path.

I have described in my now well-known book, *Sai Baba, Man of Miracles* how, one day in the Indian spring of 1965, a young white-faced woman in an ochre robe came walking through the palm grove in the Theosophical Estate and led us to Sai Baba at a house in Madras. I will not repeat the details here, but I want to look more deeply into the outward events in the hope of catching something of their eternal meaning.

After the experience of nearly three decades with the divine Avatar, this is the inner scenario that I now apperceive. When Sai Baba came on that brief visit to Madras, he was fully aware that my wife and I were living in the Theosophical Estate at Adyar, anxious to see him and planning to do so. He was aware, too, that we belonged to his flock and that it was time we came into it. No doubt he had been watching some of our steps along the way to him and perhaps even directing them. He was now nearer at hand, but how would he let us know? For this purpose he always uses whatever means are at hand.

In the small party of foreign devotees he had brought with him from Prasanti Nilayam to Madras, was the ochre-robed one. A young American by birth, she had been initiated onto the spiritual path by the great Sivananda of Rishikesh before his passing away. He had given her the spiritual name of Nirmalananda and she donned the ochre robes of the renunciant. Although she was staying at the roomy guest house in the gardens of the mica magnate of India, G. Venkateshwara Rao, where there should have been ample opportunity for quiet meditation, Sai Baba suggested to her telepathically that she should seek a quieter place at the Theosophical Society Headquarters and, when he started his busy morning of *darshan* in the garden and interviews in the big house where he was staying, which was separate from the guest house, off Nirmalananda went. By his power on the inner plane, he made sure that Nirmalananda would meet just the right person soon after she entered the Adyar Theosophical Estate. This was a woman, herself a renunciant from South America, staying temporarily at Adyar. This young South American woman knew that both Iris and I wanted very much to meet Satya Sai Baba, so when she saw me coming towards them on my bicycle through the palm grove, she stopped me, introduced Nirmalananda, told me that she was with Sai Baba in Madras and that she had come to the Estate in search of a quiet place for meditation. She suggested that I take Nirmalananda to Iris at Leadbeater Chambers, where there was probably a spare room that Nirmalananda could use.

Immediately I cancelled whatever business I was about and took the visitor straight to the Chambers where she met Iris. While the three of us sat together over coffee, Nirmalananda told us about some of her wonderful experiences with Sai Baba. She seemed to forget all about the reason for which she had come and made no further mention of a spot for meditation. Seeing our eagerness to meet Sai Baba, she was quite happy to guide us there immediately. For about a week, Iris had been fighting an attack of hepatitis and was feeling quite unwell. Under doctor's orders, she was keeping out of the kitchen where the native servants worked and carrying out her supervisory work from her office in Leadbeater Chambers. So, because of her sickness and the demands on her time that morning, she was unable to make the journey with Nirmalananda. So I went alone.

At the end of the bus ride, Nirmalananda took me straight to the front door of the big house where Swami was staying and knocked. The door was opened by Bob Raymer, the only male member of Swami's foreign party there. She introduced me to this red-headed American of about my own age, and told him that I would like to see Sai Baba. He was not hopeful, saying that Swami had finished his interviews for that morning, but he took me into a small front sitting-room while he made enquiries, and Nirmalananda left to go to the private guest house in the garden. Within a very few minutes Sai Baba came through the door into the room, asking, "Are you the man from Australia?" It was just as if he was expecting me, as no doubt he was.

While no surprise showed on his face, there must have been plenty on mine. I was nonplussed by his unique appearance and not even certain that he was the man I had come to see. People nowadays know him by photographs long before they go to him. But in those days there were no photographs. However, he soon revealed his identity by giving me the demonstration I had so much wanted to witness, that is, the power of super-consciousness over matter. By circling his hand, palm downwards, in the air, he materialised *vibhuti* (holy ash), first for two Indian gentlemen who had been waiting in the same room and then for me with the magical hand a few inches in front of my face. The demonstration over, he gave me a warm smile and, before leaving the room, told me to bring my wife. He seemed quite sure that I would do this.

I have described elsewhere how we both went, next day, and how Sai Baba demonstrated more of his supernormal powers. The first was, by standing in front of Iris, talking to her and materialising vibhuti for her, he completely cured her hepatitis. In fact, the depressed feeling that comes with hepatitis was replaced by a smile that she was unable to wipe off her face for the rest of that day. Secondly, for me he proved another power. Waving his hand in the air, he produced a small card on which was his ashram address and a small photo of his face. "You were asking for my address," he said, handing it to me. I was stunned. A few moments before he had come into the room, I had asked someone there for the address of Sai Baba's ashram. Through all his outward activities, he had been aware of my request and answered it himself. All I could say was, "Thankyou, Baba. May I go there?" "Any time you like," he replied. "It is your home."

Well, with these and other demonstrations, my wife and I were quite aware that we had met a superhuman being, perhaps a great yogi, and we were overjoyed. We had not yet, of course, become aware of his greatest miracle, his divine love, so we had an extremely limited concept of his reality. It was rather like a blind man trying to visualise an elephant by feeling only his ear or his tail. Yet he had made an indescribable but indelible impression on our hearts. Many years ago, at Shirdi, Sai Baba used to say that he drew people towards him like someone drawing a bird with a string attached to its leg. When, during the School of the Wisdom, we had read a small book called *The Incredible Sai Baba*, by Arthur Osborne, both my wife and I felt as if someone was pulling a string attached to our hearts. We did not know then that Sai Baba was back on earth in a new form. When, later, Iris asked Swami the meaning of this feeling, he told us that it was mainly because we would be coming to Sai Baba in this new form of Satya Sai. It was a kind of precognitive experience.

After that first meeting in the house in Madras, the invisible spiritual string tying us to Sai Baba was so strong that it was safe for us to travel and experience other teachers. The string would always bring the birds of our hearts back to our destined sadguru, Sri Satya Sai Baba. Yet, even so, some mental fog around me prevented me seeing clearly that here was my prophesied star, while the thought of his being an Avatar of God never entered my head.

That year, unusually for him, Sai Baba made several visits to Madras. Sometimes I would become aware in my meditation that he had come. At other times, members of the Venkatamuni family where he usually stayed would let us know that he was present. We would drop everything to go and spend the time with him. Nothing was important enough to keep us away. We would sit with a group of close devotees in a room of the house where he was staying. We would sometimes travel with him to other houses in Madras, where he would go to give darshan to those who were at the time unable to come to him. Sometimes he would go off alone and tell us to wait. And so we would, even if he did not return till midnight. But the hours in between were not wasted. They provided delightful *satsang*, with stories from devotees of long-standing. Stories about wonderful experiences with Sai Baba came to our ears and helped our growing concept of the spiritual amplitude of our guru. Then the return of Swami brought an ever greater reward through his smile, his shining eyes, perhaps a little pat and word of affection, or even sometimes the wave of his small brown hand to produce a gift as a token of his love.

Among the many things of revealing interest that we heard from his lips, was his description of a former life we had lived together. We were both boys, very close friends, living in a community in India where small boats were used for fishing and other purposes. He suggested that in this life we had been connected with the parents, or possibly the grandparents, of Shirdi Sai Baba. But the main point he made was, on one occasion, Iris saved my life from drowning. I was so grateful to my good comrade for this that I promised to seek him out in every future life and give him whatever help I could. Perhaps in this there was a feeling of deep friendship as well as gratitude. In this life, Swami said, our paths had crossed several times and we had been close to each other but we had not met until the right time. Since then, he went on, it has been a good partnership. "There had only been the two of you, but now there are three of us," he concluded.

I think our lives together as boys in India must have been the one before the present incarnation and Swami's revelation of it explained a number of things. It explained, for instance, why when I first saw her, I had the feeling of familiarity and the strong desire to see her again. Also it explains why she mistook me for an Indian as we stood outside the door of the yoga school in Sydney, and why sometimes, when she was sitting in *padmasana*, she would look down and see the folded legs of an Indian boy instead of her own. Swami's statement about our paths crossing many times indicated how his watchful eye had been on us in the years before we met him. Twice in northern England, when I was there in the army and Iris was living there, our paths had crossed and we had come very near to meeting each other. Then, later, we had lived very near to each other in Sydney and attended the same yoga school for several years without meeting. We did not, at first, understand his remark about there now being three of us, but later on we realised its deep truth and knew that he was the most important of the three.

When Sai Baba was not in Madras, to fill the shining hours with joy and a feeling of fulfillment, life flattened out to the routine of our Theosophical life at Adyar. But this too had its highlights of interest. I did not accept the position of editor of *The Theosophist*, which the President offered to me. I wanted to be free to travel. The great visit to Puttaparti had still to be made and there were several spiritual centres in southern India which I must investigate for the book I was planning to write on the spiritual teachers, sacred places and ashrams of Independent India. In the meantime I continued my studies of spiritual philosophy in the great library at Adyar, through many fine lectures given in the Headquarters Hall and by attending any promising lectures given outside the perimeters of the Theosophical Estate. These were from some of India's brilliant spiritual teachers who spoke fluent English. Three I remember with pleasure, and would like to mention here, are C.P. Ramaswami Iyer, a renowned Indian spiritual leader, Swami Chinmayananda, who gave outdoor lectures to big crowds on the *Bhagavad Gita*, and last, but not least, Swami Ranganatananda of the Ramakrishna Mission. We heard him first in the homes of our Sai friends in Madras giving what he called his 'parlour talks'. Later we heard him on Swami's platform giving a preliminary discourse to a crowd of about twenty thousand, then later he gave a series of talks at the Theosophical Society on the subject of *Adwaita Vedanta*. He was the international lecturer of the Ramakrishna Mission.

Christmas at Adyar brought with it the annual international Theosophical convention. Good speakers from a number of countries expounded on various aspects of Theosophy. Among them was the man from London who had spoken the vital words that brought me to India. I thanked him for this. His advice had already brought me an incredibly rich spiritual feast and I somehow knew that the best was yet to come.

After the convention, early in January, began a series of talks by J. Krishnamurti, known as Krishnaji by his followers. A son of a poor Brahmin family, Krishnamurti had been discovered when a boy by the great Theosophist, Bishop C.W. Leadbeater, incidentally one of the founders of the Liberal Catholic Church. Leadbeater and Dr Annie Besant, the President of the Theosophical Society, had taken the boy under their wing, providing him with a modern education in England and training him at Adyar for a special spiritual role. This was to be the vehicle of the Lord Maitreya, head of the Great White Lodge and considered the world teacher. Esoteric Theosophy teaches that the Christian message came from the Lord Maitreya through the man Jesus two thousand years ago. For some reason, the Besant-Leadbeater experiment with Krishnamurti, and their plan for a new dispensation coming through him, did not work out. After the death of Dr Annie Besant in the early 1930s, J. Krishnamurti and the Theosophical Society parted company. Instead of being a vehicle for the Lord Maitreya, Krishnaji began to lecture and teach from his own mind. Eventually, he gathered a good following in different countries of the world but almost every year he came back to India to give a series of talks in Madras. He would not now set foot in the Theosophical

Estate but gave his talks in the garden of a big house on the other side of the Adyar River. Practically everybody, including the President N. Sri Ram, living at the Theosophical Headquarters, attended Krishnaji's talks. Because of his break with the Society, a few of the old Theosophists, including Dr Taimni, would not go to hear him, but my wife and I were anxious to discover this Theosophical rebel's message to the world. So, as it was not very far away, we rode our bicycles over the Adyar Bridge to the pleasant garden where Krishnaji gave his early evening talks.

He was truly a memorable figure sitting, cross-legged, on his low platform under a great, spreading tree, his white robes contrasting with his dark skin and hair. He had the sharp, straight profile of an ancient Greek and the expression on his face suggested that he would not tolerate fools gladly. His audience, on chairs in a semicircle before him, was also under the leafy roof of the great tree. With the setting sun, an atmosphere of peace and beauty breathed over the whole scene. Krishnaji had no notes for his talk and I had the impression, then and afterwards, that he did not prepare his discourses. The words came spontaneously, but not always fluently, from some deep place within his mind. After that first talk, I thought of him with pleasure as the voice of Siva outside the gate. With words sometimes biting, he attacked the whole of mankind's established religious organisations. "Pull down your temples, burn your books, discard your gurus, don't waste your breath with mantras, forget the past entirely, your swamis and priests don't even bear mentioning. Sweep the whole dead structure aside and begin again from within yourself." These were some of the words he used to break up the old forms. The established forms of religion had become moribund, they did not lead men to the truth they sought but were chains that held them back from the spiritual truth.

One devout religious Hindu friend of ours from Madras was dismayed and disgusted at such an attack on his venerated religious practices. He stated that he would never go again to a Krishnaji talk. It seemed to me natural that any religious person who took such a verbal blitzkrieg literally would be dismayed and resentful, but I felt that Krishnaji did not mean us to take his words literally. They were simply an exaggerated statement of the words that come from the lips of many great spiritual teachers. Stated more moderately, his message would be, "Do not put all your reliance on your scriptures, or the teachings of your priests and gurus. They can only take you so far. Beyond that point you must go within and learn to know your true Self. It is within yourself that the truth and the wisdom and the love lie." This is surely the voice of Lord Siva who says to burn all forms that hold back our lives from the highest reality. Yet this rather negative approach of Krishnaji seemed to confuse many of his followers who complained that he gave them nothing to hold onto.

After hearing many of Krishnaji's talks that year in India and in future years under the same great tree and also in England and other places, I felt that the way to listen was with a mind open and still, as if in meditation. Indeed, I felt that his talks were a kind of verbal meditation in which we should forget the past, throw aside the crutches of verbiage, rituals and all other aids and dive deeply within to where the treasure lies.

Sometimes Krishnaji would talk like a Nature mystic. He would strive to lead his listeners to a deeper awareness of all things in Nature. He would plead with us to see the leaf, the flower, the tree, the bird, the spider, the cloud in a way that we had never seen them before. We had to see the reality, the divinity, the God within such objects. But he would never use such words as 'divinity' and 'God'. In fact, he seemed to avoid, as much as possible, the words and phrases in long use in spiritual teachings. It was as if he felt such currency had been debased. Some seemed to get the message from Krishnaji's iconoclastic style and content. Others followed him around the world in a desperate attempts to get his meaning. Yet a number of those who came to stay at Leadbeater Chambers during and after Krishnaji's sessions of talks, confided to me that he left them in a void. He had, they said, swept away their moorings and gave them nothing to hold onto. So it seemed to me that J. Krishnamurti was the right spiritual teacher for the few, he was not for the many. Although my wife and I felt warm love and appreciation for this handsome, earnest world teacher, we knew that he was not for us personally.

As well as sitting at the feet of a number of leading spiritual teachers during that first year in India, I was continuing my search for ultimate truth through the facilities at Adyar, both at the second School of the Wisdom conducted by Dr Taimni and at Headquarters Hall. In the latter I was continuing to study the *Upanishads* and other Indian spiritual texts under the direction of some good spiritual teachers. I still had in mind to write a book about the sacred heart of Mother India today but there were two great ashrams to the south of Madras that I wanted to visit before beginning this work. Furthermore, and more importantly, the journey to Puttaparti was still to be made. Sai Baba, I knew in my bones, would play a big part in any such book on India's spiritual life.

After Krishnaji's talks had ended and the halcyon days of January were slipping by in the tranquil oasis of the Theosophical Estate, I knew that the time was getting close for my journey. Despite the banquet of spiritual understanding I had imbibed since coming to India, despite the expansion of mental horizons it had given me, I still felt an inner emptiness, an inexplicable dissatisfaction. I needed something else. But where would I find that something?

One day, an English Theosophist, by the name of Peter Bright, came to Adyar. He regarded the late Ramana Maharshi as his spiritual guru and had just come from that great master's ashram near the sacred hill of Arunachala. But just before coming to Adyar, he had paid a quick visit to Sai Baba at Puttaparti. As it had only been a short visit, I asked him, half-jokingly, "Are you one of those who regard Sai Baba as a fake?" There was an expression of indignation in his bright blue eyes as he replied, "If Sai Baba is fake, I'll go back to beer." Peter then went to considerable trouble to soften our journey into the interior. He arranged for us to stay with wealthy friends of his in Bangalore and for us to have one of their private cars to take us to Puttaparti. "Will they lend us a bullock cart, too?" I joked. "The roads are rough, but a car will take you all the way," Peter replied.

In the upshot, Iris was unable to go, mainly because of her work. Well, there are some things in life that one has to do alone, and perhaps this is one of them, I thought, as I boarded a bus in Madras for the two hundred mile drive to Bangalore, the first leg of my historic, life-changing journey.

16. Born Again At Sixty

Cut off thy head and cast it on the ground,
trample on it long and mercilessly.
Only if you can do this may you venture
on the homeward journey.

KABIR

I HAD NOT read the dramatic hyperboles of the fifteenth-century saint Kabir when I made my first entry into Sai Baba's ashram. Brooding over the place, I was quite unaware of the fact that I was entering the operating theatre for the removal of my mental block on the homeward journey. My first thoughts were that the ashram was well named, Prasanti Nilayam, 'A Place of Great Peace'. Sai Baba's native village lay only a few hundred yards on the sunset side of his ashram. I received a smiling greeting from Sri N. Kasturi, who seemed to act as a secretarial receptionist for the ashram. He told me that he could not allot me accommodation until Swami came out of the prayer hall where he was conducting *bhajans*. Thinking that I may not get accommodation at all, I told my driver to wait outside the ashram in case I needed to go back to Bangalore with him. My valise was already unloaded, so I sat on it.

Listening to the sweet sacred music that floated from the prayer hall, I could see that what Kasturi called the prayer hall was in the largest building, in the centre of the ashram. It was a white, two-storey building with a veranda and balcony in front. Near me was a line of single-storey terraces, out of which Kasturi had come. On the side over which the sun was now dipping, were more low buildings, and on the opposite side from where I sat were two large open sheds.

Something inward must have happened to me as I sat there in the glorious peace coloured by the sunset and filled with sacred music. All I know is that there, sitting on my valise, I decided that Sai Baba was too great for just one chapter in the book I was proposing to write. The whole book must be about him. The haunting strains of *Arati* were sounding, though I did not know its name then, when Kasturi reappeared. My first words were, "I have decided to write a book on Sai Baba." I saw doubt written all over his face but he said politely, "Well, that will be nice if it happens." Perhaps his lack of faith in my statement came from the fact that others had made similar statements and promptly forgot about them. Kasturi's next words were, "Swami has told me to put you in the guest house."

He led me to the other side of the white building called the *Mandir*. Here I saw more one-storey terraces lining each side of a large brown rectangle. I did not know it then, but Swami had allotted me the best accommodation in the ashram. A broad veranda, enclosed by strong netting, led to a comfortably furnished bedroom with, behind that, a kitchen and a bathroom. The bathroom was of the Indian variety where one dips water from a large container to pour over oneself as a shower. I had grown accustomed to this at other ashrams and Leadbeater Chambers and preferred it to a shower. The toilet was of the Western type with a chain and cistern. Two other similar units opened onto the same broad veranda but these, I found, were occupied by some members of India's royal families. Before leaving me, Kasturi said a strange thing: "Swami says not to let anybody share this room unless he tells you to." Then he offered to dismiss my driver and departed. The first thing I did was to sample the bed. It was a comfortable single bed with clean sheets beneath a blanket. What luxury! What luck, I thought, and before going to the ashram canteen, I decided to enjoy an Indian bath. It had been a long day with several obstacles thrown in my path to the 'Place of Great Peace'.

The first of these had been a death in the family where I had spent the night in Bangalore. A car had been needed to take the body to Madras. It looked as if I might not get a car to go to Puttaparti. But they kindly decided to give me one even though it left them rather short of transport. Then, on the lonely road through the barren hills, where it seemed that nobody came or had come since the beginning of the world, we had a puncture. To his annoyance, the driver found that the spare wheel was also punctured. He blamed this on the other driver. He bowled one of the punctured wheels like a hoop along the road up a hill and round a corner, in the hope of finding a village where there might be a bike shop that would mend his puncture. I sat under a tree by the roadside while the hot, early February sun beat down on the empty landscape around me. Over an hour went by, no traffic passed me and my driver seemed to have vanished forever. I don't know how much later it was when I finally saw him running down the hill like a boy with a hoop. The tyre had been mended by a bike shop, as he had hoped, and we moved onward. The road became rougher until it was little more than a bush track. Sometimes it led through the sand of almost dry river beds. I felt that it was like one of the Lord's miracles that we eventually reached our destination. I recalled the saying that a searcher will always find obstacles thrown in his path in an important stretch of the spiritual journey. Perhaps the dark forces try to block his way, I thought.

In the little canteen, with slabs of stone for tables and seats, I had a good Indian curry. It was an Andhra Pradesh curry and very spicy, but I like it that way. When I took from my pocket a handful of rupees to pay for the meal, the canteen manager said, "No, no, Swami has given instructions that all your meals here should be free."

Early the next morning before breakfast, Kasturi arrived at my room with some books under his arm. He said, "When I told Swami what you had said about writing a book on him, he told me to bring you all the books in English already printed on his life and teaching. Here they are." They were Kasturi's book on the life of Sai Baba and several of his translations of Swami's discourses and writings. When I asked what I owed him for them, he replied, "Nothing. Swami says they are a gift." I felt the flow of Swami's love in all this generosity I was receiving and felt happy that he, unlike Kasturi, had faith in my statement about writing a book. I suspect, now, that he knew I was to be one of his scribes when I first met him in Madras and perhaps long before that. I looked forward to reading the books while at the ashram, where I intended to stay for about a week, but found that I did not have as much spare time as I had expected.

A flow of people began arriving at the ashram and, as most of the small terrace rooms were occupied by permanent residents, most of the visitors put down their beds on the floor of the open-sided sheds. Talking to some of them, I found that the reason for the flow, which was increasing in volume every day, was the fact that in about ten days' time a great Indian religious festival would take place. For Prasanti Nilayam, this was probably the greatest of all the main Hindu festivals. They told me that it was called Mahasivaratri, or just Sivaratri, for short. I had never heard of this but my new-found Sai friends explained that the name meant 'the great night of Siva' and, they said, as most of his Indian followers believed that Swami was an incarnation of Lord Siva this festival was especially sacred here at Prasanti Nilayam. Swami celebrates the occasion, they told me, by performing two wonderful public miracles. One of them is, they said, that Swami produces a Siva *lingam* from inside himself and the other is that he produces from an empty urn a constant flow of vibhuti sufficient to cover an almost life-sized statue of his earlier form at Shirdi, sufficient to give the statue a ritual bath of sacred ash. This is called *abhisheka*. They advised that I should stay for the festival and see these things. I made up my mind that I would certainly do so, but I had many questions to ask. "What is a Siva lingam?" I queried, "And how does Swami produce it from inside himself?"

They explained simply that a lingam was a symbolic object sacred to the Hindus, and especially to those who worshipped Siva, just as a cross is a sacred symbol to the Christians. It is an oval-shaped object something like an egg, they explained, and can be made of any hard material. On the evening of Sivaratri, I learned, Swami, sitting on a platform in public, brings a lingam, and sometimes more than one, from somewhere inside his body out through his mouth. It is often the size of a hen's egg or even larger. The material of which it is made varies, from year to year, from precious metals such as gold or silver to semi-precious or precious stones such as crystal or emerald or perhaps sapphire.

But why, I wondered, was this particular festival in honour of Lord Siva held on the eighteenth of February? My kind informants pointed out that it is not always on that date. In fact, like the Christian Easter festival, it depends on the moon. When the moon has waned to its very smallest size before beginning to wax towards a full moon, that is the time for Mahasivaratri. It seems that always on some date in February the moon decreases to its minimal size for the year. But why, I asked, does Lord Siva require the least possible amount of moon for his festival? The answer I received was something like this: Lord Siva, as well as being the god of renewal and regeneration, is also the god of the yogis, the one who helps man in his meditation. Meditation, of course, requires the controlling and transcending of the mind. It is well known that the moon, the lunar body of the heavens, has a powerful influence on man's mind, so that it is easier to control and master the mind when the moon is at its smallest size and weakest influence. You will find, they told me, that on Sivaratri night after Swami has produced the lingam, everybody, or nearly everybody, sits up all night, cross-legged on the ground, meditating in an effort to break through the shell of the mind and reach illumination. Doubtless, many achieve a spiritual experience in this way.

As the pressure of the crowd increased, one or two of the boldest asked to share my accommodation. I felt rather mean about denying them but remembered Swami's instructions. At this time it seemed to be a purely Indian festival and I was the only pale-faced Westerner moving among the Indians — that is, among the men. But there were two Western ladies, left over from the party that had come to Madras with Swami a year before. I had met them both on that occasion. One was the Swiss woman named Gabriela Steyer while the other was my ochre-robed messenger of the gods, Nirmalananda. She was a help to me again on this occasion.

Learning that I was planning to gather material from the growing crowd of devotees for the purposes of writing a book, and that I had not brought a notebook to the ashram for this purpose, she generously gave me her notebook. It was a fat one with all its pages blank. I was to fill it with miraculous stories from the Sai devotees before I left the ashram on that occasion. Nirmalananda told me that she had decided not to write anything on Sai Baba until she was Self-realised. I was to learn in the years to come that nobody writes a book after becoming Self-realised, so perhaps that is why Nirmalananda's name has not appeared among the many who have written books on Sai Baba.

In the days leading up to the two great miracles, while an estimated twenty-five thousand people gathered at the ashram, I had many fascinating talks with Indians who had spent nearly two decades with Satya Sai Baba. One of these was the crown prince of the Kingdom of Venkatagiri, which had, of course, ceased to be an official kingdom at the time of India's Independence back in 1947. The young prince was very well-read in the spiritual literature of India and taught me many things from the wealth of Indian culture and spirituality. I was somewhat startled, however, at one thing he said. "Many of us," he said, quietly and rather tentatively, "... many of us regard Sai Baba as an Avatar." I felt unable to make a comment on this. The word 'Avatar', I knew, meant 'God in human form on earth'. Fortunately I did not have to reply because a silence had descended on everybody outside their accommodation at the rear of the Mandir. Those not outside came quickly from their rooms and stood quietly with their hands before them, palms pressed together in the gesture of prayer, which Indians call the *namaste*. Then I saw the reason for the great silence and the gestures. Swami was walking across the brown sandy earth from his Mandir towards the Sanskrit school at the other end. His feet were bare, his red robe and mop of frizzy hair gleaming in the sunshine. Could this short, slight, bare-footed figure with the brown skin and shining, luminous eyes, be God on earth, I wondered? Such an idea seemed far removed from my previous concept of God the Father in Heaven. But I was determined to keep my mind open on the subject. When I returned to Adyar, I would find all the books available there on the subject of Avatara and study them. Meantime I felt there were many new things to be learned in this Place of Great Peace and great wonders.

In my book *Sai Baba, Man of Miracles*, initially inspired during this visit, I have described in detail the two public miracles Swami performed that year on Sivaratri day, so I will not repeat the descriptions here. When I saw the large statue of Shirdi Sai Baba completely smothered in vibhuti, produced by Swami's hand from a small empty urn, I wondered if this miracle had any purpose apart from demonstrating again the power of unfettered super-consciousness over matter. Perhaps, honouring his earlier form with the holy bath helped to demonstrate to the human mind that the body of Shirdi Sai had been the temple of the divine being now know as Satya Sai. I, myself, did not need any convincing on this point.

In the other great miracle, when my eyes actually witnessed the lingam come from Swami's mouth with a flash of light and fall into the white linen handkerchief he held below, I accepted that this genuine miracle had taken place, but, again, I wondered the reason for it. The next day when I saw it standing, larger than an average hen egg, on a stand that held it up like an egg-cup on the ledge against the light of a window, I wondered how such a large object could possibly come up through a human-sized gullet. Many years later I heard that Swami had told somebody that the lingam came up in molten form and then solidified in his mouth into the solid, egg-shaped lingam. This sounded reasonable, but from where came its stand? Seemingly of the same solid green stone material. Kasturi wrote that it too had come up from Swami's stomach, but I did not see it that night. Later I read of an incident that took place when a number of people were digging to prepare the foundations for the old Mandir in Puttaparti village. Swami told a hunchback helper to dig in a certain spot and there he found a large quantity of the *avudaiyars*, recognised by all the helpers as stands for holding lingams. "But where are the lingams to go into them, Swami?" they asked him. Swami patted his own stomach, saying, "In here." So perhaps the green stone avudaiyar I saw that morning was one of those dug up by the hunchback worker. From the time of that digging at Puttaparti, lingams had been produced every Mahasivaratri from Swami's stomach. These things much surely be a sign that Sai Baba is the great Lord Siva himself, I thought.

On more than one occasion, Swami has stated that his greatest miracle is his love. Before leaving Prasanti Nilayam that year, I was to enjoy a full experience of that great miracle. It was, for me, the grand finale of an interview that he gave to a number of people on the day before I left the ashram. With keen interest, I watched him materialise a number of gifts for different people in the interview room. I think that the last item he produced was a ring for me, embossed with a gold image of Shirdi Sai Baba. With joy, I realised that he could read my heart and knew of my great love for Shirdi Sai Baba. I know for sure that I was the last to be taken into the inner room where he deals with people's personal and private problems. I went in, when called, alone, somewhat shyly, hardly knowing what to expect.

First he talked to me in a voice that dripped with the sweet honey of love about my past, my present problems and several things about my future. Then something unexpected and wonderful happened. While his sweet tones continued, with the soothing solicitude of a thousand mothers, I felt a flood go through me from head to toe. It was as if I was having a holy bath, not of sacred ash, but of sacred oil. The warm oil seemed to pour inside me, drenching every cell of my body, breaking up and melting hard crusts of rigid attitudes and habits. It was a joyous, cleansing flood. Swami did not tell me what it was, but I knew without being told that it was a baptism of *prema*, or divine love, which doubtless is synonymous with the baptism of the Holy Spirit. I felt that my spiritual heart centre had been opened and that the divine child who had been lying there, in embryo, has now been born, and with the birth of the divine child, my real Self, I too had been reborn. My life would never be quite the same again.

As we all moved out of the interview room, I had a sudden desire to kneel before Swami and touch his feet. This was something that had gone very much against my grain before. It was all right for the Indians, I had thought, but not for a hard-headed independent Westerner, like myself. Now, with his consent, I knelt before him, touching his small, shapely feet with my hands and forehead. When I stood up, he did a strange thing. With his fingers gently against my body, he did a downward scraping movement, first at the front and then at the back of my body. It was as if he was scraping away the broken psychic shells shattered in the flood of prema. At subsequent meetings over the next few months, he continued doing the same thing, never giving his reason in words.

On the journey back to Adyar, I seemed to be floating in a joy tinged with sadness. Joy was there because I knew for sure now that I had found my prophesied star and, as under the star of Bethlehem, the Christ child had been born in me. Now I could operate from the warm heart centre instead of the cold centre of the head. Why, then, the tinge of sadness? Undoubtedly, it was because I felt I was leaving Sai Baba behind and in those two weeks at Prasanti Nilayam I had grown too attached to the Form. How could I live without the Form?

But when I finally walked into our rooms at Leadbeater Chambers, my heart gave a jump of joy. There he was, smiling at me from my desk. I had never seen a photo of Sai Baba before, so whence had come this neatly-framed photo of him? While I stood wondering and no longer sad, Iris appeared in the room and told me her story. It seemed that at the time I was having my initiation, my baptism of divine love at Prasanti Nilayam, she was experiencing the same thing in her heart here at Adyar. How was this possible, I wondered? But I learned through the subsequent years that Swami has this wonderful power of working on a married couple through either, as if they are one. Anyway, one result on Iris, was to make her hunt feverishly for a photo of Sai Baba. Eventually, she found several in an illustrated Indian magazine. She cut them out and framed them. Now one stood on my desk and others hung from a wall. Since then, photos of our Paramaguru have always been plentiful in our homes. They help to remind us of his omnipresence.

According to the Chinese calendar, that year, 1966, was the first Year of the Firehorse since 1906. How strange it is, I thought, that I should have been born on the Chinese Year of the Firehorse and born again of the Spirit at its next appearance on the Chinese calendar. Well, one is never too old to be born of the Spirit. From that day of our mutual initiation, in February 1966, my wife and I both accepted Sai Baba as our spiritual guru. He was also my star of destiny, but was he also an Avatar, a descent of God to earth, as some deeply perceptive Indians had said during my life-changing sojourn at Prasanti Nilayam? I began to look for books in the Adyar library that might help to throw some light on this question.

My greatest wealth is Love. People speak about my powers and my miracles, but my Love is my greatest miracle. All should share in this Love. Only then will there be oneness.

SAI BABA

With love
Baba

17. Insights And Episodes

If the doors of perception were cleansed,
man would see everything as it is — infinite.

BLAKE

THE LIBRARY AT Adyar did not give me much help in the mental acceptance of the concept of Avatara. Such a spiritual insight does not come from books. It was, I think, a scene at Brindavan, Sai Baba's ashram at Whitefield near Bangalore, that caused the opening and allowed the thin edge of the wedge of such an understanding to enter my mind. The scene is still vivid in my memory as if it were yesterday.

Swami was walking from the door of his interview room towards a small group of us in the garden. Standing near me, was a young Indian who startled me by saying boldly to Swami, "Are you God?" He was evidently determined to have the answer directly from the one concerned. Swami pointed to him and said, "*You* are God." I had slowly been coming to terms with his teaching that God is the reality within every human being but now he took the opportunity of the young man's question to make the reality of the God within all of us more specific and clear. He pointed out that we are all descents of the divine and, in a sense, we are therefore all Avatars, but we are completely unaware of this great truth. On the other hand, the ones that are called Avatars of God are completely aware of their divine identity. Being fully aware of their Godhood, they exhibit divine attributes and live divine lives. Their actions, coming from their divine centre, are not selfish or egocentric, as human actions usually are. All of an Avatar's actions are for the good of mankind. It is for that purpose, for the elevation of humanity, that he has come to earth but because his understanding is greater and his motivation different from that of the human being, he will be considered inscrutable and some of his actions will be misunderstood.

The aim of human life is to reach that inner God centre and, when an individual reaches it, he will think, understand and act as an Avatar. He will become a conscious Avatar of God instead of being, as now, an unconscious one. I was able to accept this teaching but it was as yet only in the front room of my mind. It had yet to penetrate to the inner sanctuary which we call the heart. This meant that my perceptions had to be cleansed and my spiritual perception clarified. This came about through the days, weeks and months in Swami's presence. The divine things he did and said, my musing on them and my writing about them, gradually built up to the firm, inner conviction that he could be nothing else but a great Avatar of God. Others, moving about on two legs, may be Gods with amnesia, sometimes very bad amnesia, but this small, bare-footed saint in the red-orange robe was God on earth, fully aware of his Godhood.

During the months that it took me to reach this conviction, I thought of him as my guiding star who would lead me to see the spiritual splendour hidden in the cloak of earthly life. Apropos of my belief that Swami was my promised star of heaven, I was fascinated to read something written by Dr E.B. Fanibunda, a Parsee orthodontist of Bombay, in his fine book *Vision of the Divine*. The quiet, reserved doctor tells how, on one occasion, Swami materialised for him a small medallion with an image of Shirdi Sai Baba on one side. Back home, with the aid of a microscope, he made out the small letters T.P.S. under the image. It was months before he had the opportunity to ask Swami the meaning of these letters. When he did so, Swami said quietly, "They are my trademark." On further questioning, Swami explained that the letter T stood for Tara, which meant a star, P stood for Puttaparti, and S for Sai. The 'trademark' also stood for his former incarnation and the third one yet to come. Shirdi Sai Baba was born near a village called Patri, so the letters stood for Tara Patri Sai. As in his next incarnation he will be known as Prema Sai, the letters will mean Tara Prema Sai. Thus the three small letters on the medallion signify the triple appearance of the star of heaven on earth. The old Hindu astrologer who read my horoscope when I was a schoolboy in Tasmania was not wrong when he said that I would find my star in the east.

Two things relevant to my theme happened at Adyar in the intervals between our periods with Sai Avatar. The first was something that came to me by his grace while I sat one morning under the great banyan tree. The ground under the great spreading tree was covered with sand and the many trunks coming down to the ground gave it the appearance of a natural cathedral. Occasionally, lectures were given under this tree, but on this sunny morning I sat alone there, in the leafy shade, looking through the slender columns that held up the green canopy of its roof. There seemed to be an other-worldly spiritual beauty about it. Suddenly, without warning, I was sitting in the *jyothi*, the divine Light. It was all around me and within me. The physical world did not entirely disappear but seemed as if it was pushed over to one side, some distance away, but the whole natural cathedral of the banyan tree disappeared and was replaced by the divine Light. The sunlight, that I could still discern in the world outside, seemed as weak as candlelight in comparison to the brightness, splendour and glory of the true divine Light. Yet its brightness did not hurt my eyes. It seemed to soothe them. Perhaps I was not seeing it by my natural eyes but by an inner sight of the spirit. The experience, with the inexpressible ecstasy that it brought, did not last long. I knew it had come as a gift of reassurance and encouragement from God and I thanked Him.

In hindsight, I think that perhaps this vision of reality was to help in my understanding that God was on earth and that he had work for me to do. I have thought also that if this jyothi, or Light of God, was the same as that seen by Paul on the road to Damascus, it could not have been the cause of his blindness. There was a divine reason for his blindness but its cause must have been something other than the divine Light which comes through spiritual perception, not by way of the human eyes. Anyway, for me, it was my second most powerful mandorla, coming soon after the major one I had in Swami's presence in the inner room at Prasanti Nilayam, that is, the baptism of divine Love.

The other event on the Theosophical Estate that should be reported is that I was awarded a Writer's Fellowship from the Kern Foundation in America to write the biographies of the two founders of the Theosophical Society. They were the Russian occultist, Madame H.P. Blavatsky, and Colonel H.S. Olcott, a veteran of the American Civil War. These two biographies were required as soon as possible and they entailed a good deal of reading in the Adyar library and research in the archives there. One advantage of this study was that it brought me a better understanding of the aims and spiritual purpose of the Society. Through reading the private diaries, letters, and old documents in the archives, I lost any lingering doubts I might have had about the actual existence of the Masters of the Great White Lodge. While Blavatsky and Olcott were front figures in the foundation of the Movement, behind the scenes there were two great *Mahatmas* working constantly to turn the scientific intellectual stream of last century towards spiritual shores. These two were Master Morya and Master Kuthumi Lal Singh (Master KH). In India they often visited the two founders, sometimes in their physical bodies and sometimes in their astral bodies. Among others who paid occasional visits was the Master

Hilarion. Such visits were recorded in private diaries and other written documents. Master Morya, usually called Master M, had been Helena Blavatsky's spiritual guide since her childhood in Russia. Later, Henry Olcott became his pupil also.

Another advantage was that the Fellowship's advance payment brought me some ready cash, very welcome to searchers living on the proverbial shoestring. A disadvantage, however, was that it delayed my start on the book I planned to write on Sai Baba. In the drive from Whitefield to Horsley Hills in 1967, I was in a car with Swami, Rajah Reddy driving, and the District Engineer who had made the practical arrangements of our stay at Circuit House. Somewhere along the way, Swami remarked casually to the Engineer that I was writing a book on him. The Engineer seemed very interested and asked if I had nearly finished the book. The fact was that I had not yet written a word of it. I did not confess this to the Engineer but I have no doubt that Swami knew it. I expect it was just a reminder to me to get started. So I understood that he regarded this work as important, for two reasons. The first reason was, I understood later, that writing the book would help my spiritual evolution. The second, also understood later, was that this book would open a door to the world outside India, through which Swami could draw to his feet those people who were ready for his spiritual teachings.

Swami seems to have also prepared the ground for its publication in the West. On the day that my literary agent in London received the manuscript on his desk, he had just had a telephone call from a well-known London publisher asking for a book on an esoteric subject. The agent sent them my manuscript and they published it. But before it came out, Iris and I had left India and were on our way back to Australia by way of England and America. In London I talked with the publishers and we agreed on the title, *Sai Baba, Man of Miracles*. In San Francisco, a young Sai devotee talked to me enthusiastically about the book as if he had read it. Yet it was not even in the bookshops in London by then. The fact was he had had it read to him at Prasanti Nilayam by Kasturi. I had sent a copy of the manuscript to Swami and he had told Kasturi to read a section of it every day to the young Western devotees who were there. I was happy because this showed that Swami approved of it.

Sai Baba teaches that we must be unaffected by praise or blame, which may be why he never inflated my ego by giving me a word of praise directly. Yet, one day, many years later, when Iris and I were alone with him in a room, he said something that, to me, was beyond all normal praise. We had been talking about futures and I asked him about my future. He said, quietly, "You have nothing to worry about. Your future will be illustrious because you will bring many people to the Light." That was all the praise I ever needed, or ever would need, from my beloved spiritual teacher.

During the enchanted summer days at Horsely Hills in 1967, blessed by his regular teachings, uplifted by his frequent miracles, he made an unexpected promise. He knew the year of my birth, having teleported for me a gold ten dollar coin, minted in San Francisco in that same year, 1906, so he knew, of course, that I had been sixty years old in the last November. He said, "As you are now sixty, I will give you a *Shastipoorti* when we return to Brindavan." Then he explained that this was a marriage ceremony given in India to a couple when the husband has reached the age of sixty. I was not, at first, very appreciative, but I thanked him. With further explanation, however, from him and others in our party, I found that it was meant to be a spiritual renewal of the marriage. Then its importance began to dawn on me. Marriage, I knew, from my own past experience and that of many acquaintances, is either a spiritual union or it is nothing. Generally, in the world today, it is a legalised partnership for the expression of the sex urge and the reproduction of the species. Iris and I had wanted our marriage to be a spiritual sacrament and we thought we had obtained it in the Liberal Catholic Church in Sydney. It was eight years since that ceremony had taken place and, as Swami sometimes pointed out, we were still good partners. But what could be better than a ceremony of spiritual renewal given by Sai Baba himself? This, we thought, should seal a happy partnership for the rest of our mortal lives. And perhaps even beyond that. It was beginning to be clear to us through the Sai teachings and influence that marriage is, indeed, a sacrifice. Each sacrifices not to the other but to the unity, to the one that they both are. This surely is a beginning, a good preliminary step towards that unity of all mankind in which every individual must sacrifice something of this ego for the sake of that union, that universal brotherhood. We said no more about it to Swami but hoped he would remember and keep his promise when we returned to Brindavan.

He said no more either until one day in the old bungalow at Brindavan, that stood where the Mandir now stands, he remarked, "I am marrying a young couple in the central hall here, tomorrow. I want you to come and watch closely, because after it I will give you the same ceremony for your Shastipoorti." The windows of our own room looked into this central hall but, as the crowds gathered there for the marriage, we went into the hall itself and found places as close as possible to the small stage, where the Indian ceremonies were taking place around the young bride and bridegroom.

In due course, we were sitting on that stage ourselves, with two Hindu pundits chanting Sanskrit *slokas* above our heads and Swami standing by in a motherly fashion. We could not remember all the steps in the rather intricate Hindu wedding ceremony, but Swami guided us in that. Eventually, he waved his hand and produced two rings, one with a ruby stone for me to put on my wife's finger and another with a diamond for her to put on my finger. Soon after that, three garlands of flowers seemed to appear in his hand, one I had to put on Iris and the other was for her to garland me and then the third one we held together and put over Swami's head. At the end of the ritual, a photographer appeared and took a number of photographs, which we still have. It all took about an hour and we thought that that was the end of the Shastipoorti. But, no, it went on for three days.

On the second day, there was poor feeding. Six hundred poor people from villages around came into the grounds and, guided by Sai volunteers, sat in long rows with leaf plates in front of them. With Swami supervising, a number of his devotees served a meal to the six hundred poor, while Iris and I stood by. Swami himself had provided the food on our behalf and we understood that the event was part of our spiritual blessing.

In the next day's event, we played a more active part. Sixty men and sixty women of the most needy and destitute of the poor were sitting in rows in the inner garden, men in one area and women in another. Iris gave new saris to the women and my job was to hand the new clothing to the poor old men. I don't know at what point this clothing came into Swami's bungalow. Perhaps at the same time as a silk sari he gave to Iris for the ceremony and the white silk he gave to me for the two garments the bridegroom wears. I saw clothes being brought out of the front door of his house into the portico, then the two garments for each man, that is a *kurtha* and a *dhoti*, came through the hands of a line of devotees to reach me. Then it was my job to give them to each old man along the line. I was careful to tell each one that the gift was from Sai Baba, but this did not stop them touching my feet in gratitude. After three days of meaningful rituals, with Swami's divine love and compassion breathing over all, we felt that our marriage must certainly be blessed and renewed.

About a week before the ceremony, when we were at Horsley Hills and Swami had transmuted a button rosebud into a diamond for me, he had said that he would convert it into a ring for my Shastipoorti, but instead of that he had doubled it. The stone in my wedding ring was identical to the one from the button rose, still in a small box in my room. Now that I had two identical diamonds, I thought I should offer to give one back to Swami, which I did. But his reply was, "What's two diamonds! You keep both." Some years later we asked Swami if we could have the button rose diamond made into a ring for Iris. His reply was, "Yes, of course. You are one." As the years went by, sweeping cleaner the doors of our perception and understanding, we realise more and more how very blessed we were by that powerful ceremony that came through the grace of our Paramguru. My old mother always used to say that a true marriage is made in heaven. She surely would have been pleased by this renewal of our marriage, organized and directed by the star of heaven on earth.

¶

The following story, which took place a few years later, is something from which both my wife and I learned a valuable lesson. It was a bright, sunny morning at Prasanti Nilayam and I had been fortunate enough to be sitting on the outer edge of the veranda in front of the Mandir, quite close to Swami's exit door. This position allowed me to have an uninterrupted view of the Lord's face as he came through the doorway. Eventually he appeared, paused to look along the lines of men on the veranda, give me a pleasant, half-smiling glance, and then stepped off the veranda and turned left to give *darshan* to the women's section first. I watched his slow progress around the semi-circle till he came to the end of the men's section on the far right. Then he came straight back along the outside of the veranda, stepped onto it and, turning, looked directly at me. I hoped for a smile and a few words from him. What I got was a very severe look and his words shocked me. "Why isn't your wife at darshan today?" he asked. His tone was a reprimand. I only had to turn my head slightly to see her sitting there in the first or second row, quite obvious to me and the other men on the veranda near me. I knew that Swami also could see her and felt that he had some other meaning. So I refrained from replying, "She's sitting there, Swami." Instead I kept silent. "You make sure that she comes to darshan always," he ordered, then, turning, he went through his door into his room.

When he had gone, I looked at the few men close to me, who were smiling. Jack Hislop, sitting just across the veranda from me, was, in fact, laughing. I knew that he could see my wife plainly and hoped that he might be able to throw some light on the mystery. "What do you think Swami means by that?" I asked him. He replied, "You never know what Swami means," and he continued to laugh quietly to himself. None of the other men around me offered any explanation. Obviously none of them knew what Swami meant. But when I returned to our room and told Iris about it, she knew immediately what he mean. "So that's why all the men were turning their heads to look at me," she said. "But I know what Swami meant. I was sitting there but I was not really at darshan. I was praying intensely to him, in fact, directing him to help John Gilbert. John was very sick when he called to see us this morning and I felt such compassion for him that I was trying to tell the Lord what to do. I should have left it to him and opened my heart and mind for his darshan."

Well, this incident, a shock to me and to her, gave us a sharp lesson on how to be at darshan. It is certainly not a place in which to intrude on Swami's mind with powerful prayer. The right thing is to sit quietly, as if in meditation, but yet not to meditate or concentrate on anything. It is rather like the 'receiving' state as taught in Subud. The body should be as relaxed as possible, while the mind is quiet and open to receive the blessing that Swami wants to give us in the darshan. The mind should be like the negative of a photographic film in the camera, sensitive and ready to receive whatever divine beam comes from the Lord. I know that people of my acquaintance have received wonderful things by sitting in a receptive state in the darshan line. An American woman I know, at her very first darshan, received the baptism of divine love that left her sitting with tears flooding down her cheeks and with the knowledge that she had already received what she had come for. Another woman, this one from England, received a cure for her breast cancer from one powerful beam from Swami's eyes, without his speaking one word to her. There is, in fact, a long list of heart transformations, life transmutations and divine healings of men and women from many climes and lands, of people who have been 'at darshan', not only physically, but with minds opened to receive the manna from on high.

17. Insights And Episodes

Always find a quiet corner after my darshan, where you may enter the stillness and receive the completion of my blessings. My energy goes out from me as I pass by you. If you proceed to talk with others immediately, this precious energy is dissipated and returned to me, unused by you. Rest assured that whatever my eye sees becomes vitalised and transmuted. You are changed day by day.

SAI BABA

18. Labours Of An Avatar

Every time virtue wanes in the world and vice and injustice are victorious, I become visible and thus I appear from age to age for the salvation of the righteous, the destruction of the wicked and the re-establishment of virtue.

KRISHNA
— from *The Great Initiates* by Edouard Schure

ONE DAY, MANY years ago, I said to Sai Baba, "Swamiji, the Indian scriptures say that all major Avatars are descendants of Lord Vishnu, but people say that you are an Avatar of Lord Siva. Why is that?" He smiled and replied, "It's all One. There is only One." I knew by then that his main teaching was that there is only one God and He goes by many names and appears in many forms. Yet, there are three main facets of the many-faceted one God. The Indian scriptures name these as Brahma, Vishnu and Siva. So I came to accept the idea that Sai Baba was an Avatar of the one God, with emphasis on the Siva facet.

I think of Siva as the power that destroys outworn forms and, at the same time, rejuvenates life through new forms. I think of Him, too, as the compassionate God of the yogis, He who helps them destroy the veil of Time to reveal Eternity. This Avatar's main reason for coming, therefore, must be to destroy the evil forces in the world that are clogging up the machinery of the evolution of consciousness for mankind. Seen only through the human eye, there must have been many periods during the last two thousand years when wickedness seemed to be in the ascendancy over good. But God's eye is more penetrating and he knows when the constant tug-of-war between good and evil has got out of balance and it is time for him to incarnate as man into the world of men in order to put the balance right. He must re-establish the forces of virtue in order that his cosmic drama may carry on through the centuries ahead.

But what did the divine eye see, looming in the decades ahead, when he came to earth last century as Sai Baba of Shirdi? Well, the age of scientific materialism was growing fast, taking men away from the old religious values and turning them off the ancient paths to Truth. Men were beginning to worship the false gods of materialism. This would lead, inevitably, to the holocausts of Hitler, the dark tyranny of Stalinism, the atom bomb and the threat of atomic destruction through the terrible years of the Cold War. If not stopped, this could mean the destruction of the earth and the end of God's plan for mankind. This terrible threat in the divine perspective brought down the first of the triple incarnation of the Sai Avatars.

During the 1960s, when the Cold War was at its height, we asked Swami if, in fact, a Third World War, the nuclear war, would come. His answer was very definite. "No, this Avatar has come, armed with divine omnipotence, to prevent such a thing." Our eyes must have expressed doubt that such a gigantic thing could be accomplished by this small figure in the red robe, for he said, in a voice of quiet confidence, "It is not the nature of an Avatar to fail." Other people asked him the same question and received the same answer. One of these was the Managing Editor of a well-known Bombay newspaper. He published his interview with Sai Baba and became a Sai devotee himself. Thus it was that Swami's words of assurance were put on record. But, perhaps, few people believed him. On one occasion we said to him, "Swami, we know that the people on both sides do not want a world-destroying world war, but what about the governments? They are the trouble." We were thinking especially of the government of Communist Russia.

"Yes," he agreed, "but the Governments will have to be changed. And they will be changed." In the rhythm of Siva's time drum there is the right time for everything. And so, at the right time, the world witnessed the amazing, almost unbelievable change of government in Russia. The Cold War, with its threat of nuclear annihilation, vanished overnight. The world breathed a sigh of relief, while our hearts rejoiced that the Avatar had carried out his promise.

Once, back in the years of the Cold War, Swami spoke to us about the Golden Age to come. There would, he said, be a number of small wars and other painful adjustments in the body of humanity and the world, but early in the next century we would be moving into a Golden Age, an age of relative peace and harmony in the family of mankind. "So, then, what will there be for Prema Sai to do?" we asked him. "There will be plenty to do," Swami replied, "in maintaining world peace and increasing the harmony." We knew that the very name Prema Sai meant the Sai of divine love, so if he could emanate more of this prema than Satya Sai does, the hopes for humanity were bright indeed. Yet, it is inherent in the divine plan that there must always be a degree of conflict and struggle. Conflict within the individual translates into conflict within the nations and the world. The aim of the divine work seems to be to keep that conflict within the perimeters of non-violence. Then there will be relative peace and harmony.

To bring about world changes, the Avatar works on the individual. Even to change governments, he works on the individuals in the government. His labours go on, on two levels, on the surface and beneath the surface, but most of his work is unseen — beneath the surface. That is where the transformation of the individual heart takes place. Sometimes I used to think that, though Swami has wrought a deep-seated change in many human hearts, and will, undoubtedly, bring the same transmutation to thousands more, how can he, in the time he has allotted to himself, possibly transform the billions of individuals walking the earth? But then I remembered that he does not have to do that. Jesus Christ used to liken the Kingdom of Heaven to small things, such as a grain of mustard seed that grows into a great tree, or the small leaven that the housewife puts into the dough to make it rise to a large loaf. Small but powerful things effect and create things many times their own dimensions. Ten good men in the city of Sodom could have saved its destruction, but they were not found. Divine Light and Love, born in a thousand human hearts, will transform the lives of many millions. The transmutation of the few will keep the ship of humanity on an even keel, making good and steady progress towards its divine goal. Such an Avataric labour is urgent and requires an arsenal of the weapons of peace for the forces of the Light.

In a series of lectures given by Dr Annie Besant at Adyar, India, early this century on the subject of Avatara, she expresses an idea of great interest. To me, it throws light on a great labour that the Avatar is carrying out today. She points out that the divine truths, the eternal verities for the upliftment of mankind, were revealed by God to the ancient rishis of India. There may have been lesser revelations in other parts of the world, but the rich treasure of divine knowledge and wisdom came to India. This rich treasure, these pearls of great price, were kept in India, guarded as if in a steel vessel, by the warrior caste, the Kshatriya caste of India. No invader could break in through that protective band of steel. But the *sanathana dharma*, the eternal wisdom, was meant not for India alone but for the whole of mankind. So, Avatar Krishna's purpose in destroying that Kshatriya caste in the war of Kurukshetra was twofold. First, it was to show that those who abuse power and govern wrongly, shall not govern at all. The second, and most far-reaching, purpose was to destroy the protective ring of steel that had served its purpose in time. The time had come for the spiritual treasure trove of India to be shared with the whole of mankind. In due course, the armies of foreign invaders would come in. Yet, even before they came to throw India open to the world, some individuals came and some individuals left. One who came, to drink deeply at the eternal spring, was Jesus of Nazareth. He took back with him large pitchers of the waters of life to share with the God-thirsty of Israel. From their following his directions, the eternal wisdom, or the part of it that Christ had been able to teach, went out to the people of the Western world. Thus, the lamp of the Christian era was lighted in a dark world.

A few hours earlier, in God's five-thousand-year day, streams of the divine wisdom had flowed into the countries of Asia in the footsteps of a few followers of the enlightened One, known as the Buddha. A few hours later, in the Brahmic day, a few small streams began to trickle out from India's fountain of immortality. One of these irrigating streams was Theosophy. Another, starting about the same time or a little later, was the Ramakrishna Mission. The leader of this mission, carrying Ramakrishna's teachings westward, was Swami Vivekenanda, who has now reincarnated to help in the great Avataric mission of Sai Baba. But, before Vivekenanda and his fellow apostles began their work in the West, a number of individual pioneers of the spirit had brought small vessels of the sacred waters to England, America, France and Germany. Through this, the Western writers known as Transcendentalists, came into being. These helped to widen the horizons of thought in the Western culture.

The last small streams of spiritual irrigation were made possible by the final foreign invasion, that of the British. Beginning in a small way, the British occupation and domination of Mother India, began about the middle of the eighteenth century. The British Raj brought a mixed bag to India. Among the good things in the bag, probably the best for divine purposes, was the legacy of the English language. It has not only provided a link language for many-tongued Mother India, but is now fast becoming an international language for world trade. Thus it is forging channels of communication to all countries, which the Avatar can use to spread world-wide the waters of life from the eternal fountain. Sai Baba's message is the voice of the waters of wisdom, collected and stored so long ago by the Indian rishis of old. He says, "I have not come to start a new religion, but to repair the ancient paths to Truth." All the spiritual verities needed for mankind's march to his ultimate goal are there in the heart of Mother India, awaiting distribution to the thirsting world. The time has come, the great need is here, the channels of communication are ready and Avatar Sai Baba is labouring night and day to carry out the distribution work which, as Avatar Krishna, he made possible at the dawn of this divine day.

In this mighty labour of enlightening the world, the Avatar does, of course, need human helpers. I have no doubt that these helpers are here. Some, like Vivekenanda, will have incarnated specially for that purpose. When the scales fall from your eyes, you will know if you were born as a helper or not. And, with those scales of Maya shed from your perception, you will know that Sai Baba has all the power he needs for his work. You will appreciate the truth of his statement that the only difference between a full Avatar and the omnipresent, omniscient, omnipotent God without form, is that the Avatar has a name and form. These, while making him more readily available to mankind, do not limit the amplitude of his divinity. Seeing him in the form of a man, the human mind is inclined to question whether he has those three fundamental faces of Almighty God. I have often heard him say there is only one God and He is omnipresent. Can this small man in red be omnipresent? Can he be everywhere at once? The mind questions. Yes, he is everywhere as spirit, the Holy Spirit. Many of his close devotees perceive him around them all time, often as Light. But, then, when he deems it necessary, that Light will suddenly take the subtle form of Sai Baba. This I know personally from experience.

Then, there is omniscience. Does he have all wisdom? Often men think that he does not. But then they are judging from their own limited human standpoint. They see only the present situation, and even that imperfectly. The divine consciousness sees past, present and future. It sees the whole, and sees it truly. Therefore, he, Swami, is often inscrutable and incomprehensible to us. It is important to note, moreover, that divine omniscience, together with divine compassion, often seems to inhibit or limit that other great facet of divine being, that is, omnipotence. "If he is all-powerful, why did he not answer my prayer?" somebody asks. Perhaps it was because, in his all-seeing wisdom, he knows that what you want, what you prayed for, will be bad for your spiritual welfare. He can be likened to a mother who will not give to her child what will be harmful to him, no matter how he cries and begs for it. The divine Mother, knowing what is good for your spiritual well-being and progress, puts that before any temporal, worldly benefit you may gain. And so, to the clouded human mind, Swami's power may often appear to be limited. What we should remember, too, is that the Avatar must frequently use a human agency to carry out his will.

Now, after many wonderful years in the benign influence of my shining star, Sai Baba, I have no doubts whatever about his omnipresence, his omniscience and its relation to his omnipotence. I have no doubt that he will call to himself, at the right time, all those who are ready to take a step forward into the divine Light and become his helpers. Thus, in ways that we cannot yet foresee, he will carry out his divine mission of enlightenment to the whole world, creating a new epoch for mankind. Yet, after these partial insights into the mission of the Avatar, I find that God remains a great mystery. As we grow, we will learn more until, at the ultimate level of divine consciousness, we will know as we are known.

Sometimes the Avatar comes with part of divine glory,
sometimes with a full equipment of his splendour,
sometimes for a particular task,
sometimes to transform an entire era of time.

I am beyond the search of the most intensive enquiry
and the most meticulous measurement.

My word will never fail. It must happen as I Will.

I shall certainly achieve the purpose of this Avatar.
Do not doubt it.

— FROM SAI BABA'S DISCOURSES

"Sai Mother we bow to thee."

19. His Calls Are Unique And Wonderful

Strange calls they are that bring us back to you,
Heard on paths that wind a night of darkness through.

ANONYMOUS

SAI BABA SAYS that nobody comes to him unless he calls them. Of course, they may go to the ashram without being called but if they are not ready for initiation onto the Sai path homeward, they will simply drift away from the ashram and wait until they are called. This may be later in the same life, or, possibly, in a later incarnation. His calls to people who are ready appear to be unexpected and his ways of calling are unique to each individual. They may be in strange situations when they hear the Sai metaphorical bugle call. I have not heard of any situation stranger than that of Walter and Elsie Cowan.

The names of this couple, who are now deceased, are well-known through the Sai literature. Soon after we met them in India, they told us, over dinner at a Bangalore hotel, the unique story of their first encounter with Sai Baba. They had learned the art of out-of-the-body travel a few months earlier than their first call to Swami. Their teacher had been an adept in the art and, spending a couple of months with them in their home in California, he led them in travel to various astral planes. Then, before leaving, he warned them that if they ever found themselves in a low astral plane and in some danger, they should call on their spiritual guru to come to their aid. They had told him that they had a spiritual guru in India.

So Walter and Elsie began travelling almost every night in their astral bodies to sit at the feet of a great teacher in one of the higher places. In the morning they would discuss what they had learned. For a time all went smoothly, then one night they did find themselves in a lower, murky astral plane. The light was grey and gloomy, like the classical Hades, and they began to contact beings that were most unfriendly. In fact, they seemed demonic. Full of panic, the Cowans realised that they were being blocked from their homeward path. In desperation, they called on the name of their spiritual guru, but he did not come. Again and again they called for help, but there was no sign of his form or sound of his voice. They began to think that they were lost forever in the nether worlds. Then, suddenly, a spiritual leader did appear to them. His form was nothing like their own guru. In fact, it was quite unfamiliar to them. But the demonic beings seemed to fall back and disappear at his approach and, with a voice of authority, he told Walter and Elsie to follow him. They did so and soon were out of the terrible astral regions, into the light of a rosy dawn, lighting up the landscape of Orange County below them. As their own house came in view, their spiritual rescuer disappeared. Suddenly, and with great relief, they were back in their bodies that had been waiting for them, unconscious in their beds, in the sprawling ranch house on the top of Cowan Heights.

Next day found them discussing their frightening adventure and wondering who their rescuer was. Would they ever meet him in the flesh? They sincerely hoped so because their own spiritual guru had failed them. The one who came to their aid certainly must have great power and compassion. The thing they wanted now above all else was to sit at his feet in the physical world.

It appeared like a coincidence, though they knew for certain that it was not, when a few days later they saw a photo of their rescuer and learned his name from a friend. It was not many weeks before they were sitting at his feet in the circular room at Dharmakshetra, Bombay. Among the many people in the room were my wife and I, for it was the first Sai Baba World Conference, held in Bombay in the middle of 1968. We became friends with them then and the friendship grew in strength through many mutual Sai experiences, particularly at Brindavan, Whitefield. I learned, through Walter and Elsie Cowan, both millionaires, that great worldly wealth does not deter one from the spiritual search or living a spiritual life. Spending some months as their guests at Cowan Heights, we found that Walter and Elsie had become sincere devotees of Sai Baba before they finally left their bodies.

¶

Stanley Burton of Wollongong, Australia, was a pathologist by profession but his main interest all his life had been comparative religion. Through the many religions of the world, he was seeking the answers to his questions about the meaning of life. But he failed to get the answers he sought and finally gave all his religious books away and decided, unhappily, that he had better remain an agnostic.

Soon after that decision, his health began to deteriorate badly. After some major surgical operations, he was told he should have a heart bypass, but he felt he was too old for that and decided against it. Soon after that, he was back in hospital with serious trouble in his bowel. His medical specialists said that it was necessary for him to have an operation to remove his colon. Through his long experience in the medical world, he knew that such an operation would bring him a lifestyle that he could not accept. He would prefer to die, he said. So Stanley discharged himself from the hospital and went home with two life-threatening conditions, a diseased heart and a diseased colon.

He was living at the time with his daughter, Joan Moylan, a clairvoyant, well-known and respected, in the Sai circles of Australia. He announced to Joan that he had come home to die. "You are not going to die," Joan said. "You are coming with me."

Obediently, he went with his daughter by car from Wollongong to Sydney. There, in the suburb of Greenacre, she took him to the home of Jack and Pearl Harrison. Jack and Pearl had turned their large double-garage into a Sai temple, where meetings for devotional singing and study were held every week. Joan Moylan was a member of this Sai centre. Incidentally, Jack and Pearl were grandparents of the child, Mayan Waynberg, who had been cured by Sai Baba of a disease declared by the medical specialists to be incurable. On instructions sent to her from Puttaparti, she had refused to take any medicine save Sai *vibhuti* in water. Behind the vibhuti had been Sai Baba's healing power and the child's complete faith in receiving it. Helping in the healing, no doubt, was the complete faith of her grandfather, Jack Harrison. Neither of them had seen Sai Baba in his physical body.

Well, on the day that Joan Moylan, with her father at her request, arrived at the Harrison home, Jack took them straight into the temple. On the altar was one of Swami's robes, which he had sent specially for use at this centre. Jack Harrison seated the patient in front of the altar and draped Swami's robe over his shoulders. Then, mixing some vibhuti in a glass of water, he gave it to Stanley and said, "Sip this." Stanley did so. While drinking the strangely unorthodox medicine, the pathologist heard Jack Harrison chanting some *mantra* above his head. Suddenly he felt some force draw him upward. Whether he actually went out of his body, or whether it was an uplift of consciousness, Stanley was not sure. All he knew was that he seemed to be at some high level, in a state of absolute bliss, for a long period. When he finally returned to consciousness of his body and his surroundings, after he does not know how long, he found that all his previous pains seemed to have disappeared. Moreover, he felt as if he was in 'that peace that passeth understanding'. This continued during his drive home to Wollongong. Not one symptom of his death-threatening condition returned during the days that passed. After about two weeks, the cautious scientist decided that he had better have some medical tests. The tests revealed no sign of his previous conditions. The diseases in his bowel and heart had mysteriously vanished and he was in a state of euphoric health.

Previously, Sai Baba had been merely a name, someone of no interest to him, though obviously of interest to his daughter, Joan. Now he decided that he must go over and see the great healer, to thank him personally. He told me about a strange, entirely unexpected thing that happened to him there at Prasanti Nilayam. The year was 1984 and Stanley was sitting in the front row of Sai Baba's darshan. As the great one moved slowly along the curved line towards him, Stanley felt overcome with shyness and looked down. Then he saw on the sand before him the bottom of Swami's red-orange robe with the feet protruding beneath.

Without looking up, Stanley said, "Swami, will you please bless all the sick people of Australia?"

"Yes," Swami replied, "all sick people everywhere."

Stanley, in a state of bliss, shut his eyes and went on asking questions and making requests. The answers came to him as if Swami was still in front of him but, opening his eyes, he saw that the red-robed figure was a long way away, almost to the end of the line. He must be using telepathy, Stanley thought to himself, and I am receiving his words telepathically. Then, speaking silently in his mind only, he said, "Sai Baba, if you are the great one people say you are, before you step back onto the veranda, turn around and hold up your hand in the gesture of blessing."

He watched Swami's back as he returned to the veranda and then, with a thrill of joy, saw him turn around, face the darshan line and hold up his hand in the gesture of blessing, as requested. Stanley now had no doubts about his divine healer's great spiritual status and felt overjoyed with the telepathic link that seemed to be between them. That link continued during Stanley's time at the ashram and even after he returned to Australia. Through his telepathic dialogues with Swami and study of the books containing the latter's teachings, Stanley finally found the answers to the deep questions that had been nagging him all his life. From there on till the end of his life, Stanley spent his time doing Sai work, part of which was to help his daughter, Joan, establish a Sai centre at Wollongong.

Joan's timely intervention, at his time of great crisis, not only gave him five extra years of healthy physical life but opened the door to Sai and a higher spiritual life, both here and hereafter.

¶

Colin Best, a young technician of Sydney, Australia, was beginning to feel the emptiness of his life. Working for a company that manufactured electronic equipment, he had a good, steady job. Boringly steady. The social round of worldly entertainment, that for a few years had filled his leisure hours, was now beginning to seem flat and meaningless. He felt the need to break through the circle of the ordered round into something more spiritually promising. So, from books he managed to obtain, he began to study along two avenues. One was meditation techniques, the other astral projection or travel outside the physical body. He knew no-one who could help him, so his was entirely a study from books.

For months he seemed to get nowhere in either line of endeavour. Then, one day, after about eight months, he made an unexpected breakthrough in astral projection. Finding himself outside his physical body, he was so alarmed that he went straight back into it. But he persisted, going a little further each time, until eventually he travelled right around the world. This was such a pleasant experience that he went round a second time and a third. During one of them, he called on his parents in England, where he had been born, but they seemed quite unaware of his visit. But meditation seemed to be getting him nowhere. Well, he had proved that determination and persistence could lead to success in astral projection, so he decided one evening to make a determined do-or-die effort at breaking through in meditation.

It was eight o'clock in the evening in the year 1972, he told me, when he made his desperate effort to breach the solid wall of the mind. He sat, cross-legged, on the floor in front of a full-length mirror and concentrated on the point between his two eyes. For twenty minutes nothing at all happened. Then several strange things occurred to his physical body. The first was the production of copious saliva from his mouth. When this stopped, tears began to run down his cheeks and, after that, came a tingling in his scalp, like ants crawling over it and biting, he said. The fourth was that his image in the mirror completely disappeared and a greyness took its place. Something is happening, he thought. I wonder what comes next. A strange voice near to him asked, "What do you want to happen next?"

Somewhat startled, Colin asked, "Who are you?"

"A friend."

"What is your name?"

"Peter."

"Oh," said Colin who had been brought up as a Christian, "Peter the fisherman."

"No," the voice replied, "he is on a different plane."

After a silence, Colin asked, "How do I know you are here at all? This may all be happening in my mind."

"What shall I do to prove to you that I am here?" the voice asked.

After thinking for a moment, Colin said, "Make my room smell like roses."

"Is that all?" Peter laughed, "That's easy."

But before the proof was given, something prompted Colin to ask if there was anybody on earth today who was as great as, or greater than, Jesus Christ.

"Yes," Peter replied. "There is one who is greater."

"What is his name?"

"I cannot tell you."

"Well ... well, where is he?"

"I cannot tell you that either."

"Why?"

"Because it's your search."

"My search? Well, when will I find this one?"

"In fifteen years' time."

Colin felt appalled at this statement. "I cannot wait that long," he said.

"Well, that is when you will find him," answered Peter.

Colin could think of nothing else to ask so the voice said, "We will talk at some other time," and there was no more.

Colin could think of nothing but this one, living on earth, greater than Jesus. He could not wait fifteen years. He must leave his body and find the great one, wherever he was on earth. But what country would he be in? India, surely. That was where the great yoga and spiritual teachings came from. Why wait fifteen years? He would go to India now astrally and find this great one.

So, leaving his physical body sitting cross-legged in front of the mirror, he was over India in a flash, hovering above the country looking down from his astral body. Wondering how he could possibly locate the great living being among the many millions in India, Colin suddenly had an inspiration. Remembering the halo of light he had seen around the heads of saints, of Jesus and the Virgin Mary, in the stained glass windows of the great cathedrals in England, he thought that undoubtedly this great one, for whom he was searching, would be surrounded by a bright light. So, soaring slowly in his astral form above India, he concentrated on finding this bright light.

It was not long before he spotted it, outshining the pale street lights that were just coming on as darkness feathered down gently over India. He went straight towards the light and says that within the time of a heart beat, he was there standing outside what looked to him like a temple. The light was inside, so he went in through the side wall and hovered just inside a few feet above the ground.

He says, "In front of me, sitting on a stage, was a small man dressed in a red-orange robe with a mop of fuzzy hair. Before him, sitting on the floor, were many people facing him. I noticed that the ladies were sitting on the left and the gentlemen on the right of him, as he faced them. But as soon as I came through the wall, he turned his head and looked directly at me. He invited me to come closer but some force held me back against the wall, so I told him that I could not come any closer. I knew that he was the only one that could see me because the people in the front rows were looking puzzled when he turned his head towards me. 'I can't come closer,' I told him, 'I can't move.' He smiled and turned his attention back to the people sitting on the floor in front of him. It was as if he forgot about my presence. So I went back through the temple wall and decided to come home. Then, in a split second, I found myself back in my body sitting in front of the mirror."

Standing up stiffly, he sat on his bed and began to think. Had he seen the great one that Peter had spoken of? If so, he was not able to go near him. So, perhaps Peter was right about waiting fifteen years. But how real was Peter? He had not sent the smell of roses that he promised.

Colin went into his kitchen and made a cup of coffee. Carrying it back into the bedroom, he almost dropped the cup. The room was filled with a wonderful perfume of roses. Sitting on his bed, sipping the coffee, thinking of his visit to India and the sight of the fuzzy-headed man in the red robe, he felt a wave of bliss go through him and tears began to run down his cheeks. He knew that he had seen the promised Great One but that he had to wait fifteen years before he could go to his feet.

Towards the end of his fifteen years' wait, Colin met a girl called Sue, who had similar interests to his own. They exchanged books and had some good discussions on spiritual subjects. One day, Colin wanted a certain book and Sue told him that he would find it at a certain bookshop in Sydney. Obtaining the book, he took it home and here is what happened, in his own words: "I turned a few pages and there, lo and behold, was a photo of the little fuzzy-headed figure sitting in a chair. My heart almost stopped. But now I knew his name and his address."

Within a very short time, Colin was at Prasanti Nilayam sitting at the feet of Satya Sai Baba, and seeing from the darshan line the *Poornachandra* which he identified as the temple through whose wall he had gone for his first sight of Sai Baba. It was now 1987, just fifteen years after he had tried in vain to come to the feet of the Great One. His 'first encounter' was not really an encounter, just a sight. Now, for mysterious reasons, beyond human understanding, the time was right for him to become a devotee of Lord Sai.

¶

In the story of Klaus Remme coming to Sai Baba, the first highlight is a prophecy that took place some forty-two years before Klaus sat in the darshan line at Prasanti Nilayam. Son of an orthodox medical practitioner in the Harz Mountains, Germany, Klaus seems to have been rather a wild youth. He describes himself as 'a bit of a rebel'. When he was about eighteen years of age, he received a message that a certain old medical doctor, a friend of his father's, wanted to see him. The old doctor's name was Strunkmann and Klaus told me that he was one of the first in Germany to practise alternative methods of healing. Somewhat apprehensively, Klaus went to the old doctor's house and found him on his deathbed. The words that came from the old doctor's lips were brief, surprising, and rather startling to the youth.

He said, "When you are sixty years of age, you will look into the eyes of God. Now prepare yourself by trying to live a good life."

About three days later, the old doctor died. In spite of himself, Klaus was somewhat impressed by this message and did, in fact, try to live a better life.

Many years later, Klaus was living in the Blue Mountains near Sydney in Australia. He was teaching Hatha Yoga and reading books on Yoga philosophy and other subjects connected with spirituality. He even bought a book on Sai Baba but it sat on his shelves for ten years before he opened it. But, unknown to Klaus, Swami was calling him.

Early one morning, he awoke in his bed to find Swami standing there beside it. Startled, Klaus sat up. Standing very close, Swami cupped Klaus' face in his two hands and said, "My love for you is eternal."

Impulsively, Klaus cupped Swami's face in his two hands and heard himself saying, "I love you, too, but I can't keep it up." He watched Swami leave the room, join two beings, who were waiting for him outside, and the three of them disappeared into the dawn. Answering a question later, Klaus told me that Swami's face felt quite solid, as if he was there in the flesh. He had felt a flood of love come into him at Swami's words.

Later in the same year, he was sitting in the darshan line at Prasanti Nilayam, watching the red-robed avatar making his slow but meaningful round. In front of Klaus, he stopped, and their eyes met. Klaus knew, beyond any doubt, that he was looking into the eyes of God. He had just passed his sixtieth birthday. There are two Satya Sai centres in the Blue Mountains and at the time of this writing, Klaus goes to both of them every week. He has become a sincere devotee of the Avatar.

I have come to inscribe a golden chapter in the history of humanity, wherein falsehood will fail, truth will triumph and virtue will reign. Character will confer power then, not knowledge or inventive skill or wealth. Wisdom will be enthroned in the councils of nations.

SAI BABA

20. A Reluctant Candidate

When me they fly, I am the wings,
I am the doubter and the doubt,
And I the hymn the Brahmin sings.

R.W. EMERSON

SOMETIMES WHEN THE divine homeward call comes, we are not aware of our readiness to receive it. We may try to fly from the call but such flight is unavailing. Inland from the seaside town of Kiama, just south of Sydney, New South Wales, Australia, are green rolling hills of rich pasture land. Neville Fredericks' father owned a dairy farm here, so, like the young Krishna of India, Neville spent his boyhood among the gentle cows. Neville was not without a knowledge of God in his youth, being brought up in the midst of a family whose members were pillars of the local church. After his school days, Neville followed in his father's footsteps, became a dairy farmer and went to church on Sundays. But teenage is the age of rebels and Neville's rebellion took the form of refusing to go to church. No longer, he said, could he accept the narrow creed that only through Christianity could one reach heaven. This, along with other dogmas, became unacceptable. If God made such rules, then God was not for him.

But a life among the milk pails without God had a certain emptiness. Perhaps it was this emptiness, this lack of real purpose he felt in his life, that made him decide to do community work. At a very early age, he joined the Kiama Council and was very soon elected to be its Mayor. This brought some satisfaction and, soon after this, his life was further enriched by his marriage to a beautiful local girl named Jill. In the years that followed, their marriage was blessed with three fine children, two boys and one girl. It would seem, to any casual observer, that this successful dairy farmer, with a beautiful, intelligent wife and a happy family life and holding a respected public position in the community, should feel real contentment. But, no, he still felt an inner void. Something was missing, he knew not what.

Leaving the management of his farm to his employees, he joined forces with his brother-in-law, Terry Gallagher, in the business of property development. Neville had great respect for his black-bearded brother-in-law, who had married one of Jill's younger sisters, named Alison. Not long after this, Terry and Alison, with their family of three teenage daughters, made their first trip to India to visit Satya Sai Baba. The idea of a foreign guru was repugnant to Neville. So, after their return, he says that his body language showed them that he did not want to hear anything about it and so, of course, he heard nothing. But his wife, Jill, was interested and heard a good deal from her sister.

Neville was not very pleased when he saw his wife frequently reading books about Sai Baba. He began to seen a subtle change in her and had the unhappy feeling that she might be drifting away from him. He concentrated more and more on his work, both his private business and his duties as Mayor of Kiama. Perhaps it was his heavy workload, combined with the aching inner emptiness and the worry about the possibility of losing the affections of his wife, that brought about his duodenal ulcer. As this grew worse and more painful, he resigned from his position as Mayor, but as the pressure of private business continued and the feeling that he was losing Jill grew stronger, his health problem remained. Time came when Jill let him know that she would like him to take her to Sai Baba on one of the several trips that Terry and Alison Gallagher were making.

To please her and to prevent any possible break between them, he vaguely agreed, but when the time for departure drew near, he asked her to cancel the tickets. This happened on more than one occasion. During the year 1985, Jill took a more determined line. She told him that she was booking air passages to India so that they could both be there at Sai Baba's ashram at Christmas time, when the Gallaghers would also be there. Moreover, she told him that if, in the end, he decided not to go, he would have to cancel his ticket himself. She would not do it. Furthermore, she and the two younger children would go whether Neville went or not.

Then, evidently as part of her campaign, she began reading aloud to him, each evening when they were both in bed, short passages from Sai Baba's discourses. Having no alternative but to listen, Neville began to think to himself, "Well there's nothing wrong with Sai Baba's teachings." Even so, he felt no desire to go to the ashram. Suddenly, it seemed to Neville that the Christmas season was upon them and he had to make a choice. He could cancel his air ticket and spend Christmas alone, because Jill was taking his daughter and his younger son to India with her, while the eldest son, Peter, was away from home. Neville did not relish the idea of cooking his own Christmas dinner and eating it alone, so he decided to take the plunge and go with them.

During the journey he felt depressed and morose at the thought of spending Christmas in a foreign ashram, whatever that may mean. During the stopover in Singapore, his ulcer became more painful and he could hardly walk. Though he had a strong inclination, then, to return to Australia, he found himself walking automatically with his family onto the plane for India. At Bangalore airport, a car arranged by brother-in-law, Terry, met them and took them straight to Brindavan, where Sai Baba was in residence.

Soon he was sitting, with his young son, Lawson, beside him, under the great spreading bhajan tree at Brindavan. It was Christmas morning and a big crowd was under the tree. All seemed to be watching a distant ornate gate that led into a garden beyond. After a time, the small figure of Sai Baba appeared at the gate and began to move across the bare ground towards them. It was almost as if he was floating. There was such an intense, silent interest from the crowd, that Neville became interested too. When Sai Baba reached the tree, his eyes, moving over the crowd, met Neville's eyes. "In that contact," Neville says, "it was as if two powerful beams of light came from Swami's eyes through mine into my head and set up a hammering and a buzzing there, something like the sound of a high-voltage electric current. One effect was to make my hair stand on end. At the same time, Swami's face looked very stern and unfriendly."

The experience was painful and rather frightening, as it seemed to be hostile. When Neville closed his eyes, the hissing and hammering inside his head ceased, but on the back of his eyelids there seemed to be a confused, whirling of light and energy. "It was like a photo I had seen of the surface of the sun," Neville said. When Neville again opened his eyes, Swami had moved on out of sight around the crowd. Turning to his young, fifteen-year-old son, Neville asked, "Did you see that?"

"See what?" Lawson replied in a flat monotone. Obviously he had not seen what his father had seen. So Neville thought that perhaps he was the only one who saw it. Perhaps he should not be here. Perhaps he was not ready to face Sai Baba, the Avatar. It would be better, he decided, if he left now, returned to the room that had been booked for him at the Bangalore hotel and then, as soon as possible, return to Australia. He needed, he felt, to do a course of study in spiritual literature to prepare himself for contact with this powerful Being.

Every time he shut his eyes now, the whirling picture of light and energy came onto his eyelids. Moreover, he was afraid to look at Swami's face again, in case the beams of bright light shot into his head again and made matters worse. But when Swami went back through the gate, Neville lingered for a while, mixing with the people and talking to some of them. He decided that they all were wonderful people, not only friendly but somehow loving. This, along with the joy on Jill's face, prevented his leaving that day. So, with his family, he returned to their hotel in Bangalore, still undecided whether to fly or remain to bear any further hostile threats from the man of power.

On the afternoon of the next day, that is, Boxing Day, I, the writer, was sitting beside Terry in a crowd when Swami passed by. "Where is your brother-in-law?" he asked Terry.

"Back in his hotel in Bangalore," Terry replied.

"I will see him with you and your families tomorrow morning at ten o'clock," Swami said and moved on.

This meant an interview. So when Terry and I returned to Swami's guest house, where the Gallaghers, Iris and I were all staying, he told his wife and daughters about the interview, with much resulting excitement.

They knew that Jill, with the two children, planned to come to Brindavan about eight o'clock the next morning and, not knowing the extent of Neville's inner turmoil, expected that he would come too. But next morning, Jill, along with son Lawson and daughter Jenny, arrived without Neville. They had left him at the hotel and knew he was planning to see his travel agent and arrange for a return flight to Australia at the earliest possible time. "But Swami is expecting him for an interview this morning," chorused the Gallaghers, and Iris and I felt something of their concern. Jill's face wore a sad expression. Could we contact him and stop him before he made his next move, was the big question. In those days a telephone call to Bangalore could take up to half an hour, or perhaps longer, even though it was only about twelve or thirteen miles away. But we must give it a try.

An old friend of ours, living in a cottage at Brindavan, permitted us to use her telephone. Terry made the phone call. Miracle number one, he got straight through to the hotel. Miracle number two, he caught Neville who was just on the point of leaving. It was fortunate that Terry had been the one to make the call because, Neville told me later, if anybody but his brother-in-law had made the call, he would have continued on his way to the travel agent. But, as it was, when Terry informed him that Swami was expecting him at an interview at ten o'clock, Neville surprised himself by saying, "All right, I'll catch a taxi and come out there."

So smiles returned to the faces of the two women and the children, as they sat excitedly waiting for the arrival of Neville in time for the interview. But ten o'clock drew near without any sign of Neville. At a few minutes before the hour, Terry said, "We must go in as Swami is expecting us." Before going, he asked me to keep a look out for Neville, whom I had never seen. "He is tall and blond," Terry said, "You'll know him."

So, after watching the group go up the steps and disappear through the main door of the Mandir, I turned towards the gate near the railway, knowing that Neville would come in by that route. Quite a number of people were milling about in the area but presently I saw a tall blond man, unmistakeably Australian, coming through the crowd. I moved towards him and noted that his white suit was spattered with blood stains. "Are you Neville?" I asked.

"Yes," he replied, his eyes lighting with pleasure at being recognised.

"Whatever has happened?" I asked him, looking at the blood stains and the bandages on his face.

"Oh, I had a bit of an accident," he said.

Telling him that everybody else had gone in, I took him by the arm and led him towards the Mandir. But we had only gone a few yards, when Terry came tripping down the steps and took him from me.

From several sources, I heard what happened inside the interview room. When they were all seated at ten o'clock, Swami looked at Lawson and said, "Where is your father?"

Lawson replied, "I don't know, Swami."

Swami produced vibhuti for several people and then a locket for Lawson and again asked him, "Where is your father?"

This time Lawson said, "I think he's in a taxi, coming here, Swami."

"No, he's not," Swami answered. "He's here." Then to Terry Gallagher, he said, "Go out and bring him in." It was then that I saw Terry coming down the steps of the Mandir to take Neville from me.

When the bloodstained figure of Neville stood in the doorway of the interview room, there was a loud gasp from everybody, while Jill burst into tears. Swami said, "He's been in a car accident. But for my grace, it would have been much worse. This is my blessing."

Shortly afterwards, Swami said that as Neville was shocked and confused, he should go and lie down. Then he closed the interview and said he would see them all later. My wife and I saw them come back to the guest house and go into the Gallaghers' room. Some time later,

Alison came and invited us in, saying that Neville had recovered enough to tell us all about his accident.

We saw him lying on a bed, under blankets, but he spoke coherently. He told us that he had been travelling alone in the back seat of a taxi coming from Bangalore. At one point, a bus in front of them stopped suddenly. His taxi, close behind it, tried to stop, but a big military truck close behind evidently could not stop in time. It slammed into the back of the taxi with such force that it drove the back bumper bar right through to the rear seat. The taxi was concertinaed between the bus and the truck. There being no such things as safety belts in the taxi, Neville was catapulted across the top of the forward seat, hit his face against the dashboard, which gashed his lips, and then was somehow bounced back onto the rear seat with blood streaming from his face. There was a gap where the rear door of the taxi had been and, through this, Neville climbed out and began to walk about on the road in a dazed condition.

A man came up to him and said, "Where were you going?"

Neville replied, "I was going out to see Sai Baba for an interview."

"Oh, I am a Sai devotee, come with me," the man said. In a private car, Neville was taken to a nearby hospital. There they put stitches in his gashed lips and bandaged them, then his kind Indian helper took him back to the road, hailed an auto rickshaw, put Neville in and said, "On your way to the interview." Then he gave instructions to the driver and namasted farewell to Neville.

So, with his head aching and feeling shocked and groggy, Neville finally arrived at the spot where I met him. Reflecting afterwards on what Swami could have meant by the remark 'this is my blessing', Neville remembered that when he had told his helper, at the scene of the accident, that he had been on his way to an interview with Sai Baba, he had had a feeling of pleasure and pride in this fact. Indeed, for the first time, he had really wanted to go to Baba. It was as if the shock of the accident had completely changed his outlook. So, in this way, the accident really was a blessing.

The next event of importance, in this scenario of surprises, came on New Year's Eve. A big crowd was gathering for devotional singing in the long hall near the gate to Swami's Mandir. Neville found himself jostled against his will into the very front row near to the stage, where Swami was sitting directly in front of him. Shyly, he kept his gaze on the floor where he sat cross-legged. He was praying fervently that God would come completely into his life. How desperately he needed God to fill the emptiness he had endured so long! Daring, at last, to look up, he caught Swami's eyes looking directly at him and something wholly unexpected happened. Instead of the fierce beams of light that he had thought hostile, there was a beam of divine love flowing from Swami's eyes and filling Neville's whole being. Whatever his inner block had been, it was now shattered and burned away. Tears came to his eyes and streamed down his cheeks. He began to sob like a child. He felt ashamed of this uncontrolled weeping, thinking that all eyes must be looking at him, but he soon found that nobody was looking at him. As usual, all eyes were on Swami.

The singing was going on and, after a while, Swami stood up and began to move down among the people. Neville looked down at the floor again and tried hard to stem his flow of tears. Presently he saw Swami's small feet on the floor close in front of him. Turning his tear-stained face upwards, he met the Sai gaze of complete understanding and divine mother love. In a gentle voice, he heard Swami say, "Very soon," and knew that this promise was the answer to his desperate prayer.

That New Year's Eve night, Neville was awakened in his hotel bedroom by sounds of a noisy party. It sounded like a jubilant Scottish party, in which whisky was washing the old year out to let the new one in. In his new-found state of spiritual initiation, Neville felt no sympathy for the sounds of worldly revelry. Soon after midnight, however, the noise ceased and Neville tried to go to sleep. But, before sleep, something else came. Trying to describe it, Neville says it was like a blissful current of energy going right through his body. A wonderful experience indeed! Was it another flow of divine love? Was it a visitation of the Holy Spirit? What is the difference, if any? The flow ceased for an interval, then came again. In fact, successive waves of this blissful energy continued for about two and a half hours. So tangible were they, that on one occasion, his wife, in bed beside him, happened to touch his body during one visitation. "You have just had another of them," she remarked. Neville estimates that he must have had between forty and fifty of these joy-bringing visitations during the two and a half hours of the night. He concluded that this powerful initiation was certainly Swami answering his prayer and bringing God into his life.

After only a few hours' sleep at the end of the night, he woke the next morning feeling cleansed and in a state of great peace. Driving in a taxi with his family towards Brindavan that morning, Neville felt at a higher level of consciousness. With great joy he looked forward to seeing his Lord's face again. Everything else seemed trivial. The noisy, busy traffic in the street seemed like a pageant in a dream, though beneath it all there was a radiance that was real.

Then he had an amazing experience. In the heavy traffic, his taxi was forced to stop briefly near the edge of a pavement, across which were a few shops. Neville, sitting in the rear seat on that side, saw across the pavement, in front of a shop, an old beggar standing. He must have been, Neville says, about twenty metres away. He was a pathetic old beggar, dressed in rags with one wooden leg and a crutch. Not really an unusual sight in an Indian street. But, looking at him, Neville's heart seemed to burst open and a flood of love went out towards the old beggar. At the same time, he heard himself say inwardly, "God bless you." The powerful beam of pure love that came from Neville had an effect that was amazing and miraculous. The old beggar seemed to turn into a pillar of light that whirled across the twenty metres to the side of the car, and there was the old man, standing with his two palms against the window and his face looking in through the glass, close to Neville's face.

The old man's face seemed to glow with radiance and his two shining eyes, looking into Neville's, seemed to return the same pure love that Neville had sent out. For a moment, the old Indian beggar and the young Australian business executive were one, in the unifying reality that pulses beneath the shadows of this world. Then the car moved on and, looking back through the rear window, Neville saw the old beggar hobbling back to his position by the wall. But this was only part of the mortal dream, beyond which he had seen the divine reality for a brief moment. The experience convinced Neville, he told me, of the truth of Swami's teaching that God is love and God is in everyone.

At Brindavan, he hurried from the taxi, like an eager boy, to drink more joys from the eyes of the Divine One. But Swami did not even look at him for the whole of that day. This, he said, put him in a worse state of shock than the accident had, but later he understood that this was another of the Sai lessons. We must not float away like thistledown on the winds of bhakti. We must keep one foot in the world while the other is in heaven, taking the upward step to God. In fact, human life is a mandorla.

It was soon after this that Neville told his wife that he was having no more pain from his duodenal ulcer and was feeling so well that he thought he would stop taking his tablets, which he had been taking for the condition. Later, after the two families had followed Swami back to Prasanti Nilayam, Swami said to Neville in an interview,

"I cured that spot when I looked at you." Neville was not sure whether Swami meant the powerful searing look that had come to him under the bhajan tree on the first day or the look of soul-cleansing divine love that Swami had poured into him at the meeting on New Year's Eve. Whichever it was the ulcer had completely gone and never returned.

Another important thing that Swami said to him, at an interview before they left for home, was that Neville Fredericks should do public work. Evidently that was his dharma, and certainly it had always been his inclination to do so. So, after returning to Australia, with his ulcer now gone, he was happy to rejoin the Kiama Council and was soon made Mayor again. His ambition was to serve the community by applying the spiritual principles and ethics of Sai Baba's teachings, not only to his business life, but also to his public activities as Mayor. In the latter, his path has to be watchful and delicate. Remembering his own former aversion to the idea of a foreign guru, he finds it wiser on most occasions to use the substance of the Sai teachings rather than the name Sai Baba. This can only be used when, intuitively, he feels that the time and occasion are appropriate. At home he finds it easier to conduct his life according to the Sai guidelines. Not only his wife, but all his children, are now Sai devotees. His own *sadhana* (spiritual practice) is to read, every night before going to sleep, a passage from Swami's printed discourses. At the end of a long, busy workday, he finds this practice refreshing to his mind and soul. Moreover, at times he finds passages appropriate for direct quotation in his public addresses.

Once, for instance, he was asked as Mayor to give an address at the opening of a new Benedictine Abbey for women. The nuns of this institution are recluses, doing no active welfare work and Neville knew that such a 'useless' institution would not be looked on with great public favour in his area. As Swami encourages the active spiritual life, rather than the purely contemplative one, he did not expect to find a suitable Sai Baba quotation for his speech at the opening. But, in fact, he did find one and used it. The large public gathering responded very favourably to his quotation and the Mother Abbess quoted it in the Abbey journal as being from the writings of Satya Sai Baba. Below is the passage given by the Mayor of Kiama, courageous but discriminating witness to the living Avatar.

20. *A Reluctant Candidate*

There are many ways to serve the world. You can serve, if not actively, at least by your serenity. Everyone need not do all things. Your Western heritage reveres active work, but if your being turns towards serenity and solitude, take it as the best, and do not be sorry for it. Only a small minority can delight in serenity and remain still. God has ruled it so. Otherwise, how could the world function? If stillness is your destiny, dare to be so. If you are a recluse, be a recluse, but be a recluse with God. Let each be as he is, remembering his Author, his Source.

SAI BABA

"Your bliss is my food."

21. More First Encounters

I call those who are ready to see me.
Of course, there are different levels of readiness.

SAI BABA

ANN MARIA MARTELL was lying in bed with her five-year-old son, James, crying her heart out. Her husband, a compulsive gambler, was sleeping in James' room. Their marriage had reached crisis point and that evening they had decided to part. Unfortunately for Anna Maria, she still loved her husband deeply, but it was quite impossible to live with an irresponsible gambler who brought nothing but problems, heartache and misery. The anguish of the situation was more than she could bear. If only she had someone to turn to for comfort. Little James, lying wide-eyed beside her, could not understand nor help. She thought of her mother who had died many years earlier in Uruguay, where Anna Maria had been born and educated. Poor Mother, she had been a devout Roman Catholic but was unable to practise her religion because her husband, a leading member of the Communist Party, was a complete atheist. So Anna Maria had been brought up with no religion herself. She had no God to call on but remembered that just before her mother's death, she had said to Anna Maria, "If ever you are in bad trouble, call to me and if there is any possible way of coming to you, I will do so." Now in her extremity, Anna Maria called in her mind, "Mother, Mother, if it's possible, please come and help me!" It was a cry from the heart. After that, her weeping stopped and she fell asleep.

But James, in the other half of the double bed, remained awake. Presently he saw a man appear on the other side of his mother. As he leaned over her sleeping form, James could only see the shoulders and face. The head was covered with a mop of hair, black against the white cloth that covered the man's shoulders. James was not alarmed. He had seen many apparitions before and knew that this was one. He knew also that the visitor was an Indian, though he could not have told how he knew this. As the mop-headed man leaned low over his mother's face, James could hear him saying, "Me, me, me." He had no idea what this meant. Then the man disappeared and James fell asleep.

The next morning he told his mother what he had seen. She was quite alarmed at the news. "An Indian! What was an Indian doing in my room?" she exclaimed. James could only tell her the strange words he heard: "Me, me," repeated a number of times. Anna Maria's chief worry was that her son had been seeing too many apparitions recently. Perhaps there was something wrong with his mind. So she took him to see the psychic, Joan Moylan, hoping to get some advice or help from her.

Hanging on the wall in Joan's sitting room was a photograph of Sai Baba. "That is the man who came into the bedroom," James said, pointing to the picture, "but he was wearing white, not that colour." The photo showed Swami in his red-orange robe. Joan left the room and came back with a photo of Swami in his white gown. "Yes, that's the man," James declared with conviction.

Now believing that someone called Sai Baba had come into her bedroom, Anna Maria was very mystified. She tried to find out from Joan why he should pay her such a visit. All Joan could tell her was, "Oh, he comes to collect his children." What Joan meant was that we are all his children and he comes to collect us when we are ready. But Anna Maria thought she meant that Sai Baba had come to take James away from her. The possibility of such a thing alarmed her and she felt very hostile towards this powerful being who could travel from India to Australia out of his body and enter closed rooms. Sensing her fears, Joan told Anna Maria more about Sai Baba and loaned her several books on him. Reading these, her fear and hostility changed to a growing interest. But why had Sai Baba paid his inexplicable visit to her room on that night when she had cried from the bottom of her heart to her dead mother? Did her mother somehow ask him to come? But how could he help?

About a year later, when the pain in her heart from her broken marriage was easing a little, another tragedy struck her. Her eighteen-year-old son, named Alex, who had been living in another part of Sydney was killed in a car accident. His only companion in the car, a seventeen-year-old youth named Noel, was also killed. When Anna Maria heard this shattering news, she did something which she had never done before. She sat cross-legged on the floor of her sitting room and called to Sai Baba for help. After a while she got up and telephoned to her friend, Joan Moylan. "Light a candle and put it on the floor in front of you," said Joan. This the distraught mother did and sat again on the floor, gazing into the flame. Presently she felt a hand on her shoulder but it was not Sai Baba this time. It was the dead Alex. His voice was gentle and soothing when he said, "You always taught me that death is a celebration. It is. Now stop weeping and go and help Noel's mother. She is in a very bad way." Noel was her only son.

Happy to find that her son was still alive, though dead, Anna Maria pulled herself together and went to do his bidding. In the months that followed, Anna Maria found herself coming closer and closer to Swami. The pull to visit him in India grew too strong to resist. Apart from wanting to experience his physical presence, she had two important questions to ask him. Did her dead mother send Swami to her that night and where was her son Alex now? She had had no sign from him since the night in the candlelight when he had touched her shoulder and spoken words of assurance and compassion.

She was still mentally hammering Sai Baba with her two questions when she sat in the darshan line at his ashram in the year 1988. He answered the one about the whereabouts of her son briefly but strongly. Walking straight towards her from his door, he spoke from his mind into hers so that nobody else near her could hear what he said. "He is with me. Now stop asking!" Then he went on along the line. He answered the other question in the strangely indirect way that he often uses. Standing before the woman who sat in front of Anna Maria, Swami asked her, "Where is your mother?" The woman pointed vaguely towards the chairs where the old and infirm ladies sit. Swami asked her the same question again, but this time looking above her head directly at Anna Maria. Again the woman waved her arm and pointed towards where her mother was sitting. "Over there, Swami," the woman replied. But then Swami answered his own question while his eyes looked into those of Anna Maria. "Your mother is standing right here in front of you," he said in a voice vibrant with divine mother love. In a flash, Anna Maria knew the answer to her question and the solution of her problem. Sai Baba was her Divine Mother and when she had called fervently for her mother's help, he had come to ease the burden of her great sorrow. Now she knew too the meaning of the words that young James had heard, 'Me, me'. "I am your divine eternal mother and I have answered your cry for help."

Anna Maria has now become very active in Sai service. Because she was brought up and educated in the Spanish-speaking country of Uruguay, she is able to do special work in Sydney, where there are many Spanish-speaking people from South America. Gathering them together in groups, she holds regular Sai meetings where study and discussion are held on the teachings and mission of the Avatar. About herself she says, "Every day more and more I feel his Divine Love saturating me and surrounding me like an envelope of protection."

¶

Elvin Gates should not have been startled when he saw the spirit walk through the door into the room where he was meditating. After all, he was a member of a Spiritualist church and the circle of ladies he was leading in meditation were fellow workers in that church. Elvin had seen discarnate spirits before but this phantom visitor with his shining red-orange robe and thick mop of black hair seemed a specially powerful spirit. Elvin looked at the large picture of Jesus hanging on the wall and prayed for protection in case an evil spirit had come into their circle. On instructions from Elvin, the small group had been meditating in silence with their eyes closed. But Elvin, as leader, had been keeping watch with his eyes open. Now he saw the visitor moving around the back of the circle, stopping behind each lady and raising the palm of his right hand in an upward gesture. Elvin did not understand this gesture and felt it was somehow derogatory. When the apparition came behind Elvin, he felt a firm, approving touch of a hand on his right shoulder. After that the phantom vanished.

When the meditation session was over, Elvin found that none of the ladies had been aware of the visit of the fuzzy-headed spirit. Even his wife, Rhonda, who did have some extrasensory perception, had seen nothing. Elvin described the appearance of their visitor and his movements, saying, "I don't think he thought much of you ladies but he gave me an approving pat on the shoulder."

The meditation session had taken place in a room of the Gates' private home in Sydney and when the visitors had gone, Rhonda remembered something that had happened to her a few days earlier in a bookshop. She had been looking for some books on spiritualism when from a shelf a book had fallen, hitting her on the foot. She had picked it up and looked at it, noting that it was a book on someone called Sai Baba. She had not really intended to buy it but when she got home with a few books she had purchased, she found this book on Sai Baba among them. "I must have bought it subconsciously," she said. The picture on the front of the book seemed very like the visiting spirit that Elvin had described. So she took the book and showed it to him. "Yes," he agreed, "that was the one who came."

The two strange events, one happening to each of them, aroused their interest. Was this Sai Baba trying to say something to them? Then a little later they heard that there was a film on Sai Baba being shown at the home of Dr Sara Pavan, not far away in another suburb of Sydney. They went to see the film and after that wanted nothing so much as to go to India and see Sai Baba.

Elvin, a true son of Adam, earned his living by the 'sweat of his brow' in heavy industry. Rhonda was doing clerical work with a business firm. They had not had a holiday for years and had saved enough money, they thought, to have a holiday. They inquired and found that it was just enough for tickets to India. They also found that they could get air tickets with a group leaving Sydney to go to Sai Baba's ashram early in the next year, which was 1987. So they went. During that time at the ashram, they both enjoyed group interviews with Sai Baba. Moreover, Elvin happened to be present at the interview in which Swami told a young man from Sri Lanka that he was the famous Vivekananda reborn to help in the Sai mission. The young man, buried in Maya, had been unaware of his true identity until that moment. At the same interview, Elvin received from Swami's miraculous hand a remarkable ring. On the enamel top of the ring, the largest one I have ever seen, was a picture of Satya Sai Baba. But, after handing it to Elvin, Swami took it back, blew on it and changed the picture to that of Jesus. "You prefer this form," he said to Elvin, as he gave the ring back to him. "That was true at the time," says Elvin, who still wears the ring with the picture of Jesus on it, "but now I wish it was Swami's picture."

After their return to Sydney, their healing work in the Spiritualist churches increased in strength. Now they identify the power that comes through them as that of their divine spiritual preceptor, Satya Sai Baba. My wife and I met them when they joined our Sai Baba centre in the Blue Mountains near Sydney. Their home was over an hour's car drive away but they attended our weekly meetings with commendable regularity. At the many interviews with Sai Baba that my wife and I have been blessed to receive through the years, he has always called us alone into the private room. But at our last interview, he called Elvin and Rhonda Gates into the private room at the same time, as if they were part of our family. They heard him tell me to write the book that was inside me, which is this present one, and I heard him tell them to carry on with the good healing work they were doing. So now, whatever anybody else may say, I know that Swami approves of healers who act as pure instruments of his divine power.

¶

Rocky Bugmann is a creative Swiss jeweller and a global traveller. He believes that it was a journey to Ayers Rock in Central Australia that began the opening of his psychic vision. After that he went to the Philippines to study psychic healing. While there he began to sit regularly for meditation with a group of about ten people. At every session figures dressed in white robes would appear, surrounded by white light and wearing benign expressions on their serious faces. Rocky was not sure whether they were Masters or great spirits. He could not identify any of them and nobody else in the group could see them.

One day a figure appeared who seemed more light-hearted and jovial than the other sedate-faced ones. He wore a red-orange robe and was surrounded by a golden-orange light that filled the whole room. On his head was a large crown of black hair. He held up his hand in blessing and from his palm came a beam of golden light that pierced Rocky's heart and filled him with bliss. The figure sent the beam of golden light into others in the meditation room also but none of them saw the figure or felt the joy-bringing beam. The smiling figure in the red-orange robe made a number of visits to the meditation group but Rocky was the only one who ever saw him or felt the power of the golden blessing from his upraised hand.

Longing to know the identity of this strangely appealing figure, Rocky made the journey from Baguio down to Manila to consult a famous clairvoyant of his acquaintance. This was Tati Suksmomo, wife of the Indonesian Manager of the Asian Development Bank. Rocky says she was the best clairvoyant he had ever met and never charged any money for her readings. He told her about his vision of the wonderful figure but, in order not to make it too easy for her, he did not describe the appearance of the figure. The clairvoyant closed her eyes and sat in silence for a few minutes, then she smiled happily, opened her eyes and said, "That was Sai Baba."

Rocky set off then to find a book on Sai Baba. But this was not easy in the Philippines, even in the early 1980s. Eventually he found one and knew immediately from the photo of Sai Baba on the cover that this was his visitor in the meditation session. Before he could read the book, Rocky saw a woman of his acquaintance in a wheelchair. She had recently been crippled in a bad motor accident.

Rocky compassionately gave her the book on Sai Baba, thinking that it may help her.

Strangely, after this first brief encounter with Sai Baba, Rocky's life became crowded with worldly matters. Central to this was his marriage to Stephanie, a young woman of Baguio, and his need to establish a home. About six years later, that is, in 1989, Rocky and Stephanie with their little son, Nathan, went on a tour of India. Wherever they went, Rocky says, they met someone who knew Sai Baba and saw photographs of him. It seemed that the time had come when they must go to Prasanti Nilayam. It was as if all roads were leading them there and so they went and both became Sai Baba devotees. Now they live in the Blue Mountains near Sydney and are very active members of the Satya Sai Baba centre there.

He called to me before I heard,
Before my sleeping heart was stirred;
But when I took Him at His word,
Forgiven, He lifted me.

FROM A CHRISTIAN HYMN

"Make your life a rose that speaks silently
in the language of fragrance."

22. *John Kelly And Aurobindo*

On a desperate stair my feet have trod
Armoured with boundless peace,
Bringing the fires of the splendour of God
Into the human abyss.

SRI AUROBINDO

ALTHOUGH I HAD dropped my original idea of writing a book on a number of Indian spiritual teachers, in favour of one on Sai Baba, I was still interested in investigating some of the great and famous ones. The teachings of Sri Aurobindo of Pondicherry were of special interest to me. But when not with Sai Baba, I was busy at Adyar researching material for the two commissioned biographies and starting to write my first book on Sai Baba. So I made no move to visit Pondicherry. Then, one day out of the blue, a big blond New Yorker appeared at Leadbeater Chambers. His name was John Kelly and, being a member of the Theosophical Society, he stayed for a few days at Adyar, but he was really only in transit on his way to Pondicherry. A number of psychic experiences in the past had shown him that Sri Aurobindo was really his spiritual guru. Aurobindo had, of course, left his physical body permanently some years earlier, but John wanted to spend as much time as possible at the ashram. Mother Mira, Aurobindo's great practical helper, was still alive and in charge of the Aurobindo ashram at Pondicherry. Apart from wanting her darshan, John felt, I think, that he would have closer contact with the spirit of his great Master at Pondicherry.

But on several occasions he returned to Adyar, spent some time there with my wife and me, and became our great friend. He was delighted when we took him to Sai Baba and on one occasion went to Prasanti Nilayam on his own and had some remarkable experiences there. One day, for example, he was sitting on the ground with several long lines of people while Swami moved along the line, ladling out a sweet from a bucket, carried by one of the boys, and giving it as *prasad* to each person in the line. It was a very hot day and Swami's robe clung to his back with perspiration. John happened to look up and, not far away, he saw floating above the ground, two shining, benign-faced Beings. Then he saw Swami go out of his body, rise to their level and greet them. It was, John said, like a scene in a pocket in space. It was a day of Hindu spiritual festival and the two Beings had, John thought, come from some high realm to pay their respects to the Avatar. But while this scene went on in the fourth dimension, Swami was still carrying on, in the three-dimensional world, with his perspiring job of handing out prasad to his devotees.

Perhaps only Swami and the very clairvoyant Irish-American saw the two great visitors from other realms greet Sai Baba in his subtle body. In the many years since then, I have learned that Swami can go in his subtle form to many places at the same time, while, in his physical body, he still carries on whatever work he is doing. Sai Baba has the same command of form as Krishna, illustrated in the Rasa dance, where he multiplied himself into as many forms as required to provide a partner for each of the *gopis* (milkmaids). Sai Baba is certainly not confined to the one small physical body we meet at the ashram.

It was through John's strong extrasensory perception that he first made contact with Sri Aurobindo. At the time, John was in the American army on active service in World War II. He had no idea who his astral visitor was. He thought of him only as an old man who suddenly appeared to give him advice on tactics in battles. For reasons he could not explain, he always took this old man's advice and it always proved good. It not only led to success in battle but once saved John's life and prevented the annihilation of his Company. On one occasion, he asked the old phantom military adviser his name. The reply was "Aurobindo." John had never heard such a name and thought it must be a password.

We heard this, and other accounts of his strange experiences, when we went, on his invitation, to stay with him in his flat at Pondicherry. There we had the darshan of the Mother and met many of the leading figures of the Aurobindo ashram. From them we learned a number of interesting things that gave support to John's experiences. One of these was that extra-corporeal travel was one of Aurobindo's best known Yogic powers. After what he called his 'Victory Day', 24th November, 1926, he seems to have spent a large part of his time working, out of his body, for the good of mankind.

Another thing we learned was that their great Master, Aurobindo, was completely convinced that the Allies must win World War II against the dark forces of the Nazis and thus help in God's work and prevent a long setback to the divine plan. He himself gave powerful help to the Allied cause from the invisible plane. He worked through whatever opening he could find. John Kelly was one such opening and it is fair to assume that there were a number of others. But apart from his work on the tactical plane, as illustrated through John Kelly's experiences, Aurobindo gave even more valuable help at the highest strategic levels.

One of these, as told to us at Pondicherry, seems to have been of crucial significance to the Allied victory. It happened on a day when Hitler called the Chiefs of his armed services together, after the fall of France, to decide whether Germany should invade England or attack Russia. It was a very important decision. While the men called together for the Conference were sitting in a room waiting, Hitler was in an adjacent room meditating. As related in an earlier chapter of this book, Hitler, during his youth in Vienna, had become open to the invisible worlds through the use of drugs and the practice of black magic. Whatever unseen forces may have been around him during his meditation on that crucial day, the most powerful of them seems to have been Aurobindo. Telepathically, he put the conviction into Hitler's mind that the best course was an attack on Russia. So convinced of this was Hitler, that when he went into the other room and faced his services Chiefs, he told them that he had already made up his mind. "We will deal with Russia first," he informed them and so the great attack on Russia began, instead of an invasion of England. This decision, prompted by Aurobindo, undoubtedly cost Hitler the war. I wonder now if any of the Allied leaders knew that they owed this false step in Hitler's war strategy to Sri Aurobindo.

It was not until after the war that John Kelly found out the name of his phantom helper in the battlefield. He made the discovery by seeing a photograph of Sri Aurobindo in New York. He began then to read all the literature he could find about the life of Aurobindo and to study his teachings. Although John is not of a philosophic turn of mind, the Aurobindo teachings, which have a philosophic flavour, appealed to him greatly. Moreover, his concentration on the wonderful spiritual philosophy of his guru, led to some interesting out-of-the-body experiences. Once, talking to Iris and me in the gardens at Adyar, John said, "I saw this all before, before I came here. I saw it from the air." He described how Sri Aurobindo once took him for an astral journey above the eastern coastline of India, that included not only the Aurobindo ashram at Pondicherry but also the Theosophical Estate at the mouth of the Adyar River. Altogether, John's psychic experiences with Aurobindo, along with his great love and understanding of the Aurobindo teachings, made me think that perhaps the strong link between the blue-eyed New Yorker and the benign old sage began in some former life. Support was given to this idea by something that happened at the ashram.

When the Mother of the ashram gave darshan to individuals, no words were spoken on either side. One looked silently into her eyes for as long as she wished, then after a few minutes she turned her eyes away, presented one with a flower and that was the end of the darshan. But in John Kelly's case, he told us, while he had to remain silent, the Mother talked. According to what he told us, her talk was a lecture in which she berated him strongly for the wrong things he was doing in his life. There is no doubt that she, as well as the Master, took a special interest in John Kelly's life journey.

In his flat at Pondicherry, close to the ashram, his shelves were lined with books of Aurobindo's teachings. They were all there and we used to study them together. In the evenings, John took great delight in reading aloud to us lines from Aurobindo's wonderful long poem *Savitri*. I don't know how long John would have stayed on happily with the Aurobindo followers in India, had not his ESP taken him back to New York. It was while he was staying in the Aurobindo Retreat in the Himalayas that he heard, clairaudiently, a conversation in a room in New York. From this he knew that his father had died and that John's family did not know where they could contact him. So he hastened back to New York and we did not see him again for many years.

But he had opened the Aurobindo door for us and we paid several more visits to the ashram after John had gone. There always seemed to me a special radiance about the people and the place. We were particularly interested in their education system. It had an international flavour with volunteer teachers from a number of different countries. The eagerness of the pupils to learn was in contrast to the schools I had known in the West. But perhaps the most striking feature of the Aurobindo education was its emphasis on physical education, and the way in which this seemed to promote the equality of the sexes. Boys and girls took part on equal terms in all sports and competitive activities. Football teams, for example, were made up of both boys and girls, while girls competed against boys in fencing, judo and other feats of strength and skill. Both sexes looked almost identical in their appearance and dress also. I remember when a young teenage pupil went past us along a road, dressed in white shorts and white top, with hair cut fairly short, we could not decide whether the pupil was a boy or a girl. The Women's Liberation organisations of the Western world should certainly be happy with Pondicherry.

After leaving school, members of the ashram kept up the practice of at least one sport during the rest of their lives and old people we met there certainly seemed physically fit and healthy. I used to wonder how much of Mother Mira's influence had been brought to bear on this aspect of the Aurobindo educational system. She herself had been the tennis champion of France in the very early years of this century and, though a very old lady when we met her, she still played tennis regularly.

Western influence and Western patterns of thought seem strong in the Sri Aurobindo spiritual teachings too. In fact, I see him as a point where East and West met, bringing an interesting and stimulating unity. Born in Bengal in 1872, he was sent, while a small boy, by his Anglophile father, to be educated in English schools. Without coming under any Indian influence, he remained in England until he had gone through Cambridge University. After obtaining his degree there, with high honours in the Classics, Aurobindo returned as an erudite Western scholar to his own country. Sidestepping the opportunity to join the prestigious Indian civil service, he began a career as a teacher in one of the Indian colleges. Then, too, his study of his own Indian culture began.

Almost inevitably he was drawn into the Indian Independence Movement and spent a period in gaol as a result. But in prison his time was not wasted. He continued to delve into the printed treasures of Indian spiritual lore and, he relates, had daily contact with the form of the Lord Krishna. After his release, friends warned him that he was liable to be arrested by the British authorities again and advised him to escape. But he seems to have developed an inner voice, like Socrates, and told his friends that he would go when the voice directed him to.

This eventually happened and, narrowly escaping arrest, he travelled south to Pondicherry. This was a French colonial settlement in which he was free from the danger of arrest by the British. There he continued his studies of the eternal spiritual verities enshrined in the Indian culture and in due course obtained some followers and established his ashram. Although, as we have seen, he travelled widely in his subtle body, his physical body remained for the rest of his life at Pondicherry.

His spiritual teachings are found in the many fine books that he produced during the years of his residence at the ashram. His *magnum opus*, in which the heart of his teachings are given, is the *Divine Life*. Here we see the ancient wisdom of India filtered through a fine intellect, trained in Western empirical thought. Because Aurobindo had a philosophical as well as poetic mind, his presentation of the body of eternal truths is philosophical as well as being couched in beautiful, often poetical, prose.

It has been stated by leading Theosophists that all the fundamental spiritual truths required for the present dispensation were given out to the Rishis of ancient India. Apart from those truths, found in the *Vedas*, and especially in the *Upanishads* of the *Vedas*, there is nothing new that can be said. So, all the teachings, all the expositions of the great spiritual teachers from Rama and Krishna through to Sai Baba, can be no more than re-statements of the ancient revelations. Each great teacher, of course, states this ancient wisdom in his own unique, individual way. So by these variations in style, in emphasis and the use of words, they lead us, their pupils, to a deeper and more complete understanding of that wisdom than can never be fully contained and presented in the vehicle of words. If, for example, we read the teachings of Lord Krishna, as presented in the Indian scriptures, we find they are expounding the same truths as we hear from the lips of Sai Baba today. But, because Sai Baba is using the idiom of today, people find him easier to understand and accept. His mind puts the ancient teachings in a mould suitable for the mass of people in this age.

Sri Aurobindo's mental instrument, trained through Western scientific culture to apperceive and shape the ancient verities from India's heart, gives a unique philosophic presentation, suitable, I think, only for the few and not the masses. To put my understanding of this in another way, the timeless spiritual truths were the food which, when treated in the channels of his great mind, came forth in a brilliant, unique way which make them his own individual teachings. They are an intellectual feast but not the diet for everyman. This is perhaps what Sai Baba meant when he told Doctor Bokak, according to the latter, that Aurobindo was the Avatar of the individual, while Sai Baba is the Avatar for the bulk of mankind.

There is, moreover, an interesting feature of Aurobindo's teachings that I have not found in any other system of Indian spiritual philosophy. Systems of thought, derived from the great Vedic insights, suggest that the goal of mankind is to individually throw off the bondage of earth and, having done so, to merge in the bliss of Oneness with Brahman. In other words, having learned all the hard lessons in the schoolroom of earth, the individual leaves that schoolroom forever and in his state of joyful enlightenment he reaches *Nirvana*, about which little can be said except that it is eternal happiness. The individual has escaped from, and never revisits, his old earthly schoolroom.

But Aurobindo has a different concept of man's ultimate destiny. Having evolved from human to superhuman, he does not shake the dust of his schoolroom from his feet, but remains to transmute the dust. Along with the growing number of his brothers in superhumanity, he works to transmute the very matter of earth into spirit. As science tells us today, all matter, be it gross or subtle, is simple energy vibrating in a certain way at a certain level. The aim of superhumanity will be to spiritualise all matter so that all mankind becomes liberated and enlightened. Thus the Kingdom of God will come to earth and life on earth will be as life in Heaven. This must mean, of course, the end of the divine evolutionary plan and the end of this dispensation. An advanced modern thinker has stated that God's Kingdom is already spread on the earth, but men cannot see it. Perhaps the work of supermen will be to teach their younger human brothers to see the Kingdom around them and, as they see it, so it shall become.

This Aurobindo concept of the spiritualisation and divination of matter, and thus the life of the world, seems to me to have a parallel in Christian theology. After the Crucifixion, the body of Jesus did not remain in the tomb. The tomb was empty. The physical body had been transmuted into what St Paul calls 'a spiritual body' or a 'glorified body'. Jesus Christ was called the 'first fruit'. In like manner to Him, all mankind, it is taught, will go through this transmutation in which the physical body becomes a spiritual body. The ultimate fate or destiny of mankind is to be with God through eternity in individual forms in spiritualised bodies.

The Pope of the Roman Catholic Church stated in 1951 that the Virgin Mary had now ascended bodily to the Godhead to join the Father, Son and Holy Spirit, all of whom are considered embodied, individual figures in the Christian religion. So, in this aspect, Aurobindo's teachings seem closer to Christian theology than to Vedanta.

Some of the leaders of the Aurobindo ashram at Pondicherry, whom we knew personally, had great hopes that the Mother of the ashram would manage to transmute and spiritualise her physical body and thus avoid physical death. But, though she looked a radiant figure and said herself that she could feel changes going on within her physical vehicle, she did not manage transmutation and died leaving a body behind, as all men, save Jesus Christ, have done. If this is to be man's destiny, the time is evidently not yet. And, perhaps, not for a very long time to come.

The noble work of Sri Aurobindo did, however, have its esoteric 'Victory Day'. This day, still celebrated at the ashram, was on 24th November, 1926. His followers understood that Aurobindo had been working for years to bring what he called the Krishna Consciousness to earth. On that day he announced that his goal had been achieved. Krishna Consciousness had come to earth and so this was his 'Victory Day'. On the day before his announcement, that is on the 23rd November, 1926, Avatar Sai Baba was born in India. A large number of his followers, including myself, see him as Avatar Krishna reborn. Could these two events, so close together in time and space, be merely coincidental? More likely they are facets of the same event. Krishna Consciousness, embodied on earth with the birth of Sai Baba at Puttaparti on the 23rd, perceived by the spiritual consciousness of Sri Aurobindo soon afterwards was announced by him to his ashram on the following day. Sai Baba is the focus of the Krishna Consciousness, or God Consciousness, which through his long days and nights of labour he is gradually spreading around the earth — spreading through the earth's mental sphere into the individual minds of all mankind.

A voice cried "Go where none have gone!
Dig deeper, deeper yet, till thou reach the grim
foundation stone and knock at the keyless gate."

SRI AUROBINDO

23. A Holy Mountain And A Great Sage

In the end everyone must come to Arunachala.

SRI RAMANA MAHARSHI

Benares is to the East, Mecca to the West, but explore your own heart, for there are both Rama and Allah.

KABIR

IT WAS INEVITABLE that we would at some time go to the sacred mountain of Arunachala. For one thing it was an important part of my search in sacred India, some thirty years after Paul Brunton had done his search — indeed, it is the place where Brunton found his spiritual guru. For another thing, there is a strong spiritual link between Sai Baba of Puttaparthi and the mountain that is sacred to Lord Siva. There is an ancient story in the Indian *Puranas* that tells of how Lord Siva, in the form of a pillar of fire, came to this spot south of Madras and here the pillar of light or fire solidified into the conical shaped mountain now worshipped as a Siva lingam. Many Indians consider Arunachala to be the most sacred spot in India and pilgrims from all over the country and from abroad come here to worship Siva. Sai Baba, through whom the Siva facet of Brahman shines, sometimes sends members of his flock to have darshan at this holy place. He may give them verbal instructions to go, but more often it is an inner direction.

Like Pondicherry, Arunachala is only a four-hour Indian bus journey south of Madras. Pondicherry lies on the coast and Arunachala some distance inland from there. Yet, though we felt the urge to go, we kept delaying this simple pilgrimage. Finally, it was again a human instrument that set our feet on the journey. The human instrument in this case was a handsome old Parsee lady, whom we met in the crowd that gathered around Sai Baba in Madras. Her name was Mrs Tallyarkan, known to all the sundry as Ma Tallyarkan. She had been and, though she sat at Sai Baba's feet constantly, she still was, a follower of the late Ramana Maharshi. Through the Sai circle and her occasional visits to the Theosophical Estate, we became good friends with Ma Tallyarkan. She invited us to stay with her in her bungalow, close to the sacred mountain of Arunachala, and so one day we caught the bus in Madras and made the journey south, the first of several as guest of Ma Tallyarkan.

It was a very hot day when we first looked on this conical mountain, rising steeply two thousand six hundred feet from the plain below. The Indian sun had burned almost white the cloak of grass that wrapped the steep side of the mountain. Was it, I wondered, being aided by the Siva fire still burning within? The occasional outcrops of rock and loose boulders were glistening with heat. Still, we decided that we must climb it and took one of the winding pathways that led us past caves, two of them associated with the great sage, one of India's leading modern Masters of the spirit. From a spot near the peak, we had a fine view of the country spread out around this remarkable, isolated peak. On one side, close to the hem of the mountain skirt, was the town of Tiruvanamalai with, close beside it, the Ramana Maharshi ashram of the same name as the town. Whether the Puranic story is true or not, the holy mountain has a life of its own. It seems to be clothed in a subtle, spiritual cloak, the fabric of which emanates from within the mountain and radiates within and beyond the mundane, earthly clothing of burnt-out grass and rocks.

Encircling the mountain at its foot, is a necklace of road, some eight miles in length. Along this necklace, the pilgrims make their journey, circumnavigating the mountain, travelling in a clockwise direction. It is said that a boon comes to those who make the journey and the more austere the means of travel the greater the boon. Most pilgrims walk around. Those hoping for a greater boon, do the eight-mile journey with bare feet, while those far advanced in age or suffering from physical disabilities travel by a horse-drawn vehicle or even by taxi.

One man we met on our first visit to Arunachala had done the circular sacred journey round the mountain in a remarkable way and had a truly remarkable boon. This was Dr Ezekiel, a medical practitioner of Tiruvanamalai. We met him one evening as we stood by the side of a road coming out of the town. Along the road towards us, with the beat of drum, sounding brass, and tinkling cymbals, came a group of men. There must have been a dozen of them, some carrying a canopy under which walked a man. Surely a prince must be approaching, we thought. And when the group came in front of us and stopped, we could see that he was truly a prince of the spirit. His eyes were shining, a smile lit up his radiant face and around him was the unmistakable vibration of one who has reached a high level of attainment. Iris was so overcome that she pushed in through the crowd of men around him and touched his feet. Then she stood up and moved back to join Ma Tallyarkan and myself by the side of the road. Then the procession moved on with its joyous marching music.

Ma Tallyarkan told us that it was Dr Ezekiel with a group of his devotees. From her, and from other people, we heard the story of his journey around the mountain and his boon. It seems that, lying horizontally on the ground, he rolled the whole eight miles along the circular route. When he stood up at the end of it, Lord Siva with his consort Parvati, were standing before him. With this boon of the Siva Shakti darshan, came the gift of healing. Dr Ezekiel had been an ordinary medical practitioner but now he healed with spiritual power. Miraculous healings were the result and people came to him in great crowds. His consulting rooms could not cope with this huge influx, so he took up a position near the road on the other side of Arunachala from Tiruvanamalai. It was a quiet, pleasant spot. He went there at about three o'clock each morning and droves of people surrounded him at that time. But the good, compassionate doctor did not have unlimited energy as does an Avatar. So, eventually, his vitality and healing power began to wane. Then he went away and stayed somewhere in seclusion until his good health came back. Eventually, he returned quietly to his practice in the town. Even so, drawn by his elevated spiritual level, people began to gather around him, treat him as their guru, and move about with him as we saw that evening by the roadside.

During this first visit to the holy mountain, Ma Tallyarkan took us to visit the writer Arthur Osborne and his wife in their cottage just outside the ashram proper. It was this gifted spiritual searcher from England who wrote the book *The Incredible Sai Baba* which had done so much in our lives. Among other books, he wrote one called *The Life and Teachings of Ramana Maharshi*. This concise, easily read, attractively written book I consider the best on the life and teachings of the great sage.

Arthur Osborne, who had lived many years at the Tiruvanamalai ashram, was conducting and editing the ashram's regular journal called *The Mountain Path*. This, in the days of Osborne, its founder and editor, was perhaps the best spiritual journal in India. Its title suggests that the mountain path up Arunachala is analogous to man's inner climb up the pathways of Yoga to the apex of Self-realisation. In later years, we met Arthur Osborne several times at the feet of Satya Sai Baba. I think that he must have been very near to Self-realisation when he died a few years later.

Although Arunachala was a famous place of pilgrimage, long before the appearance of Ramana Maharshi, the years he spent in close association with the holy mountain must have added considerably to its spiritual lustre. Although the sage did not come into this world with Avataric awareness of his divine identity, he attained such awareness at the early age of about sixteen and a half years. The way he broke through the earthly fetters to Self-awareness, although unique to himself, can be an inspiration and help to others. It happened this way.

He was born in December, 1879, near the southern Indian city of Madurai. His personal name was Venkataraman. His education was normal, taking him from primary school into high school before the great event that changed his life entirely. One day, in June, 1896, he suddenly felt an overwhelming conviction that he was about to die. His first reaction was the same as any boy in his mid-teens would feel. Fear, horror, panic. Then something very powerful within him enabled him to overcome this natural reaction and to use the conviction of imminent death as a meditation from which he may learn something valuable. So he lay on his back on the floor of the room and in active imagination went through the whole process of physical death. He visualised, clearly and dispassionately, all that would happen to his own body, right to its cremation. It was as if he preceded the natural death he expected by this practice of death through intense imagination and complete detachment from the earthly results. This enabled him to realise, experientially, that he was not the body, that he was not any of his material sheaths, but was, in truth, the Atman, the true Self within, the immortal Self of all, beyond the confines of time and space.

This realisation, gained by an ineffable experience of the truth, inevitably changed his life completely. He had been brought up in a family of Siva worshippers so, very soon after his experience, he set off for the place sacred to Siva, Arunachala. It was a journey of many miles but he did most of it on foot. When he reached Tiruvanamalai, he sat in the great Siva temple there, blissfully engrossed in the contemplation of his radiant Atman. He remained completely unaware of his physical vehicle and its needs. In the next few weeks, he would certainly have gone through actual physical death, had not certain compassionate holy men in the temple attended to all of his physical needs. It is stated in the Hindu spiritual teachings that after reaching Self-realisation, a person does not remain in his physical body for more than twenty-one days, but something in the young Venkataraman brought him back to the consciousness of his own physical body. He was evidently meant by divine destiny to become Ramana Maharshi, the great Rishi, a leading spiritual teacher of mankind.

Eventually he left the temple and went to a cave high on the mountain and, later, to a larger cave lower down. In both of these he spent most of his time in cross-legged silent bliss. Eventually more and more people came to sit in front of the silent figure. It seems to have been truly a Dakshinamurti scene, where the Lord Siva as a young man sits in silence in front of a semicircle of older devotees. No word is spoken. The students receive their spiritual nourishment from the all-wise, silent youth. It is a soul-to-soul contact and teaching. While those around him were satisfied and happy with the silent influence, the young Ramana Maharshi did, sometimes, break the silence to speak a few words. In later years, he moved down and took up his abode at the foot of the mountain. As his reputation had, by then, spread abroad, the crowds around him increased. Eventually, buildings were constructed and the ashram of Tiruvanamalai came into being.

Still his many followers seemed happy to sit around him in silent peace, receiving their spiritual refreshment and instruction by the wordless Dakshinamurti method. But now, the great Master answered many questions verbally, though he seems to have used as few words as possible. Reading sometimes the basic Hindu scriptures such as the *Bhagavad Gita* and the *Upanishads*, Ramana found that these only served to confirm what he already knew from within. As Socrates stated long ago, all knowledge is simply recollection. And a fully Self-realised person, or an Avatar, simply re-collects all the knowledge he needs to expound to his followers from within himself. When asked if he had ever had a spiritual guru, he gave his listeners to understand that, though he had not had one in this life, he had in a former life. It would seem that his guru in the former life had helped him to a point very near to enlightenment so that, early in this life, he was able by his own efforts to break through the veil of Maya.

A great Jnani himself, the sage of Arunachala led his followers along the pathway to Jnana or inner knowledge, but along a very specialised branch of that Yoga path. This is known as *Vichara* in Sanskrit, or, in English, Self-enquiry. This yoga is not entirely new, having been taught long ago by the famous Maharishi, Vasishta, and can be found in the scripture known as the *Yoga Vasishta*. But Ramana Maharshi's modern version of Self-enquiry comes entirely from within himself. Without the aid of scriptural guidance, it is a meditation that can be practised by anyone who feels drawn towards it.

It is set out very clearly in Osborne's book on Ramana Maharshi but I will try to give a brief description of it here.

The pupil sits as he would for any meditation exercise, that is, with a firm seat, a straight back, completely relaxed body, with mind as free as possible from emotion and thought. The eyes should be lightly closed to help maintain a still mind. After taking a few deep yogic breaths to enhance his inner calmness, the pupil asks himself the question, "Who am I?" He should make no attempt to give the answer to this question from his mind. He simply continues to mentally ask the question. If his mind wanders off into some other thought or idea, as minds are wont to do, he must stop the flow of thought and ask himself the question, "Who had this thought? Who had this idea?" Then his mind will answer, "I did." Then the pupil comes back to the question, "Who am I?" Thus, when the mind wanders, it is brought back as swiftly as possible to the one enquiry, "Who am I?" The answer may come quickly, or it may take a very long time. But, when it does, it will not be from the mind but from the spiritual heart. The meditator will not allow it to come from the mind. If the mind should attempt to give the answer, then again the meditator will ask, "Who thought this?" and thus come back to the 'I' and the question "Who am I?" The answer that comes from the heart cannot be put into words. The great Teacher said that it will come as a current of awareness, an awareness of who you are. And the truth of this cannot be put into words. Perhaps the meditator may, at first, have simply a glimpse of his inexpressible identity or he may have a full realisation of it, as Ramana Maharshi did and as some of his pupils have done since. This is the straight, short road to Self-realisation for those who are ready for it and for whom it is suitable. If an aspirant finds it unsuitable, the great sage taught, he should adopt the *bhakti marga* or the yoga of love and devotion.

One who did find it suitable and reached the goal through the yoga of Self-enquiry was Swami Lakshmana, who now, as a Self-realised teacher, runs an ashram a few miles north of Madras in India. He had hoped that his very promising Yoga pupil named Sharada would reach enlightenment by the same method. But she found it quite unsuitable for her temperament so followed the bhakti yoga and reached Self-realisation on that pathway. Now, called Sharadama, she is the Shakti, or helper, at the Lakshmana ashram. Both Swami Lakshmana and Sharadama, coming to Self-realisation by different pathways, felt the strong urge to leave their bodies, but retained them by the power of enlightened will, in order to be spiritual guides to humanity. The interesting story of these two enlightened ones can be read in the book by David Godman entitled *No Mind, I am the Self.*

Ramana Maharshi himself retained his physical body for over half a century after reaching his goal of full enlightenment, leaving it in the year 1950. During all those years, he remained at the foot of Arunachala, bring spiritual nourishment and wisdom to the thousands who came to him, not only from all parts of India, but also from many other countries. Those from Western countries included royal personages and famous authors.

The two seasons of the year that see the greatest influx of pilgrims to Arunachala are *Mahasivaratri* and *Kartikai*. Both of these seasons are considered sacred to Lord Siva. While Mahasivaratri is almost always in February, though occasionally early March, the Kartikai period is in November. During this month, the constellation of Pleiades (Kartikai to the Indians) comes into conjunction with the full moon. It is, at this time, that Lord Siva is said to manifest himself on the pinnacle of Arunachala.

My wife and I came on our last visit to the holy mountain during the Kartikai festival. The whole place seemed to be bathed in a subtle radiance, while a beacon of fire burned on the summit of the mountain. No doubt it was thought that Siva himself was within the fire. Did he not come here as a pillar of fire, from which he created the mountain in ancient times? The many people moving about at the foot of the mountain seemed to be floating in the radiant vibration. We ourselves felt almost lifted up when an old friend floated out of the crowd and anchored before us. This was Dr T.M.P. Mahadevan, Head of the Department of Higher Philosophy at Madras University. His usually serious, philosophic face was now aglow with an inner light.

My first contact with this worthy philosopher was on a public platform in Madras. He was giving a short preliminary talk to Sai Baba's discourse. I was scheduled to give the second preliminary talk, and as it was the first time that I had spoken to such a very large crowd (an estimated twenty thousand was present), I was too nervous to hear much of what the Doctor said. But Swami somehow managed to buoy up my morale and I actually enjoyed the occasion. The second meeting with Dr Mahadevan was in a room in a private house in Madras where a few people were gathered around the feet of Sai Baba. Actually both the Doctor and I were sitting on a couch with him. I saw Swami materialise for the Professor of Philosophy a gold medallion featuring a Siva lingam. Dr Mahadevan was leaving next day to attend a World Conference on Philosophy at Athens. It amused me to wonder what the great philosophers of the West would say if he told them about this materialisation. Would any of them embrace the transcendental or transpersonal philosophy that would make the phenomenon believable and acceptable? Indian philosophy, in which Mahadevan was steeped, contains, of course, the dimension of the spirit.

We met the Doctor on a number of later occasions, sometimes giving lectures at Sai Baba's Summer Courses on Spirituality and Indian Culture and occasionally talking to groups in the Theosophical Estate. We had long known, however, that Ramana Maharshi was his Sadguru and were not surprised to find him moving round the holy mountain at this time when the presence of Siva was so perceptible. He greeted us with his usual question, "How is Swamiji?" We knew, of course, that he was referring to Sai Baba, for whom he always showed a deep love and respect.

Doctor of the higher philosophy of the heart, as well as the head, this true son of spiritual India has now left the earth. Indeed, Mother Earth seemed to be anchoring him with difficulty when we last saw him on that shining night at the feet of the holy mountain.

There is no greater mystery than this, that being the Reality ourselves, we think to gain Reality, we think that there is something binding your Reality and that it must be destroyed before the Reality is gained. It is ridiculous. A day will dawn when you will yourself laugh at your effort. That which is on the day of laughter is also now.

RAMANA MAHARSHI

24. Sai Education For The Golden Age

If you are planning ahead for one year, plant a seed, for ten years, a tree, but if you are planning for a hundred years, educate the children.

CONFUCIUS

I BELIEVE THAT Sai Baba is planning ahead for more than a thousand years, so the education of the young is of tenfold importance. True it is, that in his fourteenth year, the boy Satya Narayana Raju threw away his high school books. But he was not as other children. He knew that he did not need books, that all knowledge lay within himself. He told the villagers around that he was Sai Baba and that his devotees were waiting for him. Some of the startled few had heard the name Sai Baba and understood him to be a Muslim holy man of a village called Shirdi in the Bombay area. Perhaps they did not know that he had died in 1918 and would have no idea that he promised to reincarnate in eight years. So how could they connect the boy of Puttaparti, born in 1926, with the Muslim fakir called Sai Baba? But little Satya Narayana had always been a wonder worker and now he began quoting long Sanskrit passages that he had never learned from books. It is sadly true, as Jesus of Nazareth pointed out, that a prophet has no honour in his own town, so all but a few in Puttaparti treated the teenage prophet with more hostility than faith. Still, strangely, devotees from other parts of India began to gather around him.

During the next few years, reports of his constant stream of miracles spread widely and the number of his devotees increased. I know personally, from a diary of one of those early devotees, that the young Satya Sai Baba was giving spiritual instruction to his group of followers. The instruction was the universal, eternal, spiritual truths revealed in the ancient Vedas. These truths, like the supernormal powers he exhibited, came not from books of instruction but from the awakened divine centre within the young village prophet. In fact, during the long period that I was personally associated with Swami, I never saw him read a book, yet he quoted from many of the books of scripture.

When I came to him personally, two and a half decades after the announcement of his identity, he was still teaching the eternal wisdom, but by then to crowds of many thousands, rather than the few around him in the village. Even so, his teachings were not only in words but also in the selfless life he lived and the compassion he showed to his human children. To be close to him, was to feel an accelerating change in one's understanding and character. Moreover, seeds of change were sown in the minds of the big crowds that sat around to hear his discourses. Furthermore, through the written word, seeds of Sai wisdom were being sown in wider fields. Even so, the remoulding of adult minds and lives, firmly set in wrong attitudes, is a slow business. Bhagavan Sai Baba knew this, of course, and he was also aware of the urgent need for change and reform.

I don't know at what point he decided to make the education of youth a special part of his mission to man. Perhaps he had always known that this was a part of his programme, for the flexible minds of youth are more easy to mould and direct into ways of right living. I know that he gave a great deal of creative thought to his educational plan during the sixties and launched it while we were still with him in the late sixties.

It began with the establishment of a University College for women at Anantapur, within easy reach of Puttaparti by car. I went there with him several times during the building of the College, which opened its doors in 1968. Asked why his very first educational institution was for women, Swami gave a number of interesting reasons. The young women are the mothers-to-be, he explained, and mothers are the children's first gurus. It is important that they have sound spiritual understanding and good characters for training the next generation. "As the women are, so is the nation." I have heard Western women complain that Swami gives women a secondary place, but this is not so. He simply makes it clear that the role of women in life is different from that of men, but it is equally important. Perhaps more so because the character of the women determine the quality of the nation and indeed, of mankind.

Furthermore, he states that through their intuitional understanding and receptivity, women properly trained can make more rapid progress than men on the spiritual path. Perhaps the age now coming to birth will benefit from this Sai concept of the important role of women. It is high time that they took their place as the equal partners of men, as they did long ago in ancient India.

Swami's second educational institution, a University College for men, came into being in the following year, 1969. It was first housed in a temporary building in the grounds of Swami's residence at

Brindavan, Whitefield. My wife and I were staying there at the time and Mr and Mrs Arthur Osborne were on a visit to Swami from Tiruvanamalai. He took the four of us to inspect the College a few days after it opened. I was struck by the gleaming white attire of the students, the first of that youthful army clad in white that now inhabit all his male Colleges. I think of them as the army of Light led by the many-crowned Conqueror in a robe of red. In those days, Swami usually wore a red robe, the red of the Conqueror in Revelations, of Sir Galahad's armour and of the Holy Grail itself. I saw how the students' eyes shone with a love of Swami, a love somehow clothed in veneration and reverence. Young hearts see more of the spirit than do hearts dried and hardened by time. I felt that this group in its temporary housing, academic yet winged by spirit, was the beginning of something of great importance to the world.

It was not long before this first Sai College for men moved into its permanent home, an architecturally beautiful building a short walk along the road from the gates of Brindavan. Its first Principal, Professor D. Narenda, was a loved and respected friend of ours from Madras. In the following years came more Sai University Colleges, one at Prasanti Nilayam near the ashram, and two in the north of India. But Swami's educational plan was to embrace the youth of all ages from kindergarten through to University graduation, and so he has established kindergartens, primary schools and high schools in various areas.

The building of these many educational institutions and the student hostels to go with them, all of architectural beauty, must have taken a good deal of money, the reader may conclude. So where did it come from? Surely not from some fourth dimension, like the many objects that come with a wave of the Avatar's hand. No, but it might be said that they come by a wave of the divine metaphorical hand, the hand that works unseen on the spiritual plane. There is a cosmic law that works unseen through the universe and through this world. Swami puts it this way: "If you start a truly good work, the money necessary for its establishment will come." He also teaches that the way for a rich man to take the proverbial camel through the eye of a needle and reach the spiritual kingdom of heaven is to use his money, or a good proportion of it, as a tool in the work of God. Most wealthy men worship their wealth and are tragically attached to it. That is the road to misery and unhappiness. Wealth need not be an obstacle on the spiritual road, Swami says. It is your attitude towards it that can be an obstacle. Change the attitude, cut the ties that bind you to it, and the obstacle vanishes. In fact, the obstacle may be transmuted into a help, a spur to speed on your spiritual progress.

Among the Sai followers in India and in Western countries were men and women, rich in worldly wealth and through their Lord's inspiration growing rich in the realm of the spirit. Some of these, it was, who, without being asked (for Swami will never ask for anything) donated the necessary money to launch the great Sai educational programme. They do not talk about it, they want no acknowledgement, praise or publicity. They give with selfless love of God and his divine work. Only from that pure spiritual motivation will Sai Baba accept a donation to his work. The donation then becomes a spiritual sacrifice, bringing divine grace to the giver.

So the first phase of the Sai schools came into being. But I understand that there are more to come for this is an ongoing process. Right at the beginning, the question I asked myself was: in what way do these Sai centres of learning differ from ordinary schools of the world? I know from my own experience in the teaching profession that the ordinary schools are two-dimensional. That is, they seek to train mind and body, giving no thought to the dimension of the spirit. It is true, of course, that the schools owned by the Christian churches do give some attention to religious training, but this is denominational and therefore narrow. It helps in the division rather than the unity of mankind. At least, this is the way it was in my day and I have reason to believe that it has not improved. The Sai schools, on the other hand, are three-dimensional. They recognise and seek to develop the dimension of the spirit. The spiritual instruction given is based on the universal truths, the perennial philosophy which is the foundation and groundwork of all great religions. Instead of enhancing the creation of denominations and sects intolerant of each other, it increases the flame of unity, of tolerance and understanding in the great brotherhood of humanity.

But it must not be thought that Sai Baba trains his pupils to go away from the world and seek the life of the spiritual hermit. He says that we humans must be strong, sound boats floating in the waters of the world. While we are made to be in the water, we must not let the water get into us. His plan is to train and tune the other two human dimensions, mind and body, in a way equal to that of the best world schools. A few short years have shown that scholastically and academically, the Sai students have not only equalled but surpassed the general outside standard. Regarding the physical dimension of his students, Sai Baba is doing special work. Observers from the Western world cannot fail to see that traditionally the educated professional classes in India regard manual work as somewhat demeaning. The amateur handyman, so much a part of life in the West, is unknown in the Indian culture. No doubt this outlook is born of the caste system that has maintained its rigid existence for centuries. The Sai schools are seeking to change this outlook and remove this weakness from the Indian cultural mandorla. Not only do the students of the Sai schools enjoy the well-known body building sports, seen from the playing fields of Eton to the rural playgrounds in outback Australia, but there is something more. The young men of the University Colleges, living in College hostels, are trained to cook, wait on tables and clean their own sleeping quarters without the help of servants. Where the facilities are available, they work on the land growing their own vegetables. They learn to maintain whatever motor vehicles are in use and do various types of handyman repair work. As part of their service to God in man, they go into nearby villages and do whatever jobs are necessary to raise the hygienic standards of the villages. Such jobs may include the cleaning out of dirty drains and other blocked up facilities, work traditionally done only by outcasts. In short, hands are being trained as well as heads and hearts, and self-reliant, well-rounded characters are being created. The vast majority of teachers, lecturers, professors in the educational institutions are Sai Baba devotees. Throughout the whole range of instruction, academic, technical or practical, they are able to lead their pupils along the guidelines of Sai morality, self-discipline and spirituality. Hovering over all and embracing all is the inspiration and divine love of the Avatar.

This fine example of three-dimensional, classless, humanitarian, character-building education should be an inspiration for the whole world. Indeed, a few Sai schools with similar ideals have sprung up in other parts of the world. But, no doubt, against the dead weight of blind materialism, the growth of such educational establishments throughout other countries will be very slow. Yet, fully aware of the dangers threatening the earth and her human children today, Sai Baba knows the urgency of his re-educational work. Therefore he has launched something else that has a good chance of spreading more quickly than the establishment of Sai-type schools. This is known as Education in Human Values or, usually, by its initials EHV. This is something that all men who love the good and long for peace and goodwill in the world can embrace. No matter what their nation or religion, no matter what their racial prejudice, no matter what their condition or complacency, all must agree that the application of EHV can lead to the regeneration of mankind. The only problem lies in the best practical means of applying it.

Briefly stated, this Education in Human Values is based on five pillars of wisdom. These themselves are a concentrated summation of the Sai teachings. As Swami says he has not come to start a new religion but to repair the ancient road to Truth, the five pillars may be considered guidelines in the Sai restatement of the eternal verities. In Sanskrit terms, the metaphorical pillars or guidelines are Satya, Dharma, Shanti, Prema, Ahimsa. These five foundation pillars to the edifice of divine wisdom and the pinnacle of the highest life for humanity may be considered separately and in any order. I will take Satya first.

It is the first name of our Avatar. It means the deep Truth of being and it was in search of this that I first set out on my world-wandering odyssey. All people yearn inwardly for this Truth of being, which is the Truth of God and man. Philosophers and poets seek desperately to express it in words and the music of words, but, though they blaze a wondrous trail towards it, they cannot quite capture this Truth in words or music. Nor can the artist do more than intimate the 'Light that never was on sea or land'. This deep-lying Truth beyond direct verbal statement is also intimated and suggested in the stories of the great myths and legends. These, with poetry, art and the teachings of the great Masters of spiritual wisdom, are the guides to inner Truth, not only for children but for seekers of all ages. For daily life in the world of affairs, there should always be Truth-seeking and Truth-speaking without fear or favour but with compassion. This is a golden rule of yoga.

Next we will look at the pillar with the word Prema inscribed upon it. In the English tongue we need more than one word to express the meaning of this. Anyone who has experienced pure, divine Love, which seeks nothing in return, would understand the meaning of Prema. There is plenty of so-called love in the world but it is usually contaminated with other emotions and desires. Also it is usually a bargain seeking something in return. Where does this pure selfless Love exist apart from the hearts of God-men such as Sai Baba, Christ and Krishna? If we remember that God is in every person's heart, we will know that Love is there too. But it is locked away and the key to its door is hard to find. The followers of Christ found it when one of them said, "We love one another because He first loved us." The sure key to open the door of the human heart today is the presence of Sai Baba or indeed his grace at a distance. But, for reasons explained earlier, his presence is not directly invoked for his plan of Education in Human Values. How then will we find the key to the secret door? Mainly by the same means as we sought the key to the door of Truth. Add to these instruments of inspiration, where possible, the living example of the teacher. This may indeed be the most powerful instrument.

When we work towards divine Love through study, practice and prayer, we may receive the key of divine grace unasked. We will find for sure that it leads us towards the great truth of unity, the oneness of all with the central One we call God. Love is the great magnetic power, the affinity that draws all into divine unity. The Italian poet seer, Dante, must have understood something of this when he said "My will and my desire were turned by Love, the Love that moves the sun and the other stars." Much will be required of the individual teacher in dealing with this value, which is more divine than human. But one gleam of pure Light from the beacon of Prema is the beginning of wisdom.

Let us move on, now, to the pillar marked Ahimsa. Whatever can this mean? Ahimsa simply means non-violence in thought, word and deed. Yet the application of this advanced human value is not so simple. We live in a world of violence and the fact that it is featured prominently in our mass media of communications suggests that we enjoy violence. So in this the majority of us must do a complete turnabout. You, the philosopher, may protest that in Nature, including Man, life lives on life. All the time lower forms of life are being sacrificed in order that higher forms may live. True, this is a law of Nature but any necessary killing for man's survival should be done as a sacrifice to the divine plan. It should never be done with violent feelings. Even when it is necessary to kill an enemy as, say, in war, it should never be done with the violent feelings of anger and hatred. Ideally, it should be done as a sacrificial duty with love in the heart of the slayer for the slain. "Love your enemies," said Jesus. Loving him is easier when we remember that God is in all, even in the worst and most contemptible of men, as Sai Baba teaches us. Perhaps the hardest thing for the average person, whether child or adult, is to refrain from violence in thought and in speech. If this can be attained, if thought and word can always be gentle, sweet and loving, then non-violence in deeds will follow naturally.

Prema is a close partner of Ahimsa and they should be developed together. With some understanding of the first three pillars of wisdom, we can grasp more easily the meaning and significance of the last two.

Dharma is best translated as Right Living. It means that we must put into action in our daily lives, in the home and at the workplace, the values of Truth, Selfless Love or Brotherhood and Non-violence. We must keep a watch on our thoughts, feelings, words and actions to see that they keep in line with those great spiritual values. To the extent that we fail in this, we are falling away from the divine unity which is the Truth of our being. Then we should acknowledge our failure, and ask God's forgiveness and begin again. The sacred or dharmic life is a constant upward striving, using the lessons of our failures as stepping stones to reach the ideal.

Living according to the values set forth in the first four pillars of wisdom will lead inevitably to the last in my list, that is, *Shanti* or 'the Peace that passeth all understanding'. Yet before that is reached, it is a value to live by for itself. Sai Baba says that world peace begins in the individual heart. Peace begins in the individual, spreads into the home and then into the community and from the community to the life of nations and hence to peace in the world. The greatest thing we can do individually for world peace is to strive for peace within ourselves and harmony in our own homes and communities. All peoples, whatever their religious or racial bias may be, must see that these are excellent values by which to train the young and retrain the elders. The Sai educational system of EHV is spreading throughout India and reaching out into other countries beyond India.

The five pillars of wisdom are the basis of the ethical and moral guidance in all the Sai schools from kindergarten to University Colleges. For a little over a decade from their beginning, the Sai University Colleges were affiliated to appropriate official universities within their area, but in November, 1981, the Sai University known as the Satya Sai Institute of Higher Learning, deemed University, came into being, established officially by the Government of India. Satya Sai Baba, born fifty-five years earlier in the humble village of Puttaparti, became the University's Chancellor. The Headquarters of the University is housed in a fine building that crowns a high hill overlooking the ashram and the village of Puttaparti. I see it as the outward and visible sign of the new spiritual education for the Age that is coming to birth.

The feeling of bliss and peace that comes from being at one with God is the most precious jewel available to Man. It is the pearl of great price compared with which all other joys are as dross. It is the pearl for which saints and sages the world over have striven and for which they have gladly forsaken all comforts and human attachments. It is peace and bliss beyond all telling but until we have tasted it we do not know, we cannot know it is that for which our souls have longed.

SAI BABA

The end of education is character.

SAI BABA

Prema (Divine Love) is Sai's greatest miracle.

25. The True Home

Wandering in heaven one eats the spirit energy of the Receptive and the still deeper secret within the secret, the land that is nowhere, that is the true home.

— from *THE SECRET OF THE GOLDEN FLOWER*

THE LIFE JOURNEY of every individual is a pilgrimage and a search. The destination of his pilgrimage is the place of everlasting happiness, his true home. The search on his long road home is for directions, clues, signs that will take him there. When he is consciously aware that his feet are on the home-seeking journey, the signs will come from time to time as gifts of grace to support and buoy up his faith. As the reader knows, I had my share of what may be called windows in heaven or glimpses of the Holy Grail. When the searcher comes at long last to the Grail castle, his questions will be answered and he will need to set forth no more on his outer journey in the world. The most important thing he learns is that the chalice of meaning, the bowl of all good things, called the Grail, serves the Grail king who abides in the innermost room of the castle. This Grail king is none other than man's inner God, his *atman*, his Christ, his inner spirit, his Holy Spirit, his true Self. All that the pilgrim has gained on his quest of the Grail, his knowledge, his actions, his devotion, his whole progress are meant to serve the God in the innermost recesses of the spiritual heart, the Grail king.

My own Grail castle was my 'star in the East', Sai Baba. From him I sought the answers to the questions I had been carrying in my knapsack across the lands and the years. He answered them all, not only the main ones but a long list of subsidiary questions. I will try to state here briefly, under suitable headings, the essence of his answers to some of the main human queries.

God

I had lost the Christian God of my forefathers in the academies of profane education. After years of wandering through the desert of agnosticism, I found God again at the feet of Sai Baba. But what a very different understanding of God I obtained! How much more acceptable to the emancipated mental outlook of today! Now He was not only within heaven but everywhere, within everything. The easiest place to find Him is within one's own heart and, finding Him there, one will gradually see Him everywhere. The Master of all form, God, is both with and without form. As the Christians taught, He is not only God of all power and all knowledge but the very embodiment of Love itself. Thus He is a merciful, compassionate and forgiving God. In truth, there is only this one Existence. Nothing else exists except this absolute One in his multitudinous modes of expression. From the barren desert where God was nothing but a doubt, I came to the bowl of plenty where God is everything, beyond all doubt.

Man

For as long as I can remember, this was the main question that I shouted to the unanswering skies, "What is man and what is his purpose here?" The answer, briefly stated, is that man is an undivided part of God. He is undivided in the same way as a sun ray may sometimes seem to be divided from the sun but in reality it is not divided. Man thinks that he is separate and therein lies his original and basic error. Original or basic sin is man's fundamental concept of being asunder from God. The word 'sin' is associated with the word 'asunder'. The purpose of man's life, or rather his many lives on earth, is to rediscover his unity with God. This is achieved through the evolution of his consciousness brought about by the mixture of hazards and happiness, joys and pains, glooms and gleams of earthly life. Between his lives on earth, he rests in other planes but he must return to the hard knocks of earth life that will stir the evolution of consciousness to the level of enlightenment and God-realisation. The purpose of man is to discover that he is divine and thence live the divine life. Man comes originally from God as a spark of divinity, sets off on the evolutionary journey of necessity and at long last earns his way back to God, his true home. But by then he has become a being conscious of his own divinity.

Nature

By Nature I mean everything from the grass under your feet to the farthest star, in fact, the whole of what we call Creation. Did God create all this? Is God the author of all this? Yes, being the one absolute Existence, He emanated it from Himself. And this divine emanation is not an act that is finished; it is going on all the time. We should think of God in two main modes. First there is the Being mode, the eternal, unchanging one Existence. Secondly, there is the Becoming mode. This is ever-changing, becoming something else from what it was the moment before. Within ourselves the being mode of God is our own divine inner spirit, while all the rest is his becoming mode. Within our bodies, for example, new cells are constantly being born while the old ones decay and pass into some other form. At one stage of our evolutionary journey we see Nature as something separate, this being the illusory perception that Sanskrit calls *Maya*. Further along the path, we see God not only in our own centre but at the deep centre of everything. Finally we see everything as God. We perceive Him in His becoming as well as in His being mode. Then it is that we see truly and know the oneness of all.

Knowing and accepting this deep truth of oneness in the mind is not the same as realising it within the spiritual heart. The first is having the end in view, the second is reaching the end. There is the story of a young man who travelled the world seeking a hidden treasure, the pearl beyond price. Finally he met a wise man who taught him many wonderful things. The most important and most astounding thing was that the hidden treasure was buried in his own garden back home. He had to dig for it himself but the wise man gave him valuable instructions about how to find it. Likewise, Swami has told me, and all others who drink the cup of his wisdom, that the spiritual pearl beyond price is buried in the garden of one's own heart, one's own spiritual heart. It is there that I must dig for it. So the end of the outward journey, bringing me as it did to the feet of the Avatar, the Master of all wisdom, was not the end of my journey. I had to set off on another one, perhaps even more difficult, more hazardous. Swami calls this the Inward Journey.

In truth, practically all the directions and guidance that a great teacher gives is connected with this journey towards the hidden treasure lying at your own centre. He may, and does, give help in worldly affairs, such as assisting you to find the right job or the right house to live in or finding the right marriage partner and in many other ways, yet seen in its true perspective, such help is given to further your footsteps along the inner path. Most of the great Avatar's directions apply to everybody, while a few are special to each individual.

The inward journey

For the most part, our inward journey is connected with our outward activities. It is as if while carrying out our allotted tasks, whether in office, farm or home, we keep a watch on our thoughts, words and deeds to make sure they conform to the guidelines set out in Swami's Education in Human Values. These five guidelines were set out and discussed in the previous chapter. But our inward journey is to see that we apply them to our daily lives. We watch, for example, to see how closely we are keeping to the deep concept of Truth in our words, actions, thoughts and feelings. How close to the shining beacon of Love, or unity with all, are we keeping; are we maintaining harmony and peace in our homes and among our work companions, for example? Are we guilty of any violence, if not in action then in words or thoughts? Are we failing in any way with the laws of *dharma* or right-living. To the extent we keep close to those ideals, we make good progress on the inward journey. To the extent we fail, and there will be many failures, we ask our divine Lord for forgiveness and try again. Like Jesus Christ of the Scriptures, Avatar Sai Baba is a forgiving God, the very embodiment of understanding and love.

Moreover, parallel to some of the Christian teachings, are special features of the Sai inward path. One of these is group devotional singing in which the heart of the singer is lifted up and his divine love increased by songs of praise and glory to God. In the case of the Sai devotional singing, all the names by which God is known, from Rama through Allah, through Christ to Sai Baba, are used. For Swami teaches all the names, if rightly understood, apply to the one God.

Allied to devotional singing and, indeed, part of it, is another special feature of the path call *satsang*, meaning spiritual company or a number of people gathered together for the worship of God. As well as singing His praises, they talk of His works and wonders and together study His teachings. In such gatherings great love, great joy, are engendered and the presence of the Avatar is felt. Such activities are great aids along the inward path of *bhakti* or devotion to God.

Other features of the Sai inward journey are prayer and meditation. Let us consider prayer first. Swami says we should ask for what we want, even though he knows our wants and needs before we ask him. It is said that expressing our wants in words, either silently or aloud, is really a help to the one who is praying. It makes specific what is vague and clarifies what is confused. Does Sai Baba hear and answer prayer? The experiences of many people show that he hears them in whatever language they are expressed and whatever distance over land and sea divides the body of the Avatar from the body of the one who prays. Experience and his teachings reveal that he grants individual requests in accordance with his divine wisdom. He is like a wise human mother who lovingly gives her child what it asks for, provided it does not do the child harm. Mother Sai has limitless resources and a far-seeing and all-wise perspective on what will bring spiritual harm, though temporary pleasure, to the human supplicant. We should understand, moreover, that the positive answer to some prayers, such as the prayer for healing, depends on the receptivity of the person praying. Jesus Christ called this 'faith'. Sai Baba illustrates this by the modern analogy of the electric current. There must be both the positive and the negative poles in order for the current to flow. Likewise, when Swami sends out the healing ray of his divine love, the one who seeks healing must be open to receive it. This openness, this receptivity, is what Christ called faith. Faith has been defined as a conviction of things unseen. It is a conviction because the spiritual heart, or the true Self, *knows* in a direct way not requiring any proof. The mind may doubt, as is its nature, but the spiritual heart *knows*, and that is faith. Such faith, which works in many positive ways in our lives, is the receiving end for the divine healing beam. When it is there in sufficient measure a divine healing takes place.

The highest form of prayer is that which seeks to be aware of the sunshine of God's presence without asking Him for anything in particular. This wordless prayer, or silent communion with the divine, is what is generally called meditation. Sai Baba teaches many different forms of meditation in order, I believe, for each individual among his followers to find the one that suits his particular needs the best. In the end each individual treads his own inward path, keeping within the perimeters of the general guidelines. This is also true of meditation. The individual must do his own digging in the garden of the heart to find the hidden treasure. But Swami says that the best type of meditation for this dark age, known as the *Kali Yuga*, is that known as devotional meditation. This simply means that each person should choose the divine form that he loves best. It may be Krishna or Rama or Jesus or Sai Baba or any other form that steeps him in the greatest divine love and joy. While concentrating on this to the exclusion of all other images, he should repeat the divine name associated with that form. He should continue this for the period of his meditation. Sometimes the image may seem to fade from the mind but, by continuing to repeat the name, the form will reappear. This daily session of meditation should be supplemented throughout the day by repeating the name and visualising the form in every spare moment when the mind is not occupied with the problems of the day. It is said that in this Age such a practice alone is sufficient to bring full God-realisation. In the meantime, it will help to overcome the hazards of the inward journey and bring a level of contentment to the aspirant's daily life.

Another special feature of the Sai journey to one's Centre is selfless service to others. God is in all people and we can serve Him best by serving our fellow men. Divine love can only grow in strength when it finds its expression this way. As muscles without exercise will dwindle and atrophy, so will love that is not exercised in works dedicated to God. Such works lie at the very heart of the yoga of love that he teaches. All the time-honoured yogas of the *sanathana dharma* form part of the Sai path. These are *jnana* (knowledge), *karma* (work), *bhakti* (devotion), with, as an integral part of them all, the self-disciplines of *raja yoga*. While *raja* means the king of yogas, the true monarch on the Sai homeward journey is *bhakti* or love, devotion, service to God wherever He is found. No doubt a study of the great philosophy of *vedanta* (drawn from the *Upanishads* at the end of the *Vedas*) would reveal most of the principles and insights of the Sai spiritual teachings, but there is one thing that such a study could not provide. That is, the personal influence and inspiration of the living Avatar who, like a never-ending fountain, pours out divine love to the world. Such eternal springs of love had been in the world before, notably through the forms of Krishna and Christ. Such waters of life still flow in the world but now the needs of the time have called forth another divine spring to replenish and augment the transforming waters of love. Vedanta alone, the ancient wisdom alone, cannot transform men's lives, even though they are necessary adjuncts. Swami insists that we imbibe the messages of such scriptures, but only through baptism in the shining streams of love can human souls be purified and redeemed.

Part of that eternal love is what we call divine grace. This is something that comes unexpectedly in time of great need. This reveals to us joyously that the great Father God wants his suffering, travel-weary sons back in the divine home. This is illustrated in the fable where the father comes out to meet the prodigal son and welcomes him back to the shelter of his home. Such divine grace near the end of the journey is also illustrated at the end of the *Odyssey*. The goddess

Athena, the divine form which Odysseus worships, appears to him, uses her wisdom to help him break through the final barriers into the sanctuary of his longed-for home.

Neither the outward journey through the lands, nor the inward journey to the land that is nowhere in space or time is meant to be easy. Both are journeys of evolution and growth against obstacles. At the end of the long obstacle course, a complete transformation has taken place. The little self that saw itself as separate, with its own desires of the greatest importance, has expanded to infinity, becoming the universal Self in all life. Thus the individual has found oneness in the spiritual land that is nowhere but everywhere. He has found that true home for which his soul has always longed. At the end of the long journey, the pilgrim's soul will know that, though its own efforts were necessary, it was in reality through the amazing grace of the Divine that he reached unity with the Divine in the ineffable mystery called Liberation, *Moksha* or *Nirvana*.

My will and my desire were turned by Love,
the Love that moves the sun and the other stars.

DANTE

Among the instruments or paths and conditions necessary
for Liberation, bhakti alone is supreme.

ADI SHANKARA